Rome
2007

WHAT'S NEW | WHAT'S ON | WHAT'S NEXT

www.timeout.com/rome

Contents

Rome by Area

Essentials

Published by Time Out Guides Ltd
Universal House
251 Tottenham Court Road
London W1T 7AB
Tel: + 44 (0)20 7813 3000
Fax: + 44 (0)20 7813 6001
Email: guides@timeout.com
www.timeout.com

Editorial/Managing Director Peter Fiennes
Series Editor Ruth Jarvis
Deputy Series Editor Lesley McCave
Business Manager Gareth Garner
Guides Co-ordinator Holly Pick
Accountant Kemi Olufuwa

Time Out Guides is a wholly owned subsidiary of Time Out Group Ltd.

© **Time Out Group Ltd**
Chairman Tony Elliott
Managing Director Mike Hardwick
Financial Director Richard Waterlow
Time Out Magazine Ltd MD David Pepper
Group General Manager/Director Nichola Coulthard
Time Out Communications Ltd MD David Pepper
Production Director Mark Lamond
Group Marketing Director John Luck
Group Art Director John Oakey
Group IT Director Simon Chappell

Time Out and the Time Out logo are trademarks of Time Out Group Ltd.

This edition first published in Great Britain in 2006 by Ebury Publishing

Ebury Publishing is a division of The Random House Group Ltd
Company information can be found on www.randomhouse.co.uk
10 9 8 7 6 5 4 3 2 1

Distributed in USA by Publishers Group West (www.pgw.com)
Distributed in Canada by Publishers Group Canada (www.pgcbooks.ca)
For further distribution details, see www.timeout.com

ISBN To 31 December 2006: 1-904978-78-9. From 1 January 2007: 9781904978787

A CIP catalogue record for this book is available from the British Library

Colour reprographics by Wyndeham Icon, 3 & 4 Maverton Road, London E3 2JE

Printed and bound in Germany by Appl

Papers used by Ebury Publishing are natural, recyclable products made from wood
grown in sustainable forests

Rome Shortlist

The **Time Out Rome Shortlist 2007** is one of a new series of annual guides that draws on Time Out's background as a magazine publisher to keep you current with everything that's going on in town. As well as Rome's classic sights and the best of its eating, drinking and entertainment, the guide picks out the most exciting venues to have opened in the last year, and gives a full calendar of events for September 2006 to December 2007. It also includes features on the important news, trends and openings, all compiled by locally based editors. Whether you're visiting for the first time in your life or just the first time since 2006, you'll find the *Time Out Rome Shortlist 2007* contains everything you need to know, in a portable and easy-to-use format.

The guide divides central Rome into six areas, each of which contains listings for Sights & museums, Eating & drinking, Shopping, Nightlife and Arts & leisure, along with maps pinpointing all their locations. At the front of the book are chapters rounding up each of these scenes city-wide, and giving a Shortlist of our overall picks in a variety of categories. We also include itineraries for point-to-point days out, and essentials including transport information and hotels.

Our listings use phone numbers as dialled locally from within Italy. To dial them from abroad, use your country's exit code followed by 39 (the country code for Italy) and the number given, including the initial '0'. We have given price categories by using one to four euro signs (€-€€€€), representing budget, moderate, expensive and luxury. Major credit cards are accepted unless otherwise stated. We also indicate when a venue is NEW, and give Event highlights.

All our listings are double-checked but businesses do sometimes close or change their hours or prices, so it's a good idea to call a venue before visiting. While every effort has been made to ensure accuracy, the publishers cannot accept responsibility for any errors this guide may contain.

Venues are marked on the maps using symbols numbered according to their order within the chapter and colour-coded according to the type of venue they represent:

❶ Sights & museums
❶ Eating & drinking
❶ Shopping
❶ Nightlife
❶ Arts & leisure

SHORTLIST
Online

The *Time Out Rome Shortlist 2007* is as up to date as it is possible for a printed guidebook to be. And to keep it completely current, it has a regularly updated online companion, at **www.timeout.com/rome**. Here you'll find news of the latest openings and exhibitions, as well as picks from visitors and residents – ideal for planning a trip. Time Out is the city specialist, so you'll also find travel information for more than 100 cities worldwide on our site, at www.timeout.com/travel.

Time Out Rome Shortlist 2007

EDITORIAL
Editor Ruth Jarvis
Copy Editors Simon Coppock, Sarah Thorowgood
Researchers Fulvia Angelini, Michele Sanzo
Proofreader Nicholas Royle

STUDIO
Art Director Scott Moore
Art Editor Pinelope Kourmouzoglou
Senior Designer Josephine Spencer
Graphic Designer Henry Elphick
Digital Imaging Dan Conway
Ad Make-up Jenni Prichard
Picture Editor Jael Marschner
Deputy Picture Editor Tracey Kerrigan
Picture Researcher Helen McFarland

ADVERTISING
Sales Director/Sponsorship Mark Phillips
International Sales Manager Ross Canadé
International Sales Executive Simon Davies
Advertising Sales Margherita Tedone, Julie Simonsen
Advertising Assistant Kate Staddon

MARKETING
Marketing Manager Yvonne Poon
Marketing & Publicity Manager, US Rosella Albanese
Marketing Designer Anthony Huggins

PRODUCTION
Production Manager Brendan McKeown
Production Co-ordinator Caroline Bradford

CONTRIBUTORS
This guide was researched and written by Anne Hanley, with the exception of Cinema Roma; Aperitivo time; Nuova trattoria paradiso (Lee Marshall); White Nights; Baroque Rome; Music Park; Year of Canova; See, Be Seen, Shop; Altar of Controversy; Straight is the Gate (Julia Crosse).

PHOTOGRAPHY
All photography by Gianluca Moggi, New Press Photo, except: pages 34, 43, 45, 59 Adam Eastland; page 147 The Art Archive/Vatican Museum Rome.
The following images were provided by the featured establishments/artists: pages 26, 27, 39.
Cover photograph: St Peter's Square. Credit: Daryl Benson/Masterfile.

MAPS
LS International Cartography, via Decemviri 8, 20138 Milan, Italy (www.geomaker.com)

Thanks to Fulvio Marsigliani at LS International and Michele Sanzo for their work on the maps, Fulvia Angelini, Chris Davies, Peter Douglas, Nick Draper, Taryn Walker, Patrick Welch and all contributors to past editions of *Time Out Rome*.

About Time Out

Founded in 1968, Time Out has expanded from humble London beginnings into the leading resource for those wanting to know what's happening in the world's greatest cities. As well as our influential what's-on weeklies in London, New York and Chicago, we publish more than a dozen other listings magazines in cities as varied as Beijing, Beirut and Mumbai. The magazines established Time Out's trademark style: sharp writing, informed reviewing and bang up-to-date inside knowledge of every scene.

Time Out made the natural leap into travel guides in the 1980s with the City Guide series, which now extends to over 50 destinations around the world. Written and researched by expert local writers and generously illustrated with original photography, the full-size guides cover a larger area than our Shortlist guides and include many more venue reviews, along with additional background features and a full set of maps.

Throughout this rapid growth, the company has remained proudly independent, still owned by Tony Elliott nearly four decades after he started Time Out London as a single fold-out sheet of A5 paper. This independence extends to the editorial content of all our publications, this Shortlist included. No establishment has been featured because it has advertised, and no payment has influenced any of our reviews. And, for our critics, there's definitely no such thing as a free lunch: all restaurants and bars are visited and reviewed anonymously, and Time Out always picks up the bill. For more about the company, see www.timeout.com.

Don't Miss
2007

Pantheon p73

Sights & Museums

Chaotic, fascinating, exhausting and stunning, Rome is a sight in itself. On a cloud-free day with a hint of summer in the air, and with a good vantage point from a well-placed curb-side café table, you could be forgiven for wondering why anyone would want to trade this for a dutiful traipse around a museum or archaeological site.

But Rome's cultural heritage is second to none, and the wealth, breadth and sheer beauty of its art, architecture and artefacts are great enough even to reward the visitor for giving up his or her ringside seat at the magnificent spectacle of everyday life on the streets of the Eternal City.

Enjoyment of these riches used to be hampered by strikes, endless restorations and short opening hours. Those days, thankfully, are over. Rome looks gorgeous after its millennium overhaul. And if some of the exciting new projects planned for the early years of the 21st century – MAXXI museum, designed by Zaha Hadid, is a case in point – are dragging their heels, others (such as Renzo Piano's Auditorium and, more recently, Richard Meyer's striking container for the Ara Pacis) have been unveiled to much acclaim.

Ancient sites

The heart of the ancient city, and the area with the greatest density of remains, all lies between the Capitoline, Palatine, Esquiline and Quirinal hills. Located here are the

SHORTLIST

Best ancient sites
- Colosseum (p53)
- Palatine (p57)
- Pantheon (p73)
- Roman Forum (p58)
- Circus Maximus (p53)
- Baths of Caracalla (p122)
- Trajan's Market (p55)
- Ostia Antica (p160)

Best new sights
- Auditorium – Parco della Musica (p103)
- MACRO (p103)
- MAXXI (p103)

Ancient meets modern
- Ara Pacis (p85)
- Crypta Balbi (p61)
- Basement of Palazzo Massimo alle Terme (p111)

Grand Masters
- Galleria Borghese (p92)
- Palazzo Barberini (p101)
- Capitoline Museums (p53)
- Galleria Doria Pamphili (p71)
- Vatican Museums (p150)

Charming churches
- Santa Maria in Cosmedin (p59)
- Santa Cecilia in Trastevere (p136)
- San Luigi dei Francesi (p73)
- Sant'Ivo alla Sapienza (p75)
- Santa Sabina (p123)

Perfect *piazze*
- Piazza del Campidoglio (p52)
- Campo de' Fiori (p60)
- Santa Maria in Trastevere (p136)
- Piazza Navona (p73)
- Piazza di Trevi (p102)

Green and shady spots
- Orto botanico (p133)
- Protestant (Acatholic) Cemetery (p126)
- Villa Borghese (p90)
- Villa Pamphili (p141)

Colosseum, the Roman and Imperial Fora and ancient Rome's most desirable residential area, the Palatine, where the sexual excesses of emperors and politicians were matched only by the passion with which they plotted against each other. For a more intimate glimpse of the ancient world, underground sites – such as the digs beneath the churches of San Clemente and Santi Giovanni e Paolo – allow you to stroll along ancient streets and into ancient homes.

Museums and galleries

Rome has long boasted some of the world's greatest and most venerable museums and galleries, but the last few years in particular have seen a rash of new permanent exhibits (MACRO, Crypta Balbi), and new venues for old ones (the Ara Pacis). Naturally, this being Rome, there's a preponderance of the ancient, Renaissance and baroque. But if the modern and

coffee from the airport where you left your wallet: £1

(still getting six nonstop hours of sleep: priceless)

Don't worry. MasterCard Global Service™ is available wherever you travel, in any language you speak. So just call the local toll-free number and we'll rush you a new card most anywhere in the world. For a complete list of toll-free numbers, go to www.mastercard.com.

AUSTRIA	0800-21-8235	POLAND	0-0800-111-1211
FRANCE	0-800-90-1387	SPAIN	900-97-1231
GERMANY	0800-819-1040	SWITZERLAND	0800-89-7092
GREECE	00-800-11-887-0303	UK	0800-96-4767
ITALY	800-870-866	USA	1-800-307-7309

From all other countries call collect:
1-636-722-7111

there are some things money can't buy. for peace of mind there's MasterCard®

contemporary is more your cup of tea, you'll find you are increasingly well catered for.

Where Rome – indeed, much of Italy – still lags behind is in its exhibition technique: there's little interaction, little thought for the needs of children, and a very academic and didactic approach to the explanation of exhibits. It's a minor hitch, however, for which the beauty of objects and their settings compensate.

Churches

Central Rome has more than 400 churches. Through the centuries, popes, princes and aristocrats commissioned architects and artists to build, rebuild and adorn their preferred places of worship. Motives were frequently anything but pious, but all this munificence has resulted in some of Rome's most spectacular sights.

Churches are places of worship. Though only the Vatican imposes its dress code strictly (both in St Peter's and the Vatican Museums), respect is appreciated and very short skirts or shorts are frowned upon. Many churches ask tourists to refrain from visiting during services; if you are admitted, you will be expected not to take photos, talk loudly or wander around. A supply of coins for the meters to light up the most interesting art works is always handy.

The abolition of compulsory military service in 2005 had the knock-on effect of depriving smaller churches of their supply of conscientious objectors to act as custodians; opening hours in some places, therefore, will depend on the whims and workload of the priest.

Opening hours

Opening hours are subject to seasonal change, but more often than not you'll find that timetables are considerably more generous than the winter hours (*orario*

Santa Cecilia in Trastevere p136

invernale – roughly from October to May) we give in this guide. Some of the major museums and archaeological sites, in particular, keep their doors open until as late as 11pm during summer (*orario estivo*). Check for current times at the information offices we have listed in the Resources A-Z section at the back of this guide, or at the green *Punti informativi turistici* (PIT) kiosks dotted around the city.

Note that many museums, galleries and ancient sites stop issuing tickets anything up to 75 minutes before the doors shut. Never presume that you can turn up at the last minute for a quick look around, especially in larger museums and sights.

Church opening times should be taken as rough guidelines; most open and close an hour later in summer. All but the largest churches close around noon, and remain firmly shut until late afternoon.

Monday can be frustrating for sightseeing in Rome, as many museums and sights are closed. Churches are open, though, as are some major sights (see box p148).

Tickets

Entrance to publicly owned museums and sites is free (*gratuito*) or reduced (*ridotto*) for EU citizens (and citizens of other countries with bilateral agreements) aged under 18 and over 65; check tariffs at entrances carefully. Under-25s in full-time education may also be eligible for discounts, as may journalists, teachers, motoring association members and various others. Make sure you carry various types of ID to take advantage of any savings.

Multi-entrance tickets

Rome continues to offer a large and bewilderingly complicated array of discounted tickets, although the **Roma Pass** (see box p119) has done much to simplify matters.

Orto Botanico p133

Visitors who have already 'done' the Galleria Borghese are entitled to a discount if they visit the Galleria Doria Pamphili within five days. Show your ticket and you'll be charged €5.70 instead of €8.

Another option is the go.card, which offers hefty discounts at many of Rome's major sights, as well as shops, cinemas, galleries, museums, pubs and more. The card is available to anyone aged 14-26, and is valid for one year. As this guide went to press, prices and terms were being reorganised, and the go.card was becoming part of a Europe-wide discount network for under-26s. For latest updates, consult www.go.card.org.

The following tickets can be bought (cash only) at any of the museums and archaeological sites involved or at the APT (p187), where a €1.50 booking fee is charged. Booking is also possible online or by phone through the Pierreci agency (06 3996 7700, www.pierreci.it). Reductions apply to EU citizens aged between 18 and 25; under-18s enter free. **Archeologia Card** (€20, €10 concessions, valid 7 days) covers the Colosseum, Palatine, Baths of Caracalla, Palazzo Altemps, Palazzo Massimo alle Terme, Baths of Diocletian, Crypta Balbi and Tomb of Cecilia Metella. **Museo Nazionale Romano Card** (€6, €3 concessions, valid 3 days) covers Palazzo Massimo alle Terme, Baths of Diocletian, Palazzo Altemps and Crypta Balbi. **Appia Card** (€6, €3 concessions, valid 7 days) covers both the Baths of Caracalla and the Tomb of Cecilia Metella. **Capitolini Card** (€8.50, €6.50 concessions, valid 7 days) covers the Capitoline Museums and Centrale Montemartini.

Booking

Booking is mandatory for the Domus Aurea and the Galleria Borghese, though if you turn up midweek in low season, there's little chance of being turned away.

Booking is possible for many other sites and museums, but getting through to reservation phonelines can be difficult. Booking agencies for Rome's major sights are the Pierreci agency (06 3996 7700, www.pierreci.it) and Ticketeria (06 32 810, www.ticketeria.it). They add a booking fee to ticket prices.

Tours

The Enjoy Rome agency (p187) organises walking tours of the city.

For hop-on, hop-off bus tours around most of Rome's major sights, the 110 Open (06 4695 2252, www.tram busopen.com) leaves from bay D in the square in front of the Termini railway station every 15 minutes through the day. This can be combined with the Archeobus service (p156) along the Appian Way.

Eating & Drinking

With their strong culinary traditions and almost religious dedication to the ritual of the morning coffee in the bar *sotto casa* (downstairs), Romans long resisted modernisation, for the simple reason that they didn't see how it could possibly improve their lot. When the extremes of trendiness arrived, they were a flash in the pan. What Rome now does best is good quality and warm surroundings… but at prices which, since the arrival of the euro, now outstrip many other European capitals.

Eating

The 'traditional' Roman *osteria* – with its checked tablecloths, sawdust-strewn floors, *mamma* in the kitchen and jugs of wine frothing straight out of the barrel –

seemed for quite a while to be succumbing to the steel-and-glass anonymity of the international dining experience. But Romans have ever been ones to favour flavour over flashiness, quality over quirks. However cool a place looks, in the end, it's what's on its plates that counts.

That said, glam in Rome doesn't necessarily mean sham: on the contrary, the city now has many establishments to please foodie fashion victims.

Moreover, the style invasion had the admirable knock-on effect of de-romanticising the trat. If *mamma* is still in the kitchen, it's usually because she's truly a great cook; gone, even in many of the most humble eateries, are the 'traditional' astringent olive oil and paintstripper *vino della casa*.

The other positive note is the increasing variety of the Roman dining scene. Whereas before the choice was between posh restaurants, humble trattorias, or no-frills pizzerias, today there are wine bars, salad bars, gastropubs, designer restaurants and deli-diners. The traditional categories have broadened: posh restaurants are going minimalist; new trattorias are creative rather than humble; and the unchanging pizzeria has been shaken up by the advent of gourmet emporia like Dar Poeta. Only the ethnic and international scene still leaves much to be desired.

Eating in Rome used to be a bargain. Euro-fuelled price opportunism and inflation in general have put paid to this, though the bill will still compare favourably with a similar dining experience in London.

The ritual

The standard meal running order is: *antipasto* (hors-d'oeuvre), *primo* (usually pasta, occasionally soup), *secondo* (meat or fish) with an optional *contorno* (vegetables or salad, served separately) and *dolce* (dessert). It's perfectly normal, however, to order any combination of the above, such as pasta followed by a simple *contorno*. Fixed-price meals are a rarity, though top-flight establishments occasionally offer a *menu degustazione* (taster menu). Places offering a *menu turistico* should usually be avoided.

The wine list

Most top-of-the-range restaurants have respectable wine lists, but the more humble trattorias and osterias have a limited selection. House wine is often uninspiring, but there are sometimes exceptions. More establishments are now offering a selection of wine by the glass (*al bicchiere* or *alla mescita*).

SHORTLIST

Best new eateries
- L'Arcangelo (p154)
- Glass Hostaria (p140)
- Settembrini (p154)

Gourmet delights
- Agata e Romeo (p112)
- L'Altro Mastai (p78)
- Antico Arco (p141)
- Il Convivio Troiani (p78)
- Il Pagliaccio (p68)
- Trattoria Monti (p114)
- Uno e Bino (p121)

Cheap and cheerful
- Alfredo e Ada (p75)
- Café Café (p118)
- Cantina Cantarini (p96)
- Enoteca Corsi (p78)
- Luzzi (p118)
- Sora Margherita (p69)
- Tuttifrutti (p128)
- Zampagna (p129)

Pizza palaces
- Da Francesco (p78)
- Dar Poeta (p138)
- 'Gusto (p87)
- Lo Zozzone (p78)
- Remo (p128)

Bars of the moment
- Fluid (p78)
- Freni e Frizione (p139)
- Salotto 42 (p78)
- Société Lutèce (p79)

Cake heaven
- Dagnino (p112)
- La Caffettiera (p78)
- Forno del Ghetto (p69)

Gelato to remember
- Alberto Pica (p66)
- Il Gelato di San Crispino (p103)
- Pellaccia (p154)

Eating alfresco
- Ar Galletto (p66)
- Matricianella (p89)
- San Teodoro (p60)

Where every experience is a common path for tradition and innovation, for design and architecture, for spirit and music and for all that talks of a multisensorial attitude to life.

Prices and tipping

Places that add service to the bill as a fixed item are still in the minority, so it's usually safe to assume it isn't included. A good rule of thumb is to leave around five per cent in a pizzeria or humble trat, and around ten in upmarket places. If service has been slack or rude, feel justified in leaving nothing – and check the bill, as the occasional restaurateur becomes strangely innumerate when dealing with tourists.

Most restaurants accept credit cards (*carte di credito*). However, if there is no sticker on the door, ask.

In this guide, we have used the € symbol to indicate price ranges. € means an extraordinarily cheap meal at €15 or less; €€ is used for anything up to €30; €€€ for up to €45; €€€€ for over €45. These prices cover a three-course meal for one, without wine.

Children, women and etiquette

Taking children into restaurants – even the smartest – is never a problem in Rome. Waiters will usually produce a high chair (*un seggiolone*), and most kitchens will keep kids happy with *pasta al pomodoro* (with tomato sauce) or *pasta in bianco* (plain, to be dressed with oil or butter and parmesan). Note that, as a rule, pizzerias are your only option before 8pm.

Though attitudes are changing, women dining alone may still occasionally attract unwelcome attention – most of it in the form of frank stares. Single diners of either sex can have trouble getting a table in cheaper places at busy times: few proprietors want to waste a table that could hold at least four diners.

Some restaurants now ban mobile phones. Smoking is illegal in all restaurants, except those with special smoking areas; these are

Alfredo e Ada p75

rare. Getting a table at weekends becomes ever more difficult: it's always a good idea to book.

Pizza

Pizza romana is thin crusted, *pizza napoletana* fluffier. Both are found here but, either way, make sure it comes from a wood-fired brick oven (*forno a legna*); pizzas from electric ovens just don't have the same flavour. Pizza toppings are usually strictly orthodox. Where they depart from the norm, it's in the name of quality rather than exoticism: don't expect pineapple. Note also that pizza is an evening thing: very few places serve it at lunchtime.

Snacks

Roman snack culture lurks in unlikely places. Any humble *alimentari* (grocer's) will put your selection from the deli counter inside the ubiquitous white Roman roll, *la rosetta*, or a slice of *pizza bianca* (plain oiled and salted pizza base), eaten as is or filled. Bars are another good bet for sandwiches and rolls.

Vegetarian

The city has few bona fide vegetarian restaurants; but, even in traditional trattorias, waiters will no longer look blank when you say *non mangio la carne* ('I don't eat meat'). Many Roman dishes, from *penne all'arrabbiata* (pasta in a tomato and chilli sauce) to *tonnarelli cacio e pepe* (thick spaghetti with crumbly sheep's cheese and black pepper) to *carciofi alla giudia* (deep-fried artichokes), are meat-free.

Wine bars

Neighbourhood *enoteche* (wine shops) and *vini e olii* (wine and oil) outlets have been around in Rome since time immemorial. Recently a number of upmarket wine bars have also sprung up (see below), offering snacks and even full meals to go with their wines.

Pasticcerie and gelaterie

Most of Rome's *pasticcerie* (cake shops) are in fact bars (see below) where freshly baked goodies can be consumed in situ with a drink.

Many bars in Rome boast a well-stocked freezer cabinet with a sign promising *produzione artigianale* (home-made ice-cream). This is often a con, the goods having been produced on the premises but from milk and pre-prepared flavourings. It doesn't necessarily mean the ice-cream will be bad though – indeed, in some cases it can be very good – but you'll need to be selective. If the colours are too bright to be real, they probably aren't. When you've exhausted the *gelato* selection, you should sample a *grattachecca*. It's the Roman version of water ice, and consists of grated ice with flavoured syrup poured over it. The city was once full of kiosks selling this treat, but now only a handful remains. They are almost always on street corners and open in summer only.

Drinking

Cafés and bars

So faint is the line between 'bar' and 'café' in Rome that the words are generally interchangeable. Bars tend to be places where you knock back your *caffè* at the counter; cafés have seating and may offer a more extensive menu.

Besides coffee, which comes in many different forms, most bars also sell *cornetti* (croissants), *tramezzini* (sandwiches) and *pizza romana* (pizza base brushed with olive oil, sliced through the middle and filled). Sandwiches and pizza can be toasted (ask, *me lo può scaldare, per favore?*).

To accompany your snack, bars generally offer *spremute* (freshly squeezed juice) and some have *frullati* (fruit shakes) and *centrifughe* (juiced fruit) too. All offer a range of sodas, juices and mineral waters. Tap water (*acqua semplice*, *acqua dal rubinetto*) is free; a glass of still or sparkling mineral water (*acqua minerale naturale* or *gassata*) costs around 30¢-50¢. Also served are wine, beer and some liqueurs, including post-prandial *digestivi* such as *amaro* (bitters, infused aromatic liqueurs) and *limoncello* (lemon liqueur).

Pubs and enoteche

Many of Rome's traditional neighbourhood bottle shops have become, at the very least, charming places to grab a drink and a slice of the *vita romana*. At best, they are chic wine bars or bars with a *dopo cena* (after-dinner) scene, offering a wide variety of drinks and a beautiful crowd for people-watching.

Rome's pubs are divided between a handful of long-standing UK-style institutions and a host of newer casual joints.

Shopping

The days when Rome's shopping districts were a succession of family-owned businesses – whether those families were greengrocers or *haute couture* Fendis – are a thing of the past, and the busy retail artery here, as in all western cities, is increasingly dominated by chains. The visitor can take comfort, however, in the fact that the majority of the chains are Italian and thus – excepting such internationally known stalwarts as Benetton, Diesel and Stefanel – a breath of fresh air in their way.

Moreover, the chain/one-off ratio here remains more healthily tipped towards the latter than elsewhere, especially once you venture off the well-beaten track. Choose your area, choose your route (p48), and you'll find that shopping in the Eternal City can still have its own very Roman flavour.

Once, this flavour included shop assistants who seemed hell-bent on either ignoring or intimidating customers. Nowadays things have improved, but it wouldn't hurt to perfect the lines *mi può aiutare, per favore?* ('can you help me please?') and *volevo solo dare un' occhiata* ('I'm just looking'); that way, you're ready for any eventuality.

Where to go

The flagship stores of all the major Italian fashion names congregate in one of the world's great window-shopping areas, on and around via Condotti, at the foot of the Spanish Steps. So well-known, concentrated and easily found are they, we have not listed them in this guide: just

SHORTLIST

Fine foods

Cool for clothes

Wine heaven

Vinyl and DVDs

Shoes

Style at home

Reading matter

follow impeccably dressed matrons and Japanese tour groups and you'll discover them all. Then when so much glamour gets too much for you, nip down via Maria de' Fiori or via Bocca di Leone where some great unfamous names survive; or along eternally hip via del Babuino with its gracious antiques shops to the great, elegant breathing space of piazza del Popolo at its far end.

The major arteries are best avoided, although even dreary via Nazionale and via del Corso have occasional gems among the cheap and not-so-cheerful dross. East of the Vatican, via Cola di Rienzo offers a smarter high-street experience with a mixture of Italian and international names for a range of budgets (Diesel and Sisley, plus Miss Sixty and Onyx, home-grown chains for demanding teenagers and older girls who can't quite bear to leave adolescence behind) as well as some top food shopping at Castroni.

Moriondo & Gariglio p80

Cobbled side streets are infinitely more rewarding. Around campo de' Fiori and across the Tiber into Trastevere, the smell of coffee mingles with sawdust as you pass workshops where furniture is being made or restored. Around piazza Navona, wood-panelled herbalists and antiques stores mingle with the chic independent designers of via del Governo Vecchio.

A stone's throw from via Nazionale, Monti is bustling with hip independent design, plus a couple of good vintage stores.

Food and markets

Just as Romans favour smaller shops over sprawling department stores (partly, admittedly, because space is so tight in the *centro storico* that there are very few department stores to be found), so they will, if they can, opt for a market rather than a supermarket for buying fresh produce.

Most districts have a market, and most are open from 6.30 or 7am until about 1.30pm Monday to Saturday. The most central are in campo de' Fiori and in via del Lavatore, beneath the walls of the Quirinale Palace; neither of these

are cheap. The markets on via Cola di Rienzo, by piazza Vittorio, in Trastevere's piazza San Cosimato and in piazza Testaccio are more realistically priced.

If market bustle is too daunting, use one of the rash of mini-markets (GS Dì per Dì, PAM, Despar) that have recently sprung up around the *centro storico*; you'll have to look carefully, however, because many are concealed behind unobtrusive doors into grand *palazzi*.

The Monday to Saturday morning market in via Sannio, just outside the Roman walls by San Giovanni in Laterano, has vast volumes of cheap clothes. On Sunday mornings, via Portuense south from the Porta Portese gate becomes a huge, seething flea market. Watch out for pickpockets and sharp traders.

What to buy where

Fresh (as opposed to long-life) milk was once sold exclusively in bars which were also labelled *latteria*; you'll now find it in most grocers and all mini-markets. Bars are also the handiest places to pick up bottled water. (Note that bars are obliged by local by-laws to provide

ORIGINAL
Murano Glass

*A myriad of colors and gracious flowing crystal
forms bedeck the shelves of this lovely shop
that is just steps away from the Trevi Fountain.
One of the most important importers
of Murano glass at highly competitive prices,
the boutique carries original Ferrari and Ducati articles
and offers worldwide shipping with UPS and Fed EX.*

*Near Fontana di Trevi
Via del Lavatore, 33 and 87 a/b
Tel. 066789860*

e-mail: muranoglass@virgilio.it

parched passersby with a free glass of tap water – *acqua dal rubinetto*.)

Stamps can be bought only in post offices or at *tabacchi* (look for shops with a white T on a blue background outside) which are the only places where you can legally buy tobacco. *Tabacchi* are also where you play the lottery and buy bus tickets, though these latter are available from most *edicole* (newspaper kiosks) too.

Newspapers are only for sale at *edicole*, though magazines are also available in some large bookshops. The *IHT* and the international edition of the *Guardian* are on newsstands at dawn; other British papers arrive mid-morning; US papers turn up later in the day, or the following morning.

All medicines – even fairly innocuous over-the-counter ones such as aspirin – are sold exclusively in pharmacies.

Paying

The city echoes with complaints about the price hikes introduced along with the euro. Whether buying a banana, a bus ticket or a bikini, if you last came to Rome with the lira you'll notice that it ain't that cheap any more, although home-grown designer names are still a little easier on the wallet.

Bargaining belongs firmly at the flea-market: in shops, prices are fixed. In theory you should be given a *scontrino* (receipt) for any purchase you make. If you aren't, then ask for it: by law, shops are required to provide one. Major credit cards are accepted just about everywhere, although it's still worth checking before getting to the till.

If you have second thoughts, most shops will take back your hasty buy, giving you a full refund or a credit note; however, they are not obliged by law to do

this. Damaged goods, on the other hand, must be replaced by the shop.

Once you've paid for your purchases, you'll usually find that your change is placed on the counter rather than in your hand. You're not being cold-shouldered: that's just the way it's done here.

Tax rebates

Non-EU residents are entitled to a sales tax (IVA) rebate on all purchases of personal goods over €155, providing they are exported unused and bought from a shop with the 'Europe Tax Free' sticker. The shop will give you a receipt and a 'Tax Free Shopping Cheque', which should be stamped by customs before your departure from Italy. For further information see www.agenziadogane.it.

Opening times

An ever-increasing number of city-centre shops stay open non-stop from 9.30 or 10am to 7.30 or 8pm, Monday to Saturday, although many independent stores still stick to the traditional 1-4pm shutdown. In the centre, more and more stores also open on Sundays.

Times given in this book are winter opening hours; in summer (approximately June to September), shops that opt for long lunches tend to reopen later, at 5pm or 5.30pm, staying open until 8-8.30pm. Most food stores close on Thursday afternoons in the winter, and on Saturday afternoons in summer. The majority of non-food shops are closed Monday mornings.

Many shops shut down for at least two weeks each summer (generally in August) and almost all are shut for two or three days around the 15 August public holiday. If you want to avoid finding a particular shop *chiuso per ferie* (closed for holidays), be sure to ring ahead.

Nightlife

A recent increase in city council arts and culture funding has had a happy knock-on effect on Rome's once-comatose nightlife scene, propelling the Eternal City towards becoming a recognised European music and dance capital.

Of course it's early days yet, and you'll need our insider information to discover where it's all happening. But hit the right spots and you'll find that a small but vibrant young artistic community is taking hold. The *centri sociali* (mega-squats) are coming up against fewer bureaucratic obstacles in their quest to dish out cutting-edge entertainment, and dancing to the best international DJs and hearing the latest bands has become a far easier task.

A great night out

Romans are a relaxed lot when it comes to nightlife. The partying might start with an evening *aperitivo* and accompanying nibbles (see box p139), but the real business of Roman nights starts late and ends late… in the morning, that is. Concerts never kick off before 10.30pm – after 11pm at weekends – and most clubs close after 4am all week. However you spend the intervening hours, end your night out in the time-honoured way: with a hot *cornetto* (croissant) and cappuccino at one of the many bars that open into the morning.

Summer splendour

Rome gives its best in the summer: you'll be spoilt for choice between

Micca Club p114

Nightlife

S H O R T L I S T

Best new
- Fake (p130)
- Micca Club (p114)

Best for live music
- Auditorium (p103)
- Spazio Boario/Villaggio Globale (p131)
- La Palma (p121)
- Teatro Palladium (p131)

Best mainstream
- Goa (p130)
- La Maison (p80)
- La Saponeria (p131)

Best alternative
- Fake (p130)
- La Palma (p121)
- Locanda Atlantide (p121)
- Metaverso (p131)
- Rialtosantambrogio (p70)
- Spazio Boario/Villaggio Globale (p131)

Best for jazz
- Classico Village (p130)
- Gregory's (p100)
- La Palma (p121)

Best areas
- Monte Testaccio (pp129-131)
- Via Libetta and the vicinity (pp129-131)
- Via della Pace and the vicinity (p80)

Best gay
- Coming Out: outside on warm evenings (p118)
- Gay Village: summer, outside and mixed (p118)
- Hangar: men only (p114)
- Muccassassina: Fridays at Qube (p121)

Best late bars
- Freni e Frizione (p139)
- Salotto 42 (p78)
- Société Lutèce (p79)
- Stardust (p141)

DON'T MISS: 2007

festivals, concerts, open-air cinema, theatre and discos, most of which come under the EstateRomana umbrella. Programme details are posted in late spring; as the festival's website seems to change address each year, it's safest to access it through the city council website (www.comune.roma.it).

Festivals to look out for include the Cornetto Free Music Festival (www.cornettoalgida.com) in June and July in the Foro Italico tennis stadium; the huge Latin American-themed Fiesta (www.fiesta.it) event at the Capannelle race track near Ciampino airport from June to August; the Jazz and Image Festival (www.villacelimontana jazz.com) in the gorgeous cool of the Villa Celimontana park from mid-June to August; the Roma Incontra il Mondo (www.villaada. org) world music festival in the Villa Ada park from late June to mid-August; and the all-free, off-beat Enzimi music and theatre festival (www.enzimi.com) held in unlikely venues around the city in September.

Where it happens

Most of Rome's nightlife is concentrated around a few easily accessible areas. Testaccio is one of Rome's liveliest quarters: just walk around the Monte Testaccio area until you find the vibe you're after. South of Testaccio off the via Ostiense, the area around via Libetta teems with trendy clubs and is poised to become even more crowded: the arrival of the Roma Tre university campus here has livened up the neighbourhood no end, and there are plans to develop the whole district as an arts hub based around the former wholesale fruit and veg market (see box p130).

Fashionistas head for the *centro storico*: spend an evening sipping wine in campo de' Fiori or the *triangolo della Pace*, which is the area west of piazza Navona, and you're automatically ensconced in trendy Roman life. The university quarter of San Lorenzo is less pretentious: drinks are cheaper, and there's always something new going on. Trastevere has lovely alleys packed with friendly, crowded bars. If you're longing for company but your Italian's weak, this is the place for you: English is the *lingua franca*.

Getting through the door

Getting into alternative, down-to-earth venues is easy enough: just join the chaotic queues at the door. But making it inside fashionable mainstream clubs can be stressful, no matter how elegantly you're dressed. Intimidating bouncers will bar your way, asking 'can I help you?' when their role is clearly to make your life difficult. Persistence and patience will usually get you in eventually.

Clubs and discobars generally charge an entrance fee at weekends but not on weekdays; sometimes you have to pay for a *tessera* (membership card) on top of, or perhaps instead of, the entrance fee. *Tessere* may be valid for a season or for a month, and in some cases they're absolutely free. Admission tickets often include a 'free' drink, but you can expect the drinks you buy thereafter to be pricey. Another popular formula is to grant 'free' admission while forcing you to buy a drink (generally expensive). To get out again you have to hand a stamped 'drink card' to the bouncer, so hold on to whatever piece of paper they give you or you'll be forced to pay twice.

Where we have not specified an admission price, entry is free.

Clubbing

Rome still has a plethora of commercial venues playing what's basically Eurodisco, even though they dress it up as 'exotic' or 'lounge'. Established fashionable venues like Goa (p130) or La Maison (p80) can always be relied on to offer good-quality DJ sets, as can newcomer Micca Club (p114). For something alternative, check out what's on at places like La Palma (p121), Fake (p130) or the tiny Metaverso (p131).

Live music

Annual attendances at live music performances have begun to outstrip those for sporting fixtures in Rome, a phenomenon that the city council puts down to the Auditorium (see box p104), a multifunctional complex that hosts classical, pop, jazz and rock events by top artists from all over the world.

But Rome's new-found live music vocation has also been spurred by a spate of openings of smallish new live clubs, and by the reopening of the huge (and, sadly, soulless) PalaLottomatica events venue in the southern suburb of EUR and the cool Teatro Palladium (p131). Strangely, the thing that is still lacking in this oh-so-outdoors city is a major venue for open-air musical events.

Centri sociali

Centri sociali were born almost three decades ago when restless youths looking for spaces in which to indulge their passion for art, music and/or politics occupied disused public buildings and renovated them, turning them into concert halls, meeting points and cinemas. Some – such as the Spazio Boario/Villaggio Globale (p131) in the holding pens of an old slaughterhouse – are located in unique buildings. Over the years they've played a key role in the city's ongoing transition from historic showcase to vibrant European capital by bringing cutting-edge artists and musicians to Rome. With more on offer elsewhere, their importance now seems to be waning, but they still have plenty to offer at bargain prices (admission is usually €4-€6). Activities are listed in the Rome pages of *La Repubblica* daily.

Gay Rome

The times seem to be a-changing for gay men and lesbians in the Bel Paese, and gay life in the Italian capital is undoubtedly becoming more mainstream. Civil unions are up for debate (albeit in the teeth of fierce Vatican pressure) and flamboyant transgender campaigner Vladimir Luxuria (www.vladimirluxuria.it) comfortably won a parliamentary seat in the 2006 elections. New organisations, venues and facilities have appeared: the historic Mario

Mieli group (www.mariomieli.org) is now flanked by the hyperactive Di'Gay Project (www.digayproject.org), which is doing an excellent job of adding yet more goodies to the social shopping trolley.

Likewise, the gay market continues to diversify and cater for distinct clienteles, with restaurants, pubs, clubs and bars attracting punters of all ages. A proliferation of mixed one-nighters also mirrors the increasing number of places where men and women can have fun under the same roof. Or, for that matter, in the open air: one of the big successes in the Roman calendar is the Gay Village (p118) each summer.

Rome's gay venues open and close at an alarming rate, so a phone call to check that the establishment still exists is a good idea before you slip into something sexy.

To enter many venues you'll need an Arcigay Uno Club Card (www.arcigay.it). This costs €14 for annual membership, though a €7 monthly version is available for out-of-towners. The card can be bought at any venue that requires it and is valid throughout Italy. Some places, though, have their own membership cards, valid only at the individual venue. In most bars you're given a printed slip on which the bar staff tick off what you consume; you pay the total amount on leaving. Be careful not to lose your slip, or you'll have to pay a stiff penalty. Where we haven't specified an admission price, entry is free.

Information

For details of upcoming events, consult the listings magazines *Trovaroma* (it comes free with *La Repubblica* on Thursdays), *Roma C'è* (weekly, on newsstands) or the trendy *Zero6* (monthly, free in shops and pubs).

Arts & Leisure

Rome's performing arts scene has bounced back after many semi-comatose decades but its rebirth, for the time being, is a bit lop-sided. In one buzzing corner of a northern suburb, the Auditorium – Parco della Musica sells more tickets each year than London's South Bank or Sydney's Opera House complex. Now the rest of Rome eagerly awaits the trickle-down effect.

The current city administration is channelling unprecedented funds into arts initiatives, though it remains to be seen whether, as time goes on, these will emerge from their somewhat institutional shells. Inside the Villa Pamphili park in the western suburb of Monteverde,

the Casa dei Teatri (06 4543 0968, www.comune.roma.it/cultura) is a centre for drama and drama-making, with a stage, spaces for workshops and study, and a library. In a villa confiscated from a local mobster, the Casa del Jazz (viale di Porta Ardeatina 55, 06 704 731, www.casadeljazz.it) is making a name for itself as a venue for jazz performers from all over the world. While the Casa del Cinema (06 423 6019, www.casadelcinema.it) inside Villa Borghese is slowly improving its programme of screenings and other film-related activities.

Where to go

Delightfully, democratically eclectic, the Renzo Piano-designed

Auditorium p103

Auditorium has overcome the problem of filling seats with a programme that ranges from symphonies to soul, from jazz to jugglers, encouraging citizens who had never set foot in a classical music venue in their lives to think again about their relationship with the performing arts.

Opera fares less well, and despite two glorious locations, continues to languish. The drab exterior of the 19th-century Teatro dell'Opera gives way to a beautiful and harmonious interior with a good-sized stage and perfect acoustics. And in summer the breathtaking majesty of the Baths of Caracalla makes for a unique backdrop and setting for lyrical productions. It's the productions themselves that often lack any lustre.

Theatre and dance, too, are still badly in need of a kick-start. The Teatro Olimpico (06 326 5991, wwwteatroolimpico.it) tries bravely

S H O R T L I S T

Eclectic programming
- Auditorium – Parco della Musica (p103)
- Teatro Palladium (p131)

Gorgeous settings
- Baths of Caracalla: summer opera season (p122)
- Palazzo del Quirinale: Sunday morning concerts (p101)
- Roman theatre in Ostia Antica (p160)
- Teatro dell'Opera (p115)

Fabulous festivals
- Estate Romana (p38)
- RomaEuropa Festival (p35)

Sporting fixtures
- Football at the Stadio Olimpico (p103)
- Jogging in the Circus Maximus (p53)
- Rugby at the Stadio Flaminio (p103)

Stadio Olimpico p103

to entice contemporary dance acts to the city; the Teatro India (06 5530 0894, www.teatrodiroma.net) is more experimental than most; while the Teatro Palladium has an adventurous music and prose programme.

Theatre and dance listings can be found in the local press. See also the useful (Italian-only) website www.tuttoteatro.com.

Summer salvation

But the encouraging signs stop there, and an increasingly sophisticated local theatre-going public has learnt that salvation comes mainly with the warm weather and its festivals.

Most of Rome's summertime festivals take place under the Estate Romana umbrella. This overwhelming event-fest runs from June to September and provides such quantities of entertainment of all descriptions that it's difficult to know where to start. The city council website (www.comune.roma.it) posts a complete programme in the late spring.

The Auditorium offers a full summer programme of quality crowd-pleasers, including international orchestras and classical/popular crossovers in its outside *cavea* seating area.

Prestigious productions of both Greek and Roman classics, as well as concerts and ballets, are staged in the wonderfully preserved Roman theatre in the ruins of Ostia Antica (for information call 06 6840 00345) from mid July to mid August. The seats are stone, so make sure you bring your own cushion – and mosquito repellent.

In autumn, the RomaEuropa Festival (800 795 525, www.roma europa.net) swings into action. Promoted by the French Academy, its programme includes multimedia events, concerts and happenings in classic and alternative venues all over the city.

The silver screen

Rome is attempting to put itself on the international cinema map with its very own film festival, the first of which takes place in October 2006. However, the chances of its doing anything that Venice doesn't already do far better are slim.

Meanwhile, the voice dubbing industry retains its stranglehold in Italy and opportunities for seeing films in anything but Italian, though greatly increased over the past few years, remain relatively infrequent. Look out for 'v.o.' (*versione originale*) in newspaper listings.

The sporting life

If the arts don't move you, there is always sport, which for most Italians is synonymous with *calcio* (football or soccer).

Roma (www.asromacalcio.it) and Lazio (www.sslazio.it) both play at the Stadio Olimpico. Tickets can be bought directly from the Stadio Olimpico box office or online from either of the club's websites (ten per cent commission is added).

With Italy finally shuffling out of its role as standing joke in the Six Nations tournament, a strong rugby subculture is emerging too. Home games are played at the Stadio Flaminio (viale Tiziano, 06 3685 7309, www.federugby.it), which is near the Auditorium in the northern suburbs.

Teatro dell'Opera p115

Calendar

Christmas crib, piazza San Pietro

Rome's ten annual public holidays are positively measly next to the 150 days that those dedicated loafers, the ancient Romans, allowed themselves for R&R. Nowadays, a public holiday with clement weather is seen by many Romans as an opportunity for fleeing the city; it brings as many out-of-towners in.

The Roman calender offers many independently run arts festivals, especially during summer, and mayor Walter Veltroni has lavished even more cultural riches on the city in recent years. Watch local press and wall posters for the occasional huge free concert, and also for major exhibitions which tend to be announced shortly before the opening date. The cultural heritage ministry site (www.beniculturali.it) and the Rome city council site

(www.comune.roma.it) are also useful sources of information.

Dates highlighted in bold are public holidays.

September 2006

8-9 **La Notte Bianca**
www.lanottebianca.it
Rome's traditional all-night party lasts two nights this year, with a pre-event on 8 Sept and the real thing on 9 Sept (see box p39).

30-27 Nov **RomaEuropa Festival**
Various locations
www.romaeuropa.net
Rome's most prestigious performing arts festival.

October 2006

Ongoing RomaEuropa Festival

6-28 Feb 2007 **Bonnard-Matisse & the Mediterranean Sea**
Il Vittoriano

New Year in piazza Navona

13-21 **Cinema – Festa Internazionale di Roma**
Auditorium – Parco della Musica and other venues
www.romacinemafest.org
The first edition of Rome's new cinema festival (see box right).

Late Oct **Mostra dell'Antiquariato**
Via de' Coronari
Antique fair in this street packed with antique dealers.

November 2006

Ongoing RomaEuropa Festival, Bonnard-Matisse & the Mediterranean Sea

1-2 **All Saints/All Souls**
Cimitero del Verano, piazzale del Verano
Romans visit family graves; pope says mass in Verano cemetery on All Souls.

16-31 Dec **Laocoön: The Origins of the Vatican Museums**
Vatican Museums
Major exhibition celebrating the 500th anniversary of the founding of the Vatican Museums.

December 2006

Ongoing Bonnard-Matisse & the Mediterranean Sea, Laocoön: The Origins of the Vatican Museums

8 **Immacolata Concezione**
Piazza di Spagna
Pope conducts a service in piazza di Spagna; firemen place a wreath high up on the statue of the Virgin.

25-26 **Christmas & Boxing Day**
Nativity scenes in churches; Christmas fair in piazza Navona; pope's *Urbi et Orbis* message in St Peter's Square on 25.

31 **New Year's Eve**
Free concert in piazza del Popolo; much street partying.

January 2007

Ongoing Bonnard-Matisse & the Mediterranean Sea

1 **Capodanno (New Year's Day)**

Cine Roma

The first edition of **Cinema – Festa Internazionale di Roma** (left) was announced with much tub-thumping but few hard facts in January 2006. Welcomed by local cineastes, the festival is being viewed more sceptically by pundits. Opening only a fortnight after the end of the Venice–Toronto–San Sebastian logjam, Rome is unlikely to attract the most prestigious international premières.

According to the festival mission statement, however, this is not the organisers' intention. The festival is instead to 'reinvent the public for film festivals' by reaching out to ordinary Romans. The 14 world premières in the main competition will be judged by a popular jury of 50 local film-goers; another section will be devoted to the 'craft of the actor' – a deliberate rejection of the directorial slant of most 'serious' film festivals.

The festival will spread from its main HQ in the Auditorium – Parco della Musica (p103) to take in other cinemas in the Villa Borghese area, including the council-funded Casa del Cinema (p30). Each day's programme will culminate in a gala première of a big-budget film due to be released in Italy in the following months. Other sections include a catch-all sidebar called Extra, which promises 'an international selection of thematic and stylistic trends in filmmaking'; and Alice nella città (Alice in the City), aimed at children and young teens.
■ www.romacinemafest.org

6 Epifania – La Befana
Piazza Navona
Old witch brings Epiphany treats for all the children.

17 Sant'Eusebio
Sant'Eusebio, via Napoleone III
Animal lovers have pets blessed.

February 2007

Ongoing Bonnard-Matisse & the Mediterranean Sea

10-20 Carnevale
Around city centre
Kids dress up and throw confetti in the run-up to Lent.

March 2007

9 Feast of Santa Francesca Romana
Monastero Oblate di Santa Francesca Romana, via Teatro di Marcello 32 & 40
Rare opportunity to visit the medieval nunnery; Romans have cars blessed at Santa Francesca Romana church in Roman Forum.

Mid Mar Maratona della Città di Roma
Around city centre
www.maratonadiroma.it
There's a 5km fun-run for those not up to the whole 42km.

16 Palazzo Massimo alle Colonne
Corso Vittorio Emanuele 141
Once-a-year opening of the patrician palace, 8am-1pm.

19 Feast of San Giuseppe
Around via Trionfale
Partying and the eating of batter balls mark St Joseph's Day.

Late Mar Giornate FAI
Various locations
www.fondoambiente.it
For one weekend each spring institutional and private owners of historic properties to reveal their spectacular interiors, usually off-limits to the public.

Late Mar Mostra delle Azalee
Piazza di Spagna

Some 3,000 vases of azaleas decorate the Spanish Steps.

April 2007

1-9 Holy Week
Vatican, Colosseum
Palm Sunday mass at St Peter's; pope's *Via Crucis* at Colosseum on Good Friday.

8-9 Easter Sunday & Monday

Apr-May FotoGrafia
Various locations
www.fotografiafestival.it
International festival of photography.

Early-mid Apr Settimana della Cultura
www.beniculturali.it
For one week, admission to state-owned museums is free and many usually closed sites open.

21 Natale di Roma
Campidoglio
Rome celebrates its 2,760th birthday with an immense firework display.

25 Liberation Day

May 2007

Ongoing FotoGrafia

1 Primo Maggio
Piazza San Giovanni
www.primomaggio.com
Trade unions organise a huge, free rock concert for May Day.

Mid May-mid June Rome Literature Festival
Basilica di Massenzio, Roman Forum
Book presentations and readings, spread out over a month.

June 2007

Ongoing Rome Literature Festival

Early June-end Sept Estate Romana
Various locations
www.comune.roma.it
Piazze, palazzi and parks come alive with music, and films are shown on outdoor screens. Many events are free.

White Nights

There's no English translation for *notte bianca*. The French toss and turn over the course of a *nuit blanche*; Italians might count sheep, the national debt or their blessings; Anglo-Saxons just suffer 'a sleepless night'. As you lie in your noisy hotel room, you might be forgiven for thinking that every night is a *notte bianca* in Rome, which has to be one of the loudest, as well as the most vibrant, places on the planet.

But the city has institutionalised the inevitable and, in September, declares an unforgettable, wide-awake, sleepless-in-Rome sort of night, when nobody goes to bed and nobody tells you to shut up or stop partying; the city positively encourages its 2.6 million *cittadini* to get out on to the street and have some fun.

Paris began the fashion, and Rome soon latched on – as did other cities including Brussels and Madrid. Despite a tropical downpour and a national power

grid collapse during Rome's first edition in 2003, the initiative proved a massive success. So much so that one night isn't enough to contain the plethora of events planned for 2006, when the sleepless 'night' runs straight through from Friday 8 September until breakfast time on Sunday.

Museums and art galleries throw open their doors so you can admire Roman sculpture at 3am or stand on the torchlit battlements of Castel Sant'Angelo from which Tosca threw herself. You can watch the moon come up over the Colosseum, or greet the dawn listening to a whole symphony orchestra playing on the Gianicolo hill.

The city council website lists the literally hundreds of events that will be taking place, ranging from poetry readings to gallery openings, wine tastings, firework displays, tango spectaculars and rock concerts.

■ www.lanottebianca.it

23 Feast of San Giovanni
Piazza di San Giovanni in Laterano
Pope leads candlelit procession to St
John's basilica.

29 Santi Pietro e Paolo
Basilica di San Paolo fuori le Mura
Street fair outside St Paul's basilica
and mass at St Peter's for feast day
of Rome's patron saints.

July 2007

Ongoing Estate Romana

Mid July **Alta Roma**
Venues vary
www.altaroma.it
Collections by Roman and international
designers, showcased against historical
backdrops over four days.

Mid July **Festa di Noantri**
Piazza Santa Maria in Trastevere,
piazza Mastai
Two weeks of arts events, street
performances and fairground
attractions.

August 2007

Ongoing Estate Romana

1 Festa delle Catene
San Pietro in Vincoli, piazza
di San Pietro in Vincoli
Chains that bound St Peter are
displayed in a special mass.

**5 Festa della Madonna
della Neve**
Santa Maria Maggiore, piazza
Santa Maria Maggiore
A blizzard of rose petals flutters
down on festive mass-goers.

10 Notte di San Lorenzo
San Lorenzo in Panisperna,
via Panisperna 90
Nuns distribute bread and candles
on this, the night of shooting stars.

15 Ferragosto
Rome closes down for the feast of the
Assumption.

September 2007

Ongoing Estate Romana

7-6 Jan 2008 **Rothko**
Palazzo delle Esposizioni,
via Nazionale 194
www.palaexpo.it
Exhibition space reopens after an interminable refurbishment with a major
exhibit of works by Mark Rothko.

Early Sept **La Notte Bianca**
www.lanottebianca.it
Rome's all-night party (see box p39).

Sept-Nov **RomaEuropa Festival**
Various locations
www.romaeuropa.net
Rome's most prestigious performing
arts festival.

October 2007

Ongoing Rothko,
RomaEuropa Festival

Late Oct **Mostra dell'
Antiquariato**
Via de' Coronari
Held in a street that's packed with
antique dealers, this antiques fair lasts
a fortnight.

November 2007

Ongoing Rothko,
RomaEuropa Festival

1-2 All Saints/All Souls
Cimitero del Verano, piazzale
del Verano
Romans visit family graves; pope says
mass in Verano cemetery on All Souls.

December 2007

Ongoing Rothko

8 Immacolata Concezione
Piazza di Spagna
Pope conducts service in piazza di
Spagna; firemen place a wreath high
up on the statue of the Virgin.

25-26 Christmas & Boxing Day
Nativity scenes in churches; Christmas
fair in piazza Navona; pope's *Urbi et
Orbis* message in St Peter's Square on 25.

31 New Year's Eve
Free concert in piazza del Popolo; much
street partying.

Itineraries

Santa Maria in Aracoeli p59

The Seven Hills

Millennia of attrition and deposits have taken their topographical toll and Rome just isn't as hilly as it was. But the magnificent seven remain and today, as in antiquity, each retains its own flavour. In ancient times wheeled vehicles were banned during daylight and Romans thought nothing of covering all seven in a day, which is still feasible if you set off early and only make brief stops. But, unless you take a marathon-runner approach to sightseeing, we recommend taking two days, particularly if there's a good show on at the Scuderie. End your first day at the Capitoline Museums, then pick up next morning in the Roman Forum. And make the route easier by hopping on a bus every now and then.

There's something very stately – even awe-inspiring – about the airy **Quirinal (Quirinale) Hill** (p100), once the site of important Roman temples. These gave way to a papal summer palace that, when the low-lying Vatican proved insalubrious and too hard to defend against attack, became the pontiff's main residence. Italy's head of state still resides in Palazzo del Quirinale (p101), which overlooks a square graced by Imperial-era statues of the gods Castor and Pollux. The view over Rome's rooftops is stunning, especially at sunset.

The Quirinale has such an imposing aura that it is generally referred to simply as *il colle* (the hill). If a prime minister is reported to be 'going up the hill', his days in office are numbered; if 'the hill' issues a pronouncement, it will be

Roman Forum p58

something momentous. Visit on a Sunday morning if you want to go inside the presidential palace, but two glorious churches on via del Quirinale – Bernini's Sant'Andrea al Quirinale (p102) and Borromini's San Carlino alle Quattro Fontane (p101) – make the hike worthwhile at any time, as do the excellent exhibitions in the Scuderie Papali al Quirinale (p102).

Equally important in ancient times, and still the seat of a city council that stamps SPQR – *senatus populusque romanus* – on rubbish bins and drain covers, the **Capitoline (Campidoglio) Hill** (p52) is a 20-minute walk to the south (or take bus 40, 60, 64, 70 or 170 from nearby via Nazionale to piazza Venezia). There were temples here to Jupiter Capitolinus and Juno Moneta. The latter stood where the church of Santa Maria in Aracoeli (p59) now stands, at the head of a daunting flight of steps. The former was nearer piazza del Campidoglio, which still looks much as Michelangelo designed it in the 1530s. On the south-east side is Palazzo del Senatorio, Rome's city hall. Flanking this are the stately Capitoline Museums (p53). If you're gasping for a drink, the cafés in the museum (you can reach them without entering the museums) and half-way up the Vittoriano monument (p59) in **piazza Venezia** have marvellous views.

It's a glorious hike from here through the Roman Forum (p58) to the **Palatine (Palatino) Hill** (p57), where the movers and shakers of ancient Rome partied and schemed in their Hollywood-style spreads. It's a green and pleasant these days, offering more extraordinary views, plus ruins and the Museo Palatino, which charts Rome's birth pangs from the time of Remus and Romulus. (Keep your ticket to the Palatine: it's valid for the Colosseum too, allowing you to hop straight to the head of the interminable queue.) Picnicking isn't strictly allowed, but if you're discreet and take your rubbish home, this is a wonderful place to break for lunch.

As the crow flies, it's no distance at all from here to the Aventine and Caelian Hills; on the ground, it's more complicated. Exit from the Palatine on the via di San Gregorio (east) side. In ten minutes, you can walk to the Circus Maximus (p53); the Aventine rises beyond. (Buses 75 and 271 do the same route.) A flash district of wealthy *plebs* in Roman times, the green, exclusive **Aventine (Aventino) Hill** still has some of the Eternal City's highest real-estate prices. It also has a lovely park (Parco Savello, p122), a spectacular church (Santa Sabina, p123) and a keyhole, at the HQ of the Knights of Malta in piazza dei Cavalieri di Malta, through which you can see three sovereign territories: the Knights', Italy and the Vatican.

In the second century BC, a brave group of *plebs* holed up on the Aventine in an attempt to get parliamentary government restored to Rome. In 1924 150 politicians stormed out of Mussolini's lower house and 'withdrew to the Aventine' in protest over the assassination of an opposition MP. Italian MPs with their hackles up still threaten to head Aventino-wards from time to time, though it doesn't usually last for long.

The **Caelian (Celio) Hill** also lies across via di San Gregorio from the Palatine, and straight up the other side. Every bit as green as it was in ancient and medieval times, when it was filled with vegetable gardens and orchards, this hill is now rather wild and unkempt. However, you'll soon hit Clivio Scauro, which leads past the towering San Gregorio Magno (p117); Santi Giovanni e Paolo (p117), with its Roman street and homes excavated beneath; and on to the welcome cool of the verdant Villa Celimontana park (p115).

Backtrack to via di San Gregorio and pick up the 75 bus to reach the highest point of the **Esquiline (Esquilino) Hill** (p105), with basilica Santa Maria Maggiore (p111) on its apex. This spot has long been dominated by women: before Mary unseated her, the goddess Juno was worshipped here. The rather seedy Esquiline district, city hall tells us, is undergoing a renaissance. It still has some way to go. But the area around Santa Maria Maggiore definitely has its charms, especially in the shape of the sister churches of Santa Prassede and Santa Pudenziana (p112).

Tired of hills? Well, you'll miss nothing if you skip the **Viminal (Viminale) Hill**. For Italians, *il Viminale* is synonymous with the interior ministry, with all the implications of chaos and graft that have accrued to the term. The ministry's drear 1920s *palazzo* stands out from streets of similar drear *palazzi* only by virtue of its immense size. And there's not even a view to redeem it.

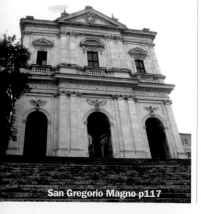

San Gregorio Magno p117

Sant'Ivo alla Sapienza p75

Rome & the Baroque

Baroque was what came after the severe classically inspired lines of the Renaissance: an extraordinary, exuberant reflection of the Catholic church having survived, and triumphed over, the Reformation.

In Rome, the baroque is all about Bs: Bernini, Borromini – great architects and sworn rivals – and Barberini, the millionaire aristocratic family (its heraldic symbol was a fat little honey bee) that produced Pope Urban VIII, who paid for most of it. Gian Lorenzo Bernini (1598-1680) – architect, sculptor, painter and playwright – designed half of baroque Rome: the exuberant, theatrical, grandiose half. Tortured, febrile Francesco Borromini (1599-1667), with his twisting architectural forms, ended up killing himself, but only after he had designed some of the greatest ecclesiastical buildings of the 17th century.

The following itinerary can be done in one long, rushed day, but splitting it over two days – aiming to get as far as San Carlino on the first and leaving the second for a leisurely stroll around the Palazzo Barberini and St Peter's – may prove more satisfying.

In either case start at **Piazza Navona** (p73), which is the great set piece of baroque Rome – an elongated oval, plonked on top of a Roman running track built by the Emperor Diocletian. The backdrop for a hundred movies, the piazza is one of the most heart-stoppingly romantic places in the universe. A market place in medieval times, the piazza was earmarked for

Fountain of the Four Rivers p73

development by another powerful baroque dynasty, the Doria Pamphilis, who settled a family member on the throne of St Peter as Innocent X. Their crest has a dove holding an olive twig: there's one atop Bernini's central obelisk extravaganza; one on the Doria Pamphilis' palace (now the Brazilian embassy); and many more on street furniture around the piazza.

Local lore holds piazza Navona to be the fulcrum of Bernini and Borromini's rivalry. At the square's centre, Bernini's magnificent Four Rivers fountain symbolises the four corners of the then-known world to which the sculptor's patrons, the Jesuits, were sending missionaries. It stands directly in front of Borromini's glorious church of Sant'Agnese in Agone (p73). On the church side of the fountain, a figure representing the Americas raises his arm as if to shield his eyes from the façade before him. The story is, in fact, nonsense: Bernini's fountain was finished before Borromini's church was planned, but legend has scant time for chronology.

East of the piazza, at the end of a beautiful porticoed courtyard off **corso Rinascimento**, stands Borromini's tiny, hallucinogenic church of Sant'Ivo alla Sapienza (p75). If the erratic opening hours prevent you peeking inside, console yourself with a coffee at nearby Bar Sant'Eustachio (p76).

At the southern end of corso Rinascimento stands the great bulk of Sant'Andrea della Valle (p63), by Carlo Rainaldi, Carlo Fontana and Borromini's uncle, Carlo Maderno – architects who bridged the gap between Renaissance and baroque.

Beyond bus-choked largo Argentina, **via del Plebiscito** leads to the vast, ornate church of Il Gesù (p61), the Jesuit HQ. Bernini would drop by here to pray before going to work in piazza Navona. If you skipped coffee, bolster your blood-sugar level with a hearty lunch on via del Gesù at the Enoteca Corsi (p78).

Turn right at the end of via del Gesù and then head north on Via Sant'Ignazio into the perfect, theatrical **piazza Sant'Ignazio**. Here stands Sant'Ignazio di Loyola (p75), a masterpiece by Andrea Pozzo. The church has a famous trompe l'oeil ceiling, and an ingenious circular canvas to disguise the fact that the proposed dome was never built. Clued-in visitors bring mirrors to examine the flying saints and cherubs without straining their necks.

Follow via Caravita to via del Corso, cross the road, and follow the tourists streaming through the narrow alleys towards the **Trevi Fountain** (p102), built long after Bernini and Borromini were dead, and the baroque declining into the rococo. Bernini was commissioned to build what was to be Rome's biggest and most spectacular fountain, but plans were put on hold by the death of Urban VIII; architect Niccolo Salvi finally got the job, and Clement XIII the satisfaction of unveiling it in 1762. Rome's finest ice-cream is served at Il Gelato di San Crispino (p103), just a couple of blocks away.

The water that supplies the Trevi also supplied the Palazzo del Quirinale (p101) on the hill above. Climb **via della Dataria** to admire the grand façade and the toy-town uniforms of the presidential horseguards. Bernini's splendid ceremonial entrance was added to what is essentially a Renaissance palace.

Across the square is the jewel-like Sant'Andrea al Quirinale (p102), another Bernini masterpiece, but a tiny one dashed off while the architect was busy with St Peter's. **Via del Quirinale** leads down the side of the palace to glorious San Carlino alle Quattro Fontane (p101). This was Borromini's first major commission, and the building he was most proud of. On this minuscule hilltop site, Borromini created an illusion of vast height, width and depth with a cunning, squashed oval dome, tapering columns and tricky coffering.

Via delle Quattro Fontane drops sharply north-west past the family seat of Urban VIII. Palazzo Barberini (p101) is now home to one of the state's finest collections of baroque art, with astonishingly life-like family portrait busts by Bernini. Maderno drew up the original palace plans and Bernini designed the rectangular staircase. Borromini took up the challenge and produced an even more elegant oval staircase. But the truly jaw-dropping treasure of the palace is on the ceiling of the magnificent throne room: Pietro da Cortona's *Triumph of Divine Providence*, one of the largest paintings in the world. The road ends in **piazza Barberini**, at the centre of which sits Bernini's Triton fountain.

The 62 bus goes from here to St Peter's. En route, in **corso Vittorio Emanuele**, it passes Chiesa Nuova (p71) with more massive works by Pietro da Cortona. The undulating brickwork façade of the Oratorio dei Filippini was designed by Borromini. In front of **St Peter's** (p147) is Bernini's ultimate stage set: the colonnade, with its triple rows of columns arranged in such a way that they seem to dissolve into a single line. All around, Barberini bees buzz on what, in the end, became Bernini's basilica.

ITINERARIES

Shop till You Drop

Rome's main shopping arteries – via Nazionale, via del Corso, via Cola di Rienzo – are crammed with retail outlets, which may be a welcome change from the brands you're used to (if, of course, you ignore the odd Body Shop/Zara/Benetton) but still exude that samey high-street feel.

The grid of streets between the Spanish Steps and via del Corso offers something a little different, if only in terms of atmosphere and price tags: the Big Guns of Italian fashion – from Prada to Dolce and Gabbana, from Fendi to Valentino – are all here.

The one-off and the quirky, the fascinating and the far-out, however, lurk down narrower alleys and in further-flung areas… parts of the city that are no less densely trafficked, of course, but do, undoubtedly, have more of a special, Roman feel.

Whether you'll manage the following itinerary in a morning depends on your stamina, and how long you spend in each shop. And remember: if it's Monday morning, forget it. Most of Rome's non-food shops are shut.

Bus-choked **largo Argentina** is a good place to begin some alternative shopping. First, get your bearings: the huge Feltrinelli bookshop on this square has maps and books in English. Cut south from here through the Ghetto to the **Forno del Ghetto** (p69) for a piece of *pizza* – no, not what you think of as pizza, but instead a thick slab of crumbly cake packed with dried and candied fruits: nibbled en route, it will keep energy levels high.

Heading west, cross via Arenula and take **via dei Giubbonari** – the medieval 'street of the jacket-makers' and still packed with

clothing retailers of all styles
and for all budgets. The road
ends in **campo de' Fiori**, where
the morning produce market
(Mon-Sat) is Rome's most central
and colourful, though definitely
not its cheapest.

From here, it's a short hop to
via dei Pettinari to check out
the wonderful shoes in glorious
colours at Borini (p69), or to **via
Monserrato** where the Tuscan-
country-meets-slick-urban designs
of Ilaria Miani (p69) stand out
among the slew of elegant interior
design and antique shops.

North out of campo de' Fiori,
take a deep breath and brave the
streaming traffic to cross corso
Vittorio, and make for **via del
Governo Vecchio**. Along this
narrow alley are very chic second-
hand clothes emporia, over-the-top
costume-jewellery makers and
some of Rome's most interesting
small-scale fashion designers. Look
out in particular for Arsenale (p79)
and Maga Morgana (p80); neither
of them is cheap but they're both

good places to get yourself an
outfit that's destined to become
a party conversation piece.

Via del Governo Vecchio segues
into via dei Banchi Nuovi which,
at its river end, hits **via dei
Coronari**, the centre of Rome's
antique trade. It's high-end stuff,
but the furniture and geegaws,
mixed with tiny shops selling
fabulous fabric, make for great
window-shopping as you strike
out west towards the top end of
piazza Navona.

For an abrupt change of mood,
and a taste of retail opportunities
offered by neighbourhood Rome,
pick up a 30 Express bus (heading
south) and stay on it until you
reach via Marmorata. Welcome to
Testaccio. Now *di moda*, Testaccio
was considered very hard-bitten a
couple of decades ago. Its produce
market in **piazza Testaccio**
(early-1.30pm Mon-Sat) is vibrant
and earthy... and considerably
cheaper than campo de' Fiori. The
north-western aisle of the market
has been colonised by shoe stalls:
mixed in with the tat are sales
samples and last year's models
of major footwear names, all at
extremely low prices. There are
more men's shoes on Saturdays.
In the surrounding streets, more
shoe shops have sprung up, making
this Rome's footwear hub.

By this time you'll be dropping.
Take heart: Testaccio is full of
excellent eateries. Alternatively,
make a pilgrimage to one last shop:
Volpetti (p129) is a temple to Italian
gastronomic delicacies, and the
perfect place to put together
ingredients for a truly gourmet
picnic. The gardens in **piazza
Santa Maria Liberatrice** are a
pretty, noisy, bustling spot in which
to eat it. And if the mother ship is
shut by the time you reach it, you
can always nip round the corner to
Volpetti's snack bar in via Volta.

ITINERARIES

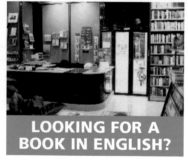

Rome by Area

Colosseum

Centro

Centro archeologico

This is where Rome began: in the space of a few centuries, a cluster of grass huts had grown into the heart of a superpower extending from Spain to Asia Minor. It was here that that the Republic – and later the Empire – was run and justice administered in grandiose buildings around richly decorated public squares (the **Roman Forum**); that magnificent palaces (the **Palatine**) overlooked the hustle and bustle of life below; that imposing temples dominated the most sacred of Rome's seven hills (the **Capitoline**); and that successive emperors strove to assert their own particular importance and munificence (the **Imperial Fora**). Here, too, emperors kept public discontent at bay with gory diversions and heart-stopping sports at the **Colosseum** and the **Circus Maximus**.

The Capitoline (Campidoglio) was the site of the two major temples, to Jupiter Capitolinus – chunks of which are visible inside the **Capitoline Museum** – and Juno Moneta, 'giver of advice'. The latter, where the church of **Santa Maria in Aracoeli** now stands, housed the sacred Capitoline geese, whose honking raised the alarm when the Gauls attacked Rome in 390 BC.

The gorgeous piazza that now tops the Capitoline was designed in the 1530s by Michelangelo; the best approach is via the steps called the *cordonata*, also by Michelangelo, with two giant Roman statues of the mythical twins Castor and Pollux at the top. The building directly opposite is Rome's city hall; on either side are the *palazzi* housing the Capitoline museums. The equestrian statue of Marcus Aurelius in the centre is a computer-generated copy; the second-century gilded bronze original is inside the museum.

The *cordonata* leads down to piazza Venezia. Dominating this dizzying roundabout is the **Vittoriano**, a piece of nationalistic kitsch that outdoes anything dreamed up by the ancients.

Sights & museums

Capitoline Museums
Piazza del Campidoglio 1 (06 6710 2071/www.museicapitolini.org). **Open** 9am-8pm Tue-Sun. **Admission** €8. **Map** p54 A2 ❶

Flanking Michelangelo's piazza del Campidoglio, the Capitoline Museums (Musei capitolini) are the oldest museums in the world, opened to the public in 1734, though the collection was begun in 1471 by Pope Sixtus IV. His successors continued to add ancient sculptures and, later, paintings.

Entry is through the Palazzo dei Conservatori (to the right at the top of the steps). The courtyard contains some parts of a colossal statue of Constantine that originally stood in the Basilica of Maxentius in the Roman Forum. Inside, ancient works – which include Rome's famous symbol, the much-reproduced fourth-century BC Etruscan she-wolf and suckling twins (added in the Renaissance) – are mixed with statues by the baroque genius Gianlorenzo Bernini.

NEW In a smart new section on the first floor, the second-century statue of Marcus Aurelius has finally been given a suitably grand space. You can also see chunks of the temple of Jupiter here.

The second-floor gallery contains paintings by greats such as Titian, Tintoretto and Caravaggio. Across the piazza (or through the underground Tabularium, the ancient Capitoline archive building), the Palazzo Nuovo houses one of Europe's greatest collections of ancient sculpture, including the coy *Capitoline Venus*, the *Dying Gaul* and countless portrait busts of emperors and their families.

Circus Maximus
Via del Circo Massimo. **Map** p54 B4 ❷

Little of the actual structure remains at the Circus Maximus, ancient Rome's major chariot-racing venue, but it's still possible to visualise the flat base of the long basin as the racetrack, and the sloping sides as the stands. At the southern end are some brick remains of the original seating (the tower is medieval). The oldest and largest of Rome's ancient arenas, the Circus Maximus hosted chariot races from at least the fourth century BC. It was rebuilt by Julius Caesar to hold as many as 300,000 people. Races involved up to 12 rigs of four horses each; the circus was also flooded for mock sea battles.

Colosseum
Piazza del Colosseo (06 700 5469/ 06 3996 7700). **Open** 9am-sunset daily. **Admission** (incl Palatine) €9; €6.50 reductions. No credit cards. **Map** p54 C3 ❸

Notes: If the queue is daunting, buy your tickets at the Palatine and enter directly. During special exhibitions, admission is €11.

Built in AD 72 by Emperor Vespasian, il Colosseo hosted gory battles between combinations of gladiators, slaves, prisoners and wild animals of all descriptions. Properly known as the Amphitheatrum Flavium, the building was later known as the Colosseum not because it was big, but because of a gold-plated colossal statue, now lost, that stood alongside. The arena was about 500 metres (a third of a mile) in circumference and could seat over 50,000 people. Nowhere in the world was there a larger setting for mass slaughter. In the 100 days of carnage held to inaugurate the amphitheatre

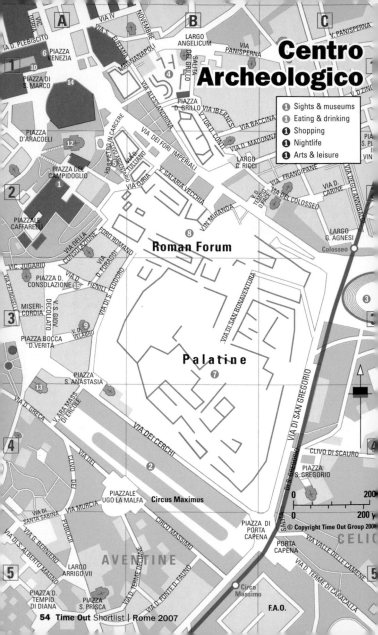

Centro Archeologico

A   **B**   **C**

- ❶ Sights & museums
- ❶ Eating & drinking
- ❶ Shopping
- ❶ Nightlife
- ❶ Arts & leisure

Roman Forum

Palatine

Circus Maximus

AVENTINE

© Copyright Time Out Group 2006

in AD 80, some 5,000 beasts perished. Sometimes, animals got to kill people: a common sentence in the Roman criminal justice system was *damnatio ad bestias*, where miscreants were turned loose, unarmed, into the arena. After the fall of the Roman Empire authorities banned games here and the Colosseum became a quarry for stone and marble to build Roman *palazzi*. The pockmarks on the Colosseum's masonry date from the ninth century, when the lead clamps holding the stones together were pillaged. This irreverence didn't stop until the mid 18th century, when the Colosseum was consecrated as a church.

Standing beside the Colosseum, Constantine's triumphal arch was erected in AD 315, shortly before the emperor abandoned the city for Byzantium.

Imperial Fora & Trajan's Market

Visitors' centre *via dei Fori Imperiali (06 679 7786/06 679 7702)*. **Open** *Visitors' centre* 9.30am-6pm daily. No credit cards. **Map** p54 B1 ❹

Trajan's Market *via IV Novembre 94 (06 679 0048/06 679 1620)*. **Open** (lower site only) 9am-2pm Tue-Sun. **Admission** €3. No credit cards. **Note**: Excavations and restoration work mean that timetables for opening and guided tours of this area can vary from week to week, and parts can be closed off temporarily. However, all the fora and much of Trajan's market are visible from the pavement of via dei Fori Imperiali.

Excavations carried out in the Imperial Fora in the 1990s opened up massive amounts of archaeological space, but the work is far from over. The great hemicycle in the upper area of Trajan's markets will become the Museo dei Fori Imperiali, a bells-and-whistles multimedia museum.

As existing fora became too small to cope with the growing city, emperors combined philanthropy with propaganda and created new ones of their own to what is now known collectively as the *Fori imperiali* (Imperial Fora).

Along the via dei Fori Imperiali (sliced cavalierly through the ruins by Mussolini) are five separate fora, each built by a different emperor.

Most impressive is Trajan's forum, at the piazza Venezia end of via dei Fori Imperiali. Laid out in the early second century AD, it is dominated by Trajan's column (AD 113), with detailed spiralling reliefs showing victories over Dacia (modern-day Romania). The rectangular foundation to the south of Trajan's column, where several imposing granite columns still stand, was the basilica Ulpia, an administrative building.

The most distinctive feature of the forum complex is the multi-storey brick crescent to the south-east of the basilica Ulpia. This great hemicycle, forming part of the *Mercati di Traiano* (Trajan's market), was built in AD 107. Entering from via IV Novembre, the first room is the Great Hall, a large space possibly used for the corn dole in antiquity. To the south of the Great Hall are the open-air terraces at the top of the great hemicycle. To the east of the Great Hall, stairs lead down to the so-called via Biberatica, an ancient street flanked by well-preserved shops. The shops here were probably *tabernae* (bars), hence the name (*bibere* is Latin for 'to drink'). More stairs lead down through the various layers of the great hemicycle, where most of the 150 shops or offices are still in perfect condition, many with doorjambs still showing the grooves where shutters were slid into place when the working day was over.

Across the road from Trajan's forum, Caesar's forum was the first of the *Fori imperiali*, built in 51BC by Julius Caesar. Three columns of the Venus Generatrix temple have been rebuilt. Back on the same side as Trajan's forum, August's forum was inaugurated in 2 BC, where three columns from the temple of Mars Ultor still stand, as does the towering wall separating the forum from the sprawling Suburra slum behind. Nerva's forum

ROME BY AREA

GiNa
eat & drink

restaurant

italian bistrò

wine & cocktail bar

tea room

sweets & ice cream

pic nic basket

music lounge

private party

Via San Sebastianello 7/A
(Next to Spanish Steps)
www.ginaroma.com
tel. 0039.06.678.02.51
Open 7/7 no stop 11 a.m 11 p.m

GiNa

eat & drink

(AD 97) lies mainly beneath via dei Fori Imperiali. On the south side of the road, Vespasian's forum (AD 75) was home to the temple of peace, part of which is now incorporated into the church of Santi Cosma e Damiano. Maps placed on a wall here by Mussolini show how Rome ruled the world.

Mamertine Prison

Clivio Argentario 1 (06 679 2902).
Open 9am-5pm daily. **Admission** donation expected. **Map** p54 A2 ⑤
Anyone thought to pose a threat to the security of the ancient Roman state was thrown into the Mamertine Prison, a dank, oppressive underground dungeon, squashed between the Roman Forum and the present-day via dei Fori Imperiali. The prison's most famous inmates, legend has it, were Saints Peter and Paul. Peter head-butted the wall in the ground-level room leaving his features impressed on the rock, and caused a miraculous well to bubble up.

Museo di Palazzo Venezia

Via del Plebiscito 118 (06 6999 4243).
Open 8.30am-7.30pm Tue-Sun.
Admission *Museum* €4; €2 reductions. *Exhibitions* varies.
Map p54 A1 ⑥

This collection contains a hotchpotch of anything from terracotta models by baroque sculptor Gianlorenzo Bernini for the angels that now grace Ponte Sant'Angelo, to medieval decorative art. Major exhibitions are staged regularly; they often give access to the huge Sala del Mappamondo, used by Mussolini as his office.

The Palatine

Via di San Gregorio 30/piazza di Santa Maria Nova 53 (06 699 0110/ 06 3996 7700). **Open** 9am-sunset daily. **Admission** (incl Colosseum) €9; €6.50 reductions. No credit cards.
Map p54 B3 ⑦
Note: When special exhibitions are being held in the Colosseum, admission costs €11.

Legend relates that a basket holding twin babes Romulus and Remus was found in the swampy area near the Tiber to the west of here. In 753 BC, having murdered his brother, Romulus scaled the Palatine hill and founded Rome. In fact, archeological evidence shows that proto-Romans had settled on Il Palatino a century – or maybe much more – before that. Later, the Palatine became the Beverly Hills of

The view from the Campidoglio

ROME BY AREA

the ancient city, where the movers and shakers built their palaces. With Rome's decline it became a rural backwater ; in the 1540s, much of the hill was bought by Cardinal Alessandro Farnese, who turned it into a pleasure villa and garden. His gardens – the Horti farnesiani – are still a lovely leafy place to wander on a hot day. Beneath the gardens is the Cryptoporticus, a semi-subterranean tunnel built by Nero. South and south-east from the gardens are the remains of vast imperial dwellings, including Emperor Domitian's Domus Augustana, with what may have been a private stadium in the garden. Next door, the Museo Palatino charts the history of the Palatine from the eighth century BC.

Roman Forum

Entrances from via dei Fori Imperiali, piazza del Colosseo & via di San Teodoro (06 700 5469/06 3996 7700). **Open** 9am-1hr before sunset daily. **Admission** free. **Map** p54 B2 ❽

During the early years of the Republic, this was an open space with shops and a few temples, and it sufficed; but by the second century BC ever-conquering Rome needed to give an impression of authority and wealth. Out went the food stalls; in came the law courts, offices and immense public buildings with grandiose decorations. The *Foro romano* remained the symbolic heart of the empire, and emperors continued to embellish it until the fourth century AD. Entering from the Colosseum, the Forum is framed by the Arch of Titus (AD 81), built to celebrate the sack of Jerusalem. To the right are the towering ruins of the basilica di Massenzio, completed in 312. Along the via Sacra, the Forum's high street, are (right) the great columns of the Temple of Antoninus and Faustina; the giant Basilica Emilia (right) – once a bustling place for administration, courts and business; the Curia, the home of the Senate, which was begun in 45 BC by Julius Caesar; and the Arch of Septimius Severus, built in AD 203. Beside the arch are the remains of an Imperial rostra, from which Mark Antony supposedly asked the Romans to lend him their ears.

San Giorgio in Velabro

Via del Velabro 19 (06 6920 4534). **Open** 10am-12.30pm, 4-6.30pm daily. **Map** p54 A3 ❾

This austere little church of the fifth century has 16 Roman columns pilfered from the Palatine and the Aventine hills in its nave, and pieces of an eighth- or ninth-century choir incorporated into the walls. In the apse is a much-restored 13th-century fresco of St George. Outside to the left is the Arco degli Argentari, built in AD 204; it was a gate on the road between the main Forum and the *forum boarium* (cattle market) along which moneychangers (*argenteri*) plied their trade.

San Marco

Piazza San Marco (06 679 5205). **Open** 8am-12.30pm, 4-7pm daily. **Map** p54 A1 ❿

Founded, tradition says, in AD 336 on the site of the house where St Mark the Evangelist stayed, this church was rebuilt by Pope Paul II in the 15th century, when neighbouring Palazzo Venezia was constructed. San Marco then gained its baroque look in the mid 18th century. Remaining from earlier manifestations are the 11th-century bell tower and, in the apse, a ninth-century mosaic of Christ. The portico has the gravestone of Vanozza Catanei, mother of the notorious Cesare and Lucrezia Borgia.

San Nicola in Carcere

Via del Teatro di Marcello 46 (06 6830 7198). **Open** 7am-noon, 4-7pm Mon-Sat; 9.30am-1pm Sun, holidays. **Map** p54 A3 ⓫

The 12th-century San Nicola was built over three Roman temples, dating from the second and third centuries BC; a guide (donation appreciated) takes you down to these. On the outside of the church, six columns from the Temple of Janus can be seen on the left; the ones on the right are from the Temple of Spes (Hope).

Roman Forum

Santa Maria in Aracoeli

Piazza del Campidoglio 4 (06 679 8155). **Open** 9am-12.30pm, 2.30-5.30pm daily. **Map** p54 A2 ⑫

Up a daunting flight of 120 marble steps, the romanesque Aracoeli ('altar of heaven') stands on the site of an ancient temple to Juno Moneta. The current basilica-form church was designed in the late 13th century. The first chapel on the right has scenes by Pinturicchio from the life of St Francis of Assisi's helpmate St Bernardino (1486). To the left of the altar, a round chapel contains relics of St Helena, mother of the Emperor Constantine. At the back of the transept, the Chapel of the Holy Child contains a venerated disease-healing *bambinello*, which is often whisked to the bedside of moribund Romans.

Santa Maria in Cosmedin & the Mouth of Truth

Piazza della Bocca della Verità 18 (06 678 1419). **Open** 9am-5pm daily. **Map** p54 A4 ⑬

Built in the sixth century and enlarged in the eighth, Santa Maria was embellished with a glorious Cosmati-work floor, throne and choir in the 11th-13th centuries. The altar is a Roman bathtub; in the sacristy is a fragment of an eighth-century mosaic of the Holy Family, brought here from the original St Peter's. The church is better known as the *bocca della verità* (the mouth of truth), after the great stone mask of a man with a gaping mouth on the portico wall – in fact, it is probably an ancient drain cover. Anyone who lies while their hand is in the mouth will have that hand bitten off, according to legend. It was reportedly used by Roman husbands to determine the fidelity of their wives. On the little green opposite stand the first-century BC temples of Hercules (round) and Portunus (square).

Vittoriano

Piazza Venezia (06 699 1718). **Open** *Monument* 9.30am-4pm daily. *Museo Centrale del Risorgimento* 9.30am-6.30pm daily. *Complesso del Vittoriano* (06 678 0664; for exhibitions only) 9.30am-7.30pm Mon-Thur; 9.30am-11.30pm Fri-Sat; 9.30am-8.30pm Sun. **Admission** free. *Exhibitions* varies. No credit cards. **Map** p54 A1 ⑭

Variously known as 'the wedding cake' and 'the typewriter', this eyesore of a monument to united Italy, constructed between 1885 and 1911, contains exhibits on the struggle to unify the country, and stages good temporary art shows. Best of all, you can climb to the top for a 360-degree view over Rome from the only spot where the spectacle isn't marred by the Vittoriano itself. You can also admire charmingly kitsch art nouveau propaganda mosaics in the colonnade. There's a very pleasant outdoor café halfway up.

Event highlights The Complesso will host an exhibition entitled 'Bonnard, Matisse and the Mediterranean' from 6 Oct 2006 to 28 Feb 2007.

Eating & drinking

San Teodoro

Via dei Fienili 49-51 (06 678 0933). **Meals served** 1-3.30pm, 7.45pm-12.30am Mon-Sat. Closed 1wk Dec; 2wks Jan; 1wk Easter; 10 days Aug. **€€€€. Map** p54 A3 ⑮

Of a summer's evening, there are few better places in Rome for an alfresco meal than this seafood-oriented restaurant around the back of the Forum, in the prettiest of residential squares. Come prepared to splash out, though. Some dishes are pure *cucina romana*; others, like the *tonnarelli San Teodoro* (with shrimps, courgettes and cherry tomatoes) are lighter and more creative.

The Ghetto & Campo de' Fiori

The area that stretches south from busy corso Vittorio Emanuele (aka corso Vittorio) to the Tiber has tightly wedged buildings, narrow cobbled alleys and a mixture of graceful Renaissance columns and chunky blocks of ancient travertine: the perfect backdrop to everyday Roman street life.

It's an area of contrasts: campo de' Fiori – with its lively morning market and livelier partying

crowds at night – stands next to solemn, dignified piazza Farnese with its grand Palazzo Farnese, partly designed by Michelangelo. Top-end antique dealers in via Giulia rub along with craftsmen plying their trades in streets with names (via dei Leutari – lutemakers; via dei Cappellari – hatmakers) that recall the jobs of their medieval ancestors. In ancient times, this was the *Campus martius* (field of war), where Roman males did physical jerks to stay fighting fit. Packed with theatres, it was also where ancient Romans headed for low-brow fun. After barbarian hordes rampaged through Rome in the fifth and sixth centuries, the area fell into ruin. By the late Middle Ages, it was densely populated and insalubrious. But when the pope made the Vatican – just across the river – his main residence in the mid 15th century the area's fortunes improved.

In the south-east, largo Argentina is a polluted transport hub with a chunk of ancient Rome at its heart: visible when you peer over the railings are columns, altars and foundations from four temples, dating from the mid third century BC to c100 BC.

On the southern side of the square lies the Ghetto: its picture-postcard alleys mask a sorrowful history. Rome's Jews occupy a unique place in the story of the diaspora, having maintained a presence in the city uninterrupted for over 2,000 years, which makes them Europe's oldest Jewish community. But the Ghetto was walled off from the rest of the city in 1556, remaining that way until the 1870s, and in 1943 over 1,000 Jews were deported to Auschwitz. In piazza Mattei stands the delicate Turtle Fountain, erected overnight in the 1580s, though the turtles may have been an afterthought.

Sights & museums

Crypta Balbi

*Via delle Botteghe Oscure 31 (06
678 0167).* **Open** 9am-7.30pm Tue-
Sun. **Admission** €7; €3.50 reductions.
No credit cards. **Map** p65 E4 ⑯
Note: There is an extra charge of
€2 during special exhibitions.

The Crypta Balbi displays one of
Rome's more interesting recent archaeological finds, combines the best of the
ancient with state-of-the-art technolo-
gy and is packed with displays, maps
and models that explain (in English)
Rome's evolution from a bellicose pre-
Imperial era, to early Christian times
and on through the dim Middle Ages.

Galleria Spada

*Piazza Capo di Ferro 3 (06 687
4896/www.galleriaborghese.it).* **Open**
8.30am-7.30pm Tue-Sun. **Admission**
€5; €2.50 reductions. No credit cards.
Map p64 C4 ⑰

This gem of a palace was acquired
by art collector Cardinal Bernardino
Spada in 1632; the walls are crammed
with paintings. There are some impressive names here: Domenichino,
Guercino, Guido Reni plus the father-
daughter Gentileschi duo, Orazio and
Artemisia. The main attraction of the
museum, however, is the Borromini
Perspective: At weekends, guides take
visitors to a courtyard where perspective trickery makes a 9m-long (30ft)
colonnade look much longer.

Il Gesù

Piazza del Gesù (06 697 001). **Open**
Church 6.30am-12.30pm, 4-7.30pm
daily. *Loyola's rooms* 4-6pm Mon-Sat;
10am-noon Sun. **Map** p65 E3 ⑱

The Gesù, built in 1568-84, is the flagship church of the Jesuits, and was
designed to involve the congregation
as closely as possible in services, with
a nave unobstructed by aisles. One of
Rome's great baroque masterpieces –

The Mouth of Truth p59

ROME BY AREA

SENSUS ||| FARNESE

RESTAURANT

Amid antique fountains and charming squares within Rome's Renaissance golden triangle, a new culinary experience is born. Sensus Farnese arrives in town offering a vast range of exquisite wines, with the commitment of bringing back the best of traditional Italian flavour to your dish. You will be able to follow up the preparation of your meal through our open kitchen in the new exclusive, elegant and sober tendency restaurant created just for you in the heart of Rome.

ROMA, VICOLO DEL GIGLIO, 22 - TEL. 06.6877966
s.farnese@ergonitalia.com - www.ergonfood.com

Triumph in the Name of Jesus by Il Baciccia (1676-79) – decorates the ceiling of the nave. On the left is the ornate chapel of Sant'Ignazio (1696). Above the altar is what was long believed to be the biggest lump of lapis lazuli in the world; in fact, it's covered concrete. Outside the church, at piazza del Gesù 45, you can visit St Ignatius' rooms.

Museo Barracco di Scultura Antica

Corso Vittorio 166 (06 6880 6848/ 06 687 5657). No credit cards. **Map** p64 C3 ⑲
Note: Closed at time of writing; due to reopen summer 2006.

This small collection of mainly pre-Roman art was amassed in the first half of the 20th century by Giovani Barracco. Don't miss the copy of the *Wounded Bitch* by the fourth-century BC sculptor Lysippus, on the second floor.

Museo Ebraica di Roma

Lungotevere Cenci (06 6840 0661/ www.museoebraico.roma.it). **Open** 10am-5pm Mon-Thur, Sun; 9am-2pm Fri. Closed on Jewish holidays. **Admission** €7.50; €3 reductions. No credit cards. **Map** p65 E5 ⑳
As well as luxurious crowns, Torah mantles and silverware, this museum presents vivid reminders of the persecution suffered by Rome's Jews at various times through history: copies of the 16th-century papal edicts that banned Jews from many activities, and heart-rending relics from the concentration camps.

NEW Now refurbished and extended, the museum has recently been able to display a collection of exquisite carvings from long-gone Roman synagogues.

Portico d'Ottavia

Via Portico D'Ottavia. **Map** p65 E5 ㉑
Great ancient columns and a marble frontispiece, held together with rusting iron braces, now form part of the church of Sant'Angelo in Pescheria, but they were originally the entrance of a massive colonnaded square (portico) containing temples and libraries, built in the first century AD by Emperor Augustus and dedicated to his sister Octavia. A walkway (open 9am-6pm daily) has been opened through the *forum piscarium* – the ancient fish market; it continues past a graveyard of broken columns and capitals to the Teatro di Marcello, passing by three towering columns that were part of the Temple of Apollo (433 BC).

Sant'Andrea della Valle

Corso Vittorio 6 (06 686 1339). **Open** 7.30am-noon, 4.30-7.30pm daily. **Map** p64 C3 ㉒
Designed in 1524 by Giacomo della Porta, this church was handed to over to Carlo Maderno who stretched the design upward, creating a dome that is the highest in Rome after St Peter's. Puccini set the opening act of *Tosca* in the chapel on the left.

Teatro di Marcello

Via Teatro di Marcello. **Map** p65 E5 ㉓
This is one of the strangest and most impressive sights in Rome – a Renaissance palace grafted on to an ancient theatre. Julius Caesar began building the theatre, but it was finished in 11 BC by Augustus, who named it after his favourite nephew. Originally it had three tiers and seated up to 20,000 people. Abandoned in the fourth century AD, it was turned into a fortress in the 12th century and then, in the 16th century, into a *palazzo* by the Savelli family.

Tiber Island & Ponte Rotto

Map p65 D5 ㉔
When the last Etruscan king was driven from Rome, the Romans uprooted the wheat from his fields and threw it in baskets into the river. Silt accumulated and formed an island where Aesculapius, the Roman god of medicine, founded a sanctuary in the third century BC. That's what the legend says, and the island has always had a vocation for public health. Today a hospital occupies the north end. The church of San Bartolomeo is built over the original sanctuary. Remains of the ancient building can be seen from the

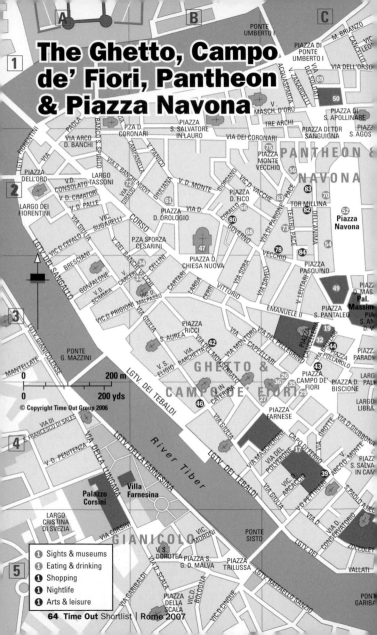

The Ghetto, Campo de' Fiori, Pantheon & Piazza Navona

PANTHEON & NAVONA

Piazza Navona

GHETTO & CAMPO DE' FIORI

River Tiber

GIANICOLO

Pal. Massim

Palazzo Corsini

Villa Farnesina

200 m

200 yds

© Copyright Time Out Group 2006

- **1** Sights & museums
- **1** Eating & drinking
- **1** Shopping
- **1** Nightlife
- **1** Arts & leisure

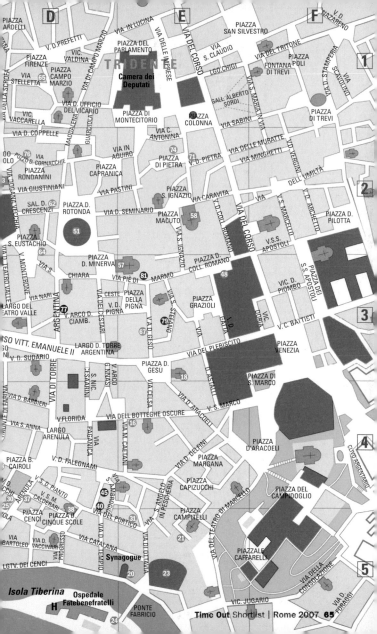

Crypta Balbi p61

riverside footpath, from where there's also a fine view over the *ponte rotto* (broken bridge). This stands on the site of the Pons aemilius, Rome's first stone bridge, built in 142 BC. It was rebuilt many times before 1598, when they gave up trying. To the east of the bridge is a tunnel in the embankment: the gaping mouth of the city's great Cloaca Maxima sewer, built in the sixth century BC.

Eating & drinking

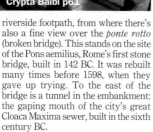

Alberto Pica
Via della Seggiola 12 (06 686 8405).
Open *Jan-Mar, Oct, Nov* 8am-2am
Mon-Sat. *Apr-Sept, Dec* 8am-2am
Mon-Sat; 4.30pm-3am Sun. Closed
2wks Aug. No credit cards. **Map**
p65 D4 ㉕
Alongside the regular bar is an excellent selection of ice-cream, among which the rice specialities stand out: *riso alla cannella* (cinnamon rice) is particularly delicious.

Antico Forno Campo de' Fiori
Campo de' Fiori 22 (06 6880 6662).
Open 7.30am-2.30pm, 4.45-8pm Mon-Sat. Closed 2wks Aug. No credit cards.
Map p64 C3 ㉖
This little bakery does by far the best takeaway sliced pizza in the campo de' Fiori and surrounding area. Their plain *pizza bianca* base is delicious in itself, but you'll thank yourself for checking out the one with *fiori di zucca* (courgette flowers) too.

Ar Galletto
Piazza Farnese 102 (06 686 1714).
Meals served 12.15-3pm, 7.30-11pm
Mon-Sat. Closed 10 days Aug. **€€**.
Map p64 C4 ㉗
You don't need to pay the inflated prices charged by other restaurants hereabouts to get a ringside view of piazza Farnese. Humbler than the competition, and Roman to its marrow, Ar Galletto serves food that is firmly in the local tradition, with dishes like *penne all'arrabbiata* or *spaghetti alle vongole* proving appetising and – for the location – well priced. It has tables on the square in summer.

Bernasconi
Piazza Cairoli 16 (06 6880 6264).
Open 7am-8.30pm Tue-Sun. Closed
Aug. No credit cards. **Map** p65 D4 ㉓

It's well worth fighting your way inside this cramped, inconspicuous bar for unbeatable chewy, yeasty *cornetti*.

Bottiglieria Il Nolano

Campo de' Fiori 11-12 (06 687 9344).
Open 6pm-2am Mon-Fri; noon-2am Sat, Sun. No credit cards. **Map** p64 C4 ㉙
This friendly bar is rustic indoors in the winter, while in warmer weather it sets old-fashioned cinema-style seats on the pavement outside. Perfect for watching the campo's colourful parade of characters.

Bruschetteria degli Angeli

Piazza B Cairoli 2A (06 6880 5789).
Open 12.30-3pm, 7.30pm-1am daily. Closed 1wk Aug. **€**. **Map** p65 D4 ㉚
The star turns here are the heavenly house *bruschette* (average €8) with a range of toppings from red chicory and bacon to grilled courgettes and mozzarella. There's also pasta, grilled steaks and a good range of draught beers. It overlooks a little park.

Da Giggetto

Via Portico d'Ottavia 21A-22 (06 686 1105/www.giggettoalportico.com).
Meals served 12.30-3pm, 7.30-11pm Tue-Sun. Closed 2wks July. **€€**. **Map** p65 E5 ㉛
This old standby in the Ghetto serves up decent versions of Roman-Jewish classics like *carciofi alla giudia* (fried artichokes) and fried *baccalà* (salt cod). The atmosphere is warm and bustling, with large tables of tourists enjoying the ambience and the plentiful helpings.

Ditirambo

Piazza della Cancelleria 74 (06 687 1626/www.ristoranteditirambo.it).
Meals served 7.30-11.30pm Mon; 1-3pm, 7.30-11.30pm Tue-Sun. Closed 3wks Aug. **€€€**. **Map** p64 C3 ㉜
This funky trattoria serves up dishes based on fresh, mainly organic ingredients. They specialise in traditional fare with a creative kick, as in the excellent pasta with rabbit, coquilles St Jacques with purée of chickpeas or veal silverside braised in coffee.

Going underground

Most visitors are pleased to find Rome is so compact and walkable, if only because it spares them having to cope with an apparently bewildering public transport system. Approached calmly, though, transport in the Eternal City is easily mastered: the metro doesn't go anywhere most tourists wish to see (why spend valuable sightseeing time down a black hole, anyway?), but buses are frequent, cheap… packed and mired in chaos.

This chaos is due in large part to the fact that the *metropolitana* (mass transit system) is woefully inadequate for a modern city. Hardly surprising when any hole dug in Rome reveals layer upon layer of history, with avid archaeologists eager to jump in.

In spring 2006, construction work began on Rome's new metro line C. Unlike A and B, this line will slice north-west to south-east, right through the most visited areas of the *centro storico* – not ferrying tourists so much as Romans, thus leaving visitors to enjoy extensive pedestrianised zones above.

This won't happen until 4.3 million cubic metres of earth have been moved (plus another 600,000 for archaeological digs), 1.6 million cubic metres of concrete poured, €3,000 million spent and 30 stations built along 25km (15 miles) of track.

All this, authorities say, will have been achieved by 2013. At which Romans smile knowing smiles and wish their grandchildren the joy of it.

Campo de' Fiori p60

Il Goccetto

Via dei Banchi Vecchi 14 (06 686 4268). **Open** 11.30am-2.30pm, 6.30-11pm Mon-Sat. Closed 1wk Jan, 3wks Aug. **Map** p64 B3 ③③

One of the more serious *centro storico* wine bars, with dark wood-clad walls and a cosy, private-club feel. Wine is the main point here, with a satisfying range by the glass from €3.50.

Il Pagliaccio

Via dei Banchi Vecchi 129A (06 6880 9595/www.ristoranteilpagliaccio.it). **Meals served** 8-10.30pm Tue; 1-2.30pm, 8-10.30pm Wed-Sat. Closed 2wks Aug; 1wk Jan. €€€€. **Map** p64 B3 ③④

Anthony Genovese's *centro storico* restaurant offers one of the best-value gourmet dinners in Rome. The chef's risk-taking approach is clearly illustrated in an *antipasto* of small fried fish served with tomato and basil ice cream and coriander-flavoured cucumber jelly. But his skill is equally evident in less pyrotechnic dishes like the *gnocchi* with lamb and two varieties of wild mushoom. Leave plenty of space for the excellent desserts.

La Vineria

Campo de' Fiori 15 (06 6880 3268). **Open** 9am-2am Mon-Sat. Closed 2wks Aug. **Map** p64 C4 ③⑤

The longest-running wine bar on the campo, La Vineria is where Romans flock to chat and plan the evening ahead over good wines by the glass starting at a remarkably cheap €1.50.

Le Piramidi

Vicolo del Gallo 11 (06 687 9061). **Open** 10.30am-midnight Tue-Sun. Closed 3wks Aug. €. No credit cards. **Map** p64 C4 ③⑥

Le Piramidi makes for a welcome change from takeaway pizza if you're in the mood for nothing more than a quick snack. The range of Middle Eastern takeaway fare is small, but it's all fresh, cheap and tasty.

Mad Jack's

Via Arenula 20 (06 6880 8223). **Open** 4pm-2am Mon-Thur; 4pm-3am Fri, Sat; 11.30am-2am Sun. Closed 1wk Aug. **Map** p65 D4 ③⑦

This formulaic but reliable Irish pub is packed at night and at weekends with crowds of young Italians and Anglos

spilling out on to the pavement. The beverages of choice are beer and cider (on draught and of various types) but there's wine and cocktails too.

Sora Margherita

Piazza delle Cinque Scole 30 (06 687 4216). **Meals served** 12.30 3pm Tue Thur, Sun; 12.30-3pm, 8-10.30pm Fri, Sat. Closed Aug. **€€**. No credit cards. **Map** p65 D5 ⊕

Sora Margherita is not for health freaks, but no one argues with serious Roman Jewish cooking at these prices. The classic pasta and meat dishes on offer include a superlative *pasta e fagioli* (with beans), *tonnarelli cacio e pepe* (pasta with cheese and pepper) and *ossobuco* washed down with rough-and-ready house wine.

Shopping

Borini

Via dei Pettinari 86 (06 687 5670). **Open** 3.30-7.30pm Mon; 9am-1pm, 3.30-7.30pm Tue-Sat. Closed 3wks Aug. **Map** p64 C4 ⊕

Franco Borini's shop is busily chaotic, with piles of shoes inside the peeling walls. His elegant but durable shoes follow fashion trends religiously and come at prices that won't make you wince as you reach for your cash.

Forno del Ghetto

Via Portico d'Ottavia 1 (06 687 8637). **Open** 8am-7.30pm Mon-Thur, Sun; 8am-sunset Fri. Closed 3wks Aug & Jewish holidays. No credit cards. **Map** p65 D4 ⊕

Run by three dour ladies, this tiny shop has no sign but is immediately recognisable by the line of slavering regulars outside. Among other goodies, they come for the unforgettable damson and ricotta tarts, or the equally wonderful chocolate and ricotta version.

Ibiz

Via dei Chiavari 39 (06 6830 7297). **Open** 9.30am-7.30pm Mon-Sat. Closed 2wks Aug. **Map** p64 C4 ⊕

Ibiz bags are made by hand in the on-site workshop: look on as you mull over which of the handbags, briefcases, backpacks and leather accessories you want to take home.

Ilaria Miani

Via Monserrato 35 (06 683 3160/ fax 06 6839 2172/www.ilariamiani. it). **Open** 3.30-7.30pm Mon; 10.30am-1.30pm, 3.30-7.30pm Tue-Sat. Closed Aug. **Map** p64 B3 ⊕

Designer Ilaria Miani is known as the creator of a certain Tuscan farmhouse style. But in her elegant shop off piazza Farnese, her furniture and interior design *objets* look anything but rustic. Pricey, but very stylish.

Loco

Via dei Baullari 22 (06 6880 8216). **Open** 3.30-8pm Mon; 10.30am-8.30pm Tue-Sat. Closed 2wks Aug. **Map** p64 C3 ⊕

If you like your shoes avant-garde, this small store decorated with copper and wood is the place. From classy to wild and eccentric, its pieces are always one step ahead of the flock.

People

Piazza Teatro di Pompeo 4A (06 687 4040). **Open** 3.30-8pm Mon; 10.30am-

Il Pagliacclo p68

2.30pm, 3.30-8pm Tue-Sat. Closed
3wks Aug. **Map** p64 C3 ④④
This tiny vintage clothes store is the
best in town. As well as quality second-
hand coats and men's suits, it sells cool
1960s- and '70s-style garments (one-of-
a-kind 'tennis' dresses, miniskirts, hipsters) designed by owners Germana and
Sara, re-using period fabrics.

Nightlife

Rialtosantambrogio

*Via Sant'Ambrogio 4 (06 6813
3640/www.rialtosantambrogio.org).*
Open times & days vary. Closed
Aug. **Admission** €3.50-€5. No
credit cards. **Map** p65 D4 ④⑤
This *centro sociale* (squat) in the Ghetto
hosts performances, art exhibitions,
live music and disco nights with
cutting-edge electronica DJs and VJs,
especially at the weekend. A meeting
point for the radical crowd.

Arts & leisure

Salus per Aquam

NEW *Via Giulia 4 (06 687 7449).*
Open 9.30am-7.30pm Mon-Sat.
Closed 3wks Aug. **Map** p64 B4 ④⑥

This gorgeous spa with a high quotient
of Rome's beautiful people in its clientele offers a mouth-watering range of
massage and beauty treatments for
men and women, plus a hammam and
hairdressing. By appointment only.

The Pantheon & Piazza Navona

Two squares – both living links
to ancient Rome – dominate this
bustling area of picturesque alleys
in the loop of the river north of
corso Vittorio Emanuele: piazza
della Rotonda – home to the
Pantheon – and magnificent
piazza Navona.

   This was part of the ancient
Campus martius, where Roman
manhood drilled for war then
retired to luxurious bathhouses to
wash off the sweat, to theatres for
entertainment and to grand temples
to dwell on notions of Empire. After
the Empire fell, the *Campus* was
prime construction territory and
every medieval wall tells a tale of
primitive recycling: grand *palazzi*

ROME BY AREA

were built from stolen marble; humbler souls constructed their little houses among the ruins. It's still a democratic area, where mink-coated contessas mingle with pensioners, craftsmen and tradesmen. After dark, smart restaurants and hip bars fill to bursting, especially around **Santa Maria della Pace**.

When corso Vittorio was hacked through the medieval fabric in the 1870s, only the most grandiose of homes – like Palazzo Massimo at No.141, its curved façade following the stands in Domitian's odeon (small theatre) – were spared.

To the east of the Pantheon, the **Galleria Doria Pamphili** contains one of Rome's finest art collections, while the charmingly rococo piazza Sant'Ignazio looks like a stage set. In neighbouring piazza di Pietra, the columns of the Temple of Hadrian can be seen embedded in the walls of Rome's ex stock exchange.

West of piazza Navona, piazza Pasquino is home to a severely truncated classical statue; for centuries, Romans have let off steam by pinning satirical verse (*pasquinate*) to this sculpture. Further north, elegant, antique-shop-lined via dei Coronari was once the haunt of pilgrim-fleecing rosary-makers (*coronari*).

Sights & museums

Chiesa Nuova/Santa Maria in Vallicella

Piazza della Chiesa Nuova (06 687 5289). **Open** 8am-noon, 4.30-7pm daily. **Map** p64 B2 ➐
Filippo Neri (1515-95) was a wealthy Florentine who abandoned commerce to live among the poor in Rome. He founded the Oratorian order in 1544. In 1575 work began on the order's head-quarters, the Chiesa Nuova. Neri wanted a large, simple building; the walls

were covered with the exuberant frescoes and multicoloured marbles only after his death. Pietro da Cortona painted the *Assumption of the Virgin* (1650) in the apse, Rubens the *Virgin and Child* (1608) over the altar.

Galleria Doria Pamphili

Piazza del Collegio Romano 2 (06 679 7323/www.doriapamphilj.it). **Open** 10am-5pm Mon-Wed, Fri-Sun. **Admission** €8; €5.70 reductions. No credit cards. **Map** p65 E3 ➒
The entrance to this magnificent private gallery is through state apartments planned by Camillo Pamphili in the mid 16th century. The main galleries are around the central courtyard. Velázquez's portrait of the Pamphili Pope Innocent X is the highlight of the collection; there's a splendid bust by Bernini of the same pontiff next to it. At the end of the Galleria degli Specchi are four small rooms ordered by century. In the 17th-century room, Caravaggio is represented by the *Rest on the Flight into Egypt* and the *Penitent Magdalene*; the 16th-century room includes such works as Titian's shameless *Salome* and a *Portrait of Two Men* by Raphael.

Museo di Roma

Palazzo Braschi, via di San Pantaleo 10 (06 6710 8346/www.museodiroma. comune.roma.it). **Open** 9am-7pm Tue-Sun. **Admission** €6.20; €3.10 reductions. No credit cards. **Map** p64 C3 ➒
Note: For special exhibitions tickets cost €8 (€6.50 reductions) .
A rotating collection recounts the evolution of the city from the Middle Ages to the early 20th century. Sculpture, clothing, furniture and photographs help to put the city's monuments in a human context.
Event highlights 'Habemus Papam – Papal Elections from the Renaissance to the 20th Century' (from 4 Oct 2006-6 Jan 2007).

Palazzo Altemps

Piazza Sant'Apollinare 48 (06 687 2719). **Open** 9am-7.45pm Tue-Sun.

IL BACARO ROMA

sfizi ai fornel.

Via degli Spagnoli,
Roma
tel. 06.6872554
06.6864110
www.ilbacaro.com
**OPEN
TO LATE NIGHT**
(closed Sunday)
Reservations advisable

Admission €7; €3.50 reductions.
No credit cards. **Map** p64 C1 ⑩
Note: Tickets cost €2 extra if there
is a special exhibition on.

The 15th- to 16th-century Palazzo
Altemps houses part of the state-
owned stock of Roman treasures: gems
of classical statuary purchased from
the Boncompagni-Ludovisi, Altemps
and Mattei families. The Ludovisis
liked 'fixing' statues: an *Athena with
Serpent* (Room 9) was revamped in the
17th century by Alessandro Algardi,
who also 'improved' the *Hermes
Loghios* in Room 19. Room 21 has the
Ludovisi Throne, the museum's greatest treasure, a fifth-century BC work
from Magna Grecia… though some
believe it to be a fake.

Pantheon

Piazza della Rotonda (06 6830 0230).
Open 8.30am-7.30pm Mon-Sat; 9am-
6pm Sun; 9am-1pm public holidays.
Map p65 D2 ⑪
The Pantheon was built by Hadrian in
AD 119-128 as a temple to the most
important deities; the inscription on the
pediment records a Pantheon built 100
years before by General Marcus
Agrippa (which confused historians for
centuries). Its fine state of preservation
is due to the building's conversion to a
church in 608, though its bronze
cladding was purloined over the
centuries: part is now in Bernini's
baldacchino in St Peter's. The bronze
doors are the original Roman ones.
Inside, the Pantheon's glory lies in its
dimensions. The diameter of the hemi-
spherical dome is exactly equal to the
height of the building. At the centre of
the dome is the oculus, a circular hole
9m (30ft) in diameter, a symbolic link
between the temple and the heavens.
Until the 18th century the portico was
used as a market: supports for the
stalls were inserted into the notches
still visible in the columns.

Piazza Navona

Map p64 C2 ⑫
This tremendous theatrical space owes
its shape to an ancient athletics stadium, built in AD 86 by Emperor
Domitian. Just north of the piazza, at
piazza di Tor Sanguigna 16, remains of
the original arena are visible from the
street. The piazza acquired its current
form in the mid 17th century. The
central Fountain of the Four Rivers,
finished in 1651, is one of the most
extravagant masterpieces designed by
Bernini. Its main figures represent the
longest rivers of the four continents
known at the time; Ganges of Asia, Nile
of Africa, Danube of Europe and Plata
of the Americas, all with appropriate
flora. The figure of the Nile is veiled,
because its source was unknown.

San Luigi dei Francesi

*Piazza San Luigi dei Francesi (06 688
271).* **Open** 8.30am-12.30pm, 3.30-7pm
Mon-Wed, Fri-Sun; 8.30am-12.30pm
Thur. **Map** p65 D2 ⑬
Completed in 1589, San Luigi/St Louis
is the church of Rome's French community. In the fifth chapel on the left
are Caravaggio's spectacular scenes
from the life of St Matthew (1600-02).
But don't overlook lovely frescoes of St
Cecilia by Domenichino (1615-17), in
the second chapel on the right.

Sant'Agnese in Agone

Piazza Navona (06 6819 2134).
Open 9am-noon, 4-7pm Tue-Sat;
9am-1pm, 4-8pm Sun. **Map** p64 C2 ⑭
Legend says that teenage St Agnes
was cast naked into the stadium of
Domitian around AD 304 when she
refused to renounce Christ and marry
a powerful local. Her pagan persecutors chopped her head off (and the
implausibly small skull is still here),
supposedly on the exact spot where the
church now stands. Begun in 1652 the
church was given its splendidly fluid
concave façade by Borromini.

Sant'Agostino

Piazza Sant'Agostino (06 6880 1962).
Open 8am-noon, 4.30-7.30pm daily.
Map p64 C1 ⑮
This 15th-century church has one of
the earliest Renaissance façades in
Rome, made of travertine filched from
the Colosseum. Inside, the third column

Bar Sant'Eustachio p76

on the left bears a fresco of Isaiah by Raphael (1512), while the first chapel on the left has Caravaggio's depiction of the grubbiest pilgrims ever, presenting themselves at the feet of the startlingly beautiful *Madonna of the Pilgrims* (1604).

Santa Maria della Pace

Vicolo del Arco della Pace 5 (06 686 1156). **Open** 10am-12.45pm Tue-Fri. **Map** p64 C2 ⑤⑤

Built in 1482, Santa Maria della Pace was given its theatrical baroque façade by Pietro da Cortona in 1656. Just inside the door is Raphael's *Sybils* (1514). There's a beautifully harmonious cloister by Bramante, his first work after arriving in Rome in the early 16th century; exhibitions are often held here.

Santa Maria sopra Minerva

Piazza della Minerva 42 (06 679 3926). **Open** 7am-7pm Mon-Sat; 8am-7pm Sun. **Map** p65 E3 ⑤⑦

Rome's only Gothic church was built on the site of an ancient temple of Minerva in 1280. Its best works of art are Renaissance: on the right of the transept is the Carafa chapel, with frescoes by Filippino Lippi (1457-1504). Also here is the tomb of the Carafa Pope Paul IV (1555-59), famous for enclosing the Jewish Ghetto and having loincloths painted on the nudes of Michelangelo's *Last Judgment* in the Sistine chapel. A bronze loincloth was also ordered to cover Christ's genitals on a work here by Michelangelo, a Christ holding up a cross. The *Madonna and Child*, an earlier work believed by some to be by Fra Angelico, is in the chapel to the left of the altar, close to the artistic monk's own tomb. The father of modern astronomy, Galileo Galilei, who dared suggest that the earth revolved around the sun, was tried for heresy in the adjoining monastery in 1633. In the square in front of the church is a charming marble elephant bearing an obelisk on its back, by Bernini.

Sant'Ignazio di Loyola

Piazza Sant'Ignazio (06 679 4406). **Open** 7.30am-12.30pm, 3-7.15pm daily. **Map** p65 E2 ⑤⑧

Sant'Ignazio was begun in 1626 to commemorate the canonisation of St Ignatius, the founder of the Jesuits. Trompe l'oeil columns soar above the nave, and architraves by Andrea Pozzo open to a cloudy heaven. When the monks next door claimed that a dome would rob them of light, Pozzo simply painted a dome on the ceiling. The illusion is fairly convincing if you stand on the disc set in the floor of the nave. Walk away, however, and it collapses.

Sant'Ivo alla Sapienza

Corso Rinascimento 40 (06 686 4987). **Open** 8.30am-5pm Mon-Fri; 9am-noon Sat, Sun. **Map** p64 C3 ⑤⑨

In this crowning glory of Borromini's tortured imagination, the concave façade is countered by the convex bulk of the dome, which terminates in a bizarre corkscrew spire. Inside, the convex and concave surfaces on the walls and up into the dome leave you feeling like someone spiked your cappuccino. Opening times are notoriously erratic.

Eating & drinking

Alceste al Buon Gusto

NEW *Corso Rinascimento 70 (06 686 1312).* **Meals served** 1-3pm, 8-11pm Mon-Sat. **€€€€**. **Map** p64 C2 ⑥⓪

The new Roman offshoot of an historic seaside fish restaurant, Alceste has a great location and superbly fresh seafood, especially in its delicious parade of *antipasti*. But the decor is rather boringly minimalist, and we found not only the service but also the dishes – among them the trademark *rombo con le patate* (turbot baked with potatoes) – rather tired, especially for these prices.

Alfredo e Ada

Via dei Banchi Nuovi 14 (06 687 8842). **Meals served** 1-3.30pm, 8-10.30pm Mon-Fri. Closed Aug; 1wk Dec-Jan. **€€**. No credit cards. **Map** p64 B2 ⑥①

Ada has been bustling between these eight tables since the 1940s. The day's set-price menu, chalked on a board, includes simple dishes: *spaghetti aglio e olio* (garlic and oil), perhaps, or *salsiccia con fagioli* (sausage with beans).

Armando al Pantheon

Salita de' Crescenzi 31 (06 6880 3034). **Meals served** 12.30-3pm, 7.30-11pm Mon-Fri; 12.30-3pm Sat. Closed Aug. €€. **Map** p65 D2 ⑫
Armando is a simple, no-frills trattoria, a few yards from the Pantheon, serving classics like *fettucine all'Armando* (with peas, mushrooms and tomatoes) or *ossobuco*. The only concession to changing times are the vegetarian dishes.

Bar della Pace

Via della Pace 3-7 (06 686 1216). **Open** 4pm-2am Mon; 9am-2am Tue-Sun. **Map** p64 C2 ⑬
Eternally *à la mode*, this bar has warm, antiques- and flower-filled rooms for the colder months and (pricey) pavement tables beneath the trademark ivy-clad façade.

Bar Sant'Eustachio

Piazza Sant'Eustachio 82 (06 6880 2048). **Open** 8.30am-1am daily. No credit cards. **Map** p65 D2 ⑭
This is one of the city's most famous coffee bars and its walls are plastered with celebrity testimonials. The coffee is quite extraordinary, if expensive. Try the *gran caffè*: the *schiuma* (froth) can be slurped out afterwards with spoon or fingers. Unless you specify (*amaro* means 'no sugar'), it comes very sweet.

Boccondivino

Piazza Campo Marzio 6 (06 6830 8626). **Meals served** 1-3pm, 8-11.30pm Mon-Fri; 7.30-11.30pm Sat. Closed 3wks Aug. €€€. **Map** p65 D1 ⑮
This jazzy, artsy restaurant has one of Rome's best-value sit-down lunch menus: €18 for two courses. At dinner, prices are higher and there's a more foodie slant, with dishes such as rabbit casserole with black olives, candied tomatoes and polenta medallions.

Piazza Navona p73

Wireless in the park

Cross one of Rome's larger parks any evening as dusk falls, and you'll see huddles of students on benches, their faces bathed in blue screen light. There's a *senza tetto* (homeless man) too, who charges his battered laptop in a local library then settles down for some surfing in his makeshift residence of cardboard and blankets in Villa Borghese, says Gianni Celata, chairman of Roma Wireless.

Since summer 2005, *ville* Borghese, Pamphili, Ada and Torlonia have been pilots in a city council-sponsored scheme to make huge swathes of the *centro storico* into a Wi-Fi zone. By late summer 2006, 'Hotspots' were scheduled in *piazze* around the centre and across to the Vatican. Until well into 2007, Celata says, access will remain open to all (in blithe disregard of Italy's anti-terrorism laws, which state that providers of internet access to the public must register

all their users) and, for an hour, free. 'Though all you have to do,' he reveals, 'is switch off and on again and you've got another hour.'

Going online with your laptop, palmtop or latest generation cellphone in a piazza Hotspot will take you straight to *Viaggio in Roma*, a concatenation of mini-portals containing exhaustive historical, gastronomic, retail and practical information on your immediate surroundings in Italian and, in the first phase, English and Japanese. 'German, Spanish and other languages will follow,' explains Celata.

'We're catering for a cultured traveller, not a hit-and-run tourist,' he adds. 'We aim to provide the kind of in-depth all-inclusive area-specific information that you just couldn't get into an average-sized guide book.' (But if what you really want is simply a chance to check your stocks, shares or e-mail, you can bypass the information and get straight to business.)

When it's fully up and running, the service will be *a pagamento*. Celata looks rather abashed when asked how much it will cost, admitting that enthusiasm for getting on stream meant practicalities like this had been largely overlooked. 'But it'll be small change, not a major expense,' he says. 'We might have a debit card system for habitual users.'

In the mean time, information on Rome's Hotspots and *Viaggio in Roma* will be available on the following sites:
- www.distrettoict.it
- www.romawireless.it
- www.viaggioinroma.it

ROME BY AREA

Da Francesco

Piazza del Fico 29 (06 686 4009).
Meals served *Sept-July* noon-2.50pm,
7pm-12.45am Mon, Wed-Sun; 7pm-
12.45am Tue. *Aug* 7pm-12.30am
Wed-Sun. **€€**. No credit cards.
Map p64 B2 ⑥⑥

Accept no imitations. Da Francesco is
the genuine pizzeria article: tasty pizzas; warm, traditional ambience; brisk
but friendly service; and a range of
competent, classic *primi* and *secondi*.

Enoteca Corsi

Via del Gesù 87-88 (06 679 0821).
Meals served noon-3pm Mon-Sat.
Closed 4wks Aug. **€€**. **Map** p65 E3 ⑥⑦
This 1940s wine shop was the first in
Rome to serve lunch. The daily changing menu is on a board at the entrance,
with dishes that follow the traditional
Roman culinary calendar – potato
gnocchi each Thursday and stewed
baccalà (salt cod) on a Friday. No bookings are taken, so get there early.

Fluid

*Via del Governo Vecchio 46-47
(06 683 2361/www.fluideventi.com).*
Open 6pm-2am daily. Closed 1wk
Aug. **Map** p64 B2 ⑥⑧
This ultra-sleek designer bar with
black floors, stunning chandeliers and
plasma screens is very lively, but the
crowd is not always as cool as the
interiors. DJs play live sets every night.

Il Convivio Troiani

*Vicolo dei Soldati 31 (06 686 9432/
www.ilconviviotroiani.com).* **Meals
served** 8-11pm Mon-Sat. Closed
1wk Jan; 1wk Aug. **€€€€**. **Map**
p64 C1 ⑥⑨
In an elegant, minimalist setting, the
three Troiani brothers serve ultra-
gourmet creations such as a *risotto con
funghi porcini e quaglia scaloppata*
(porcini mushrooms and quail scallops)
or sole fillets stuffed with artichokes,
served in a shallot, lemon and clam
sauce. The desserts are spectacular.

I Tre Scalini

Piazza Navona 28-32 (06 6880 1996).
Open 9am-midnight daily. Closed Jan.
Map p64 C2 ⑦⓪

This bar is famous for its *tartufo* – a
calorie-bomb chocolate ice-cream con-
coction with huge lumps of chocolate
inside. Beware: sit down inside or out,
and the price mark-up is massive.
Instead, take your ice-cream away and
enjoy it next to Bernini's fountain.

La Caffettiera

Piazza di Pietra 65 (06 679 8147).
Open *Sept-June* 7am-9pm daily.
July, Aug 7am-9pm Mon-Sat. **Map**
p65 E2 ⑦①
Politicians from the nearby parliament
buildings lounge in the sumptuous tea-
room of this temple to Neapolitan goodies, while lesser mortals bolt coffees at
the bar. The *rum babà* reigns supreme,
but ricotta lovers rave over the crunchy
sfogliatella and rich *pastiera*.

L'Altro Mastai

*Via Giraud 53 (06 6830 1296/www.
laltromastai.it).* **Meals served** 7.30-
11.30pm Tue-Sat. Closed Aug. **€€€**.
Map p64 B2 ⑦②
At this creative Italian restaurant with
elegant neo-Pompeiian decor, chef
Fabio Baldassare prepares a menu that
changes four times a year. Not a place
for a quick snack, but if you have the
time, money and appetite, you're in for
a treat. The wine list is satisfyingly
vast; the desserts are to die for.

Lo Zozzone

*Via del Teatro Pace 32 (06 6880
8575).* **Open** 9am-9pm Mon-Fri;
9am-11pm Sat. Closed Aug. **€**.
No credit cards. **Map** p64 C2 ⑦③
The 'dirty old man' serves Rome's best
pizza bianca ripiena – which, as a sign
explains, is 'White Pizza With Any
Thing You Like Inside'. Fillings range
from classics like prosciutto and mozzarella to exotic combinations. Pay at
the till for a regular (€2.50) or large (€3)
piece; then join the receipt-waving
hordes to get served.

Salotto 42

Piazza di Pietra 42 (06 678 5804).
Open 10am-2am Tue-Sat; 10am-
midnight Sun. Closed Aug. **Map**
p65 E2 ⑦④

Incredibly comfortable chairs and sofas give this place a cosy feel during the day, when a smörgåsbord of nibbles is available. By night, the sleek room becomes a gorgeous cocktail bar with a great soundtrack, excellent cocktails and a selection of books on fashion, art and design.

Société Lutèce

Piazza di Montevecchio 17 (06 6830 1472). **Open** 6pm-2am daily. Closed 2wks Aug. **Map** p64 C2 ⓰
Popular with eclectic Roman hipsters, this bar's cramped quarters cause a spill-over into the piazza. The *aperitivo* buffet is plentiful (get there early) and the vibe is decidedly laid back.

Trattoria

Via del Pozzo delle Cornacchie 25 (06 6830 1427). **Meals served** 8-11.30pm Mon-Sat. Closed 2wks Aug. **€€€**. **Map** p65 D2 ⓱
Ebullient Sicilian chef Filippo La Mantia takes Sicilian standards like caponata or pasta alla Norma and gives them his own creative twist. There's a €10-a-shot lunchtime couscous bar (noon-3pm Mon-Sat).

Shopping

Antica Erboristeria Romana

Via di Torre Argentina 15 (06 687 9493/www.anticaerboristeriaromana. com). **Open** 8.30am-1.30pm, 2.30-7.30pm Mon-Sat. Closed 2wks Aug. **Map** p65 D3 ⓱
Visit this charming 18th-century apothecary-style shop if only to admire the carved wood ceilings and banks of tiny wooden drawers – some etched with skull and crossbones – in which herbal remedies are hidden away.

Arsenale

Via del Governo Vecchio 64 (06 686 1380). **Open** 3.30-7.30pm Mon; 10am-7.30pm Tue-Sat. Closed 3wks Aug. **Map** p64 C2 ⓲
Patrizia Pieroni's wonderful garments make for great window displays – and successful party conversation pieces. They've been going down well with the boho-chic luvvie crowd for ten years.

Ditta G Poggi

Via del Gesù 74-75 (06 678 4477/www.poggi1825.it). **Open** 9am-1pm,

Lo Zozzone

4-7.30pm Mon-Sat. Closed 2wks Aug.
Map p65 E3 79
This wonderfully old-fashioned shop has been selling paints, brushes, canvases and artists' supplies of every description since 1825.

Maga Morgana

Via del Governo Vecchio 27 (06 687 9995). **Open** 10am-7.30pm Mon-Sat. **Map** p64 B2 80
Designer Luciana Iannace's quirky one-of-a-kind women's clothes include hand-knitted sweaters, skirts and dresses. Knitted and woollen items are sold down the road at via del Governo Vecchio 98 (06 687 8095).

Moriondo & Gariglio

Via del Piè di Marmo 21 (06 699 0856). **Open** 9.30am-1pm, 3.30-7.30pm daily. Closed Aug **Map** p65 E3 81
This fairytale chocolate shop with beautiful gift-boxes is especially lovely close to Christmas, when you will have to fight to get your hands on the excellent *marrons glacés*. The shop is usually closed on Saturday afternoons during June and July.

Too Much

Via Santa Maria dell'Anima 29 (06 6830 1187/www.toomuch.it). **Open** noon-midnight daily. **Map** p64 C2 82
Lovers of kitsch need look no further than Too Much: two storeys crammed floor-to-ceiling with gimmicky design and household objects.

Nightlife

Anima

Via Santa Maria dell'Anima 57 (06 6889 2806/347 850 9256). **Open** noon-4am daily. **Map** p64 C2 83
With improbable baroque-style, gilded mouldings, this small venue has a buzzing atmosphere and good drinks, and caters for a mixed crowd of all ages and nationalities. Hip hop, R&B, funk, soul and reggae.

La Maison

Vicolo dei Granari 3 (06 683 3312/ www.lamaisonroma.it). **Open** 11pm-3.30am Tue-Thur, Sun; midnight-5am Fri, Sat. Closed July-Sept. **Admission** €15. **Map** p64 C2 84
One of the clubs of choice of Rome's fashion-victims, La Maison is dressed to impress… but elegantly. Huge chandeliers, dark red walls and curvy sofas give it an opulent, courtly feeling. Surprisingly, the place is not snobbish, the music on offer is not banal and the atmosphere is truly buzzing. The doormen can be picky.

Moriondo & Gariglio

Piazza del Quirinale p100

Tridente & Borghese

The Tridente

The wedge of super-chic streets at the foot of the Spanish Steps is used to jet-set attention: as long ago as the 18th century it had a *dolce vita* all of its own… except that then it was called the Grand Tour. Thousands of English '*milords*' took lodgings in the piazza di Spagna and strayed nowhere without a trusted guide. Even today there are visitors who never make it further than the plethora of glorious fashion retailers here.

The whole area was built as a showpiece. Rome's most elegant square, piazza del Popolo, was given its oval form by architect Giuseppe Valadier in the early 19th century. It is the starting point of a much earlier three-pronged urban plan.

Leading out centrally from the square is the Tridente's main thoroughfare, the via del Corso, which passes high-street clothing retailers en route to the towering column of Marcus Aurelius (piazza Colonna) – built between AD 180 and 196 to commemorate the victories on the battlefield of that most intellectual of Roman emperors – and piazza Venezia.

Via Ripetta veers off down to the riverside, leading to Emperor Augustus' **mausoleum** and the **Ara Pacis**.

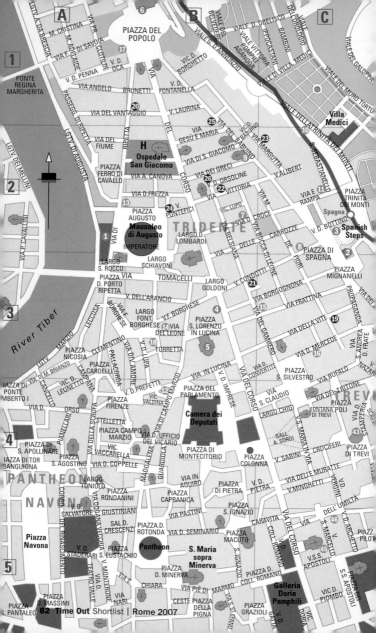

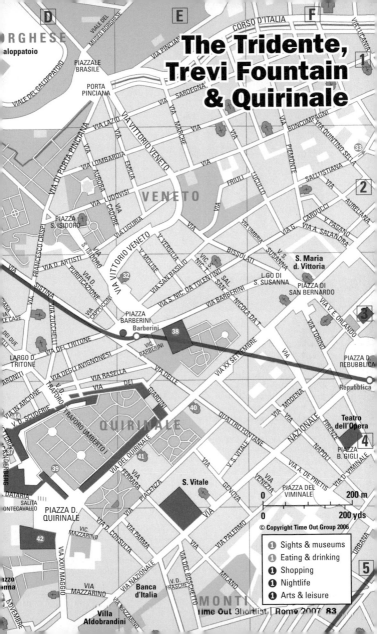

The Tridente, Trevi Fountain & Quirinale

Altar of controversy

In 2006, the wraps finally came off Richard Meier's luminous, and hugely controversial, glass structure commissioned to rehouse the most important monument of first-century Rome: the **Ara Pacis**. Intended to mark the millennium, Meier's project was held up by interminable wrangling as debate raged over whether the Eternal City needed – or indeed wanted – an enormous, futuristically modern building at its very heart.

Rome's *centro storico* remains miraculously intact, bypassed by post-war architectural horrors; but piazza Augusto Imperatore – home both to the Ara Pacis and Emperor Augustus' raggedly imposing circular mausoleum – had already enjoyed a Fascist-era makeover. *Il Duce*, who saw himself as a new Augustus, planned to occupy the mausoleum when his time was up.

Some people find that the piazza has its own kitsch charm, with its stylised frescoes of prancing fencers and tennis players, its mosaics of Romulus, Remus and the she-wolf and its aerodynamic travertine angels: the solid, rugged, four-square (but slightly farcical) face of Mussolini's tried-but-failed brave new world view.

Others – especially on the Left – have always loathed it, and have long been itching to make a change. Now, the New York-based architectural superstar's gleaming box containing the sacrificial altar makes the 1930s buildings look as antique, and as (politically) irrelevant, as the 2,000-year-old funeral mound.

Whatever you think of the building itself, there's no denying the beauty of the mausoleum-top cypress trees reflected in the banks of glass, or the colours of the lead of neighbouring church domes and stucco of older buildings played back across the transparent façade. Beyond the glass case, mottled plane trees shimmer on the embankment, while inside, the altar is seen to stunning effect.

Between lengthy halts while the guardians of the city's antiquities sent archaeologists to dig in the site, work continued at fever pitch to complete the building in time for its official handover to the city for its 2759th 'birthday' on 21 April 2006. But the work doesn't stop here. An underpass is also planned, to bury busy embankment traffic beneath an unbroken vista across the river.
■ www.richardmeier.com
■ www.arapacis.it

Piazza del Popolo p81

The third street, the chic via del Babuino, runs past a series of mouth-watering antiques shops and designer outlets to the **Spanish Steps**.

Parallel to via del Babuino, tucked in right below the Pincio hill, is via Margutta, now fondly remembered as the focus of the 1960s art scene and the setting for Gregory Peck's home in the 1953 classic *Roman Holiday*. And criss-crossing the three main arteries are streets, such as via Condotti, that have given Rome its reputation as an international fashion centre.

Sights & museums

Ara Pacis Augustae
NEW *Lungotevere in Augusta
(06 8205 9127/www.arapacis.it).*
Open 9am-7pm Tue-Sun. **Admission**
€6.50; €3 reductions. No credit cards.
Map p82 A2 ❶

The Ara Pacis ('Altar of Peace') was inaugurated in 9 BC to celebrate the security that Augustus' victories had brought. The altar was rebuilt in the early 20th century from fragments amassed through a long dig and a trawl through the world's museums. The altar itself sits inside an enclosure carved with delicately realistic reliefs. The upper band shows the ceremonies surrounding the dedication of the altar. The carved faces of Augustus and his family have all been identified. It now resides in a container designed by Richard Meier, inaugurated to much fanfare in 2006 (see box p84).

The forlorn brick cylinder next door in piazza Augusto Imperatore was originally a mausoleum covered with marble pillars and statues, begun in 28 BC. Augustus was laid to rest in the central chamber on his death in AD 14.

Keats-Shelley Memorial House
*Piazza di Spagna 26 (06 678 4235/
www.keats-shelley-house.org).*

ROME BY AREA

Keats-Shelley Memorial House p85

Open 9am-1pm, 3-6pm Mon-Fri;
11am-2pm, 3-6pm Sat. Closed 1wk Dec.
Admission €3.50. No credit cards.
Map p82 C2 ❷

The house at the bottom of the Spanish
Steps where the 25-year-old John Keats
died of tuberculosis in 1821 is crammed
with mementos: a lock of Keats' hair
and his death mask, an urn holding tiny
pieces of Shelley's charred skeleton,
and copies of documents and letters.

Piazza di Spagna & Spanish Steps

Map p82 C2 ❸

Piazza di Spagna has been a compulsory stop for visitors to Rome ever
since the 18th century when a host of
poets and musicians stayed here. The
square takes its name from the Spanish
Embassy, but it is most famous for the
Spanish Steps (Scalinata di Trinità dei
Monti), an elegant cascade down from
the church of Trinità dei Monti. The
steps (completed in 1725) were, in fact,
funded by a French diplomat. At the
foot of the stairs is a boat-shaped fountain, the *barcaccia*, designed in 1627 by
either Gian Lorenzo Bernini or his less-
famous father Pietro.

Palazzo Ruspoli-Fondazione Memmo

*Via del Corso 418 (06 6830 7344/
www.palazzoruspoli.it).* **Open** times
vary. **Admission** varies with
exhibition. No credit cards.
Map p82 B3 ❹

The palace of one of Rome's oldest
noble families is today used for touring
exhibitions of photography and art as
well as archaeology and history. The
basement rooms also often host photo-
graphic exhibitions, and admission is
sometimes free.

San Lorenzo in Lucina

*Piazza San Lorenzo in Lucina 16A
(06 687 1494).* **Open** 9am-7.30pm
daily. No credit cards. **Map** p82 B3 ❺

This 12th-century church was built
on the site of an early Christian place
of worship. (Visits to the digs cost
€2 and must be booked in advance.)
Roman columns are incorporated into
the exterior, while the 17th-century
interior contains Bernini portrait busts,
a kitsch 17th-century *Crucifixion* by
Guido Reni and a monument to the
French artist Nicolas Poussin, who
died in Rome in 1665. In the first chapel

on the right is a grill, reputed to be the one on which St Lawrence was roasted to death.

Santa Maria del Popolo

Piazza del Popolo 12 (06 361 0836).
Open 8am-1.30pm, 4.30-7.30pm Mon-Sat; 8am-7.30pm Sun. **Map** p82 B1 ❻
According to legend, Santa Maria del Popolo occupies the site of a garden in which the hated emperor Nero was buried. In 1099 Pope Paschal II built a chapel here to dispel demons still believed to haunt the spot. In 1472, Pope Sixtus IV rebuilt the chapel as a church. In the apse are Rome's first stained-glass windows (1509). The apse was designed by Bramante, while the choir ceiling and first and third chapels in the right aisle were frescoed by Pinturicchio. The Chigi Chapel was designed by Raphael for wealthy banker Agostino Chigi, and features Chigi's horoscope. The church's most-gawped-at possessions, however, are the two masterpieces by Caravaggio to the left of the main altar, showing the stories of Saints Peter and Paul.

Eating & drinking

Antica Enoteca di Via della Croce

Via della Croce 76B (06 679 0896).
Open 11.30am-1am daily. €€.
Closed 1wk Aug. **Map** p82 B2 ❼
A tasteful revamp of this wine bar has retained most of the original 1842 fittings, including the marble wine vats and a venerable wooden cash desk. There's a cold antipasto buffet at the bar, and a restaurant with tables in the long back room. It also operates as an off-licence.

Antico Caffè Greco

Via Condotti 86 (06 679 1700).
Open 10.30am-7pm Mon, Sun; 9am-7pm Tue-Sat. Closed 2wks Aug.
Map p82 C2 ❽
Founded in 1760, this venerable café was once the hangout of Casanova, Goethe, Wagner, Shelley and Byron. Today it has its sofas packed with tourists, while locals cram the foyer.

Caffè Canova-Tadolini

Via del Babuino 150A (06 3211 0702). **Open** 8am-8.30pm Mon-Sat.
Map p82 B2 ❾
Once the studio of the 19th-century sculptor Antonio Canova, this café has tables among its sculpture models and a refined and elegant old-world feel.

Ciampini al Café du Jardin

Viale Trinità dei Monti (06 678 5678).
Open *mid Mar-mid Nov* 8am-midnight daily. Closed mid Nov-mid Mar.
Map p82 C2 ❿
This open-air café near the top of the Spanish Steps is garlanded with creeper-curtained trellises, with a pond in the centre. There's a stunning view, especially at sunset.

GiNa Eat&Drink

Via San Sebastianello 7A (06 678 0251). **Open** 11am-5pm Mon; 11am-10pm Tue-Sat; 11am-8pm Sun. Closed 2wks Aug. €€. **Map** p82 C2 ⓫
This bright and artsy light-lunch and dinner bar is a good option for snacking by the Spanish Steps. The menu is homely: a couple of soups, four or five daily pasta dishes, a range of creative and gourmet salads, wine by the glass or bottle.

Gino in vicolo Rosini

Vicolo Rosini 4 (06 687 3434).
Meals served 1-2.45pm, 8-10.30pm Mon-Sat. Closed Aug. €€. No credit cards. **Map** p82 B4 ⓬
Tucked away in a hard to find lane off piazza del Parlamento, this neighbourhood osteria champions much of the lighter side of the local tradition in dishes like *tonnarelli alla ciociara* (pasta with mushrooms and tomatoes), and pasta and chickpeas in ray sauce; desserts include a classic and excellent tiramisù.

'Gusto

Piazza Augusto Imperatore 9 (06 322 6273/www.gusto.it). **Open** *Wine bar* 11.30am-2am daily. **Meals served** *Pizzeria* 1-3pm, 8pm-1am daily. *Restaurant* 12.30-3pm, 7.30pm-midnight daily. €€ **Pizzeria**. €€€ **Restaurant**. **Map** p82 A2 ⓭

ROME BY AREA

YOU KNOW
WHERE TO GO.

ROME
VIA VITTORIO VENETO 62A • +39-06-4203051

'Gusto is a multi-purpose, split-level pizzeria, restaurant and wine bar, with a kitchen shop and bookshop next door. The ground-floor pizza and salad bar is always packed; upstairs, the more expensive restaurant applies oriental techniques to Italian models, not always convincingly. The wine bar out back is buzzing and stylish, with a good selection of wines by the glass and nibbles.

Matricianella

Via del Leone 3 (06 683 2100). **Meals served** 12.30-3pm, 7.30-11pm Mon-Sat. Closed 3wks Aug. **€€€**. **Map** p82 B3 ⑭

This is a friendly, bustling place with great prices. The Roman imprint is most evident in classics such as *bucatini all'amatriciana* or *abbacchio a scottadito*, but there are plenty of more creative options. The well-chosen wine list is a model of honest pricing. Book ahead.

Palatium

NEW *Via Frattina 94 (06 6920 2132).* **Open** 11.30am-midnight Mon-Sat. Closed 2wks Aug. **€€€**. **Map** p82 C3 ⑮

Though it's backed by the regional government, this new wine bar and caterie in the heart of the fashion district is more than a PR exercise. Dedicated to the wines of Lazio – the region around Rome – it gives punters the chance to go beyond the Castelli romani clichés to explore lesser-known local wines like Cesanese or Aleatico. The upstairs restaurant (meals served 12.30-3.15pm, 8-11pm) offers light creative dishes – though it's a more expensive trip than the affordable downstairs buffet.

Pizza Ciro

Via della Mercede 43 (06 678 6015). **Meals served** 11.30am-1.30am daily. **€€**. **Map** p82 C3 ⑯

From outside it looks like a modest, touristy pizza parlour. But Ciro is in fact a huge eating factory. The pizzas (of the high-crust Neapolitan variety) are not at all bad, and *primi* such as

tubetti alla Ciro (pasta with rocket and mussels) provide a decent alternative.

Rosati

Piazza del Popolo 5 (06 322 5859). **Open** 8am-11.30pm daily. **Map** p82 A1 ⑰

This bar's art nouveau interior has remained unchanged since its original opening in 1922. Try the *Sogni romani* cocktail: orange juice with four kinds of liqueur in red and yellow – the colours of the city.

Vic's

Vicolo della Torretta 60 (06 687 1445) **Meals served** 12.30-3pm, 7.30-10.30pm Mon-Sat. Closed 2wks Aug. **€**. No credit cards. **Map** p82 B3 ⑱

This wine and salad bar offers a wide range of creative salads such as radicchio, pine nuts, sultanas and parmesan. There's pared-back Roman *osteria* decor, friendly service and a fairly priced wine list.

Shopping

Anglo-American Book Co

Via della Vite 102 (06 679 5222/ www.aab.it). **Open** 3.30-7.30pm Mon; 10am-7.30pm Tue-Sat. Closed 2wks Aug. **Map** p82 C3 ⑲

A good selection of books in English.

Buccone

Via Ripetta 19-20 (06 361 2154). **Open** 9am-8.30pm Mon-Thur; 9am-midnight Fri, Sat. Closed 3wks Aug. **Map** p82 B3 ⑳

This *enoteca* is filled from floor to arched ceiling with wines and spirits, sub-divided by region. They also serve lunch (**€€**) during the week, and dinner on Friday and Saturday.

Federico Buccellati

Via Condotti 31 (06 679 0329/ www.federicobuccellati.com). **Open** 3.15-7pm Mon; 10am-7pm Tue-Fri; 10am-6pm Sat. **Map** p82 B3 ㉑

One of the most highly regarded gold- and silversmiths in Italy, Buccellati specialises in pretty, delicate, neo-Renaissance designs.

Lake at Villa Borghese p92

Gallo
Via Vittoria 63 (06 3600 2174).
Open 3.30-7.30pm Mon; 10am-2pm,
3-7pm Tue-Sat. Closed 2wks Aug.
Map p82 B2 ❷
Gallo sells splendid socks and tights
in cotton, wool or cashmere. The
trademark stripes also feature on
scarves in the winter and lovely biki-
nis in the summer.

La Bottega del Marmoraro
Via Margutta 53B (06 320 7660).
Open 8.30am-7.30pm Mon-Sat.
No credit cards. **Map** p82 C2 ❷
A tiny space crammed with pseudo-
classical inscriptions, headless statues
and busts. The jolly *marmoraro* Enrico
Fiorentini can make to order.

La Soffitta Sotto i Portici
*Piazza Augusto Imperatore (06 3600
5345).* **Open** 9am-sunset 1st & 3rd Sun
of mth. Closed Aug. **Map** p82 B2 ❷
Street market with collectables of all
kinds, ranging from magazines to jewellery, at non-bargain prices.

TAD
*Via del Babuino 155A (06 3269 5122/
www.taditaly.com).* **Open** noon-8pm
Mon, Sun; 10.30am-7.30pm Tue-Sat.
Closed 2wks Aug. **Map** p82 B1 ❷

The concept behind this 'concept store'
is that you can shop for clothes, shoes,
flowers, household accessories, CDs,
mags and perfumes, get your hair
done, eat fusion Thai-Italian and drink
– all in one super-cool place.

The Lion Bookshop
*Via dei Greci 33 (06 3265 4007/
www.thelionbookshop.com).* **Open**
3.30-7.30pm Mon; 10am-7.30pm Tue-
Sun. Closed 1wk Aug. **Map** p82 B2 ❷
This friendly shop is great for contemporary fiction and children's books.
There's also a café, which doubles as a
gallery space.

Via Veneto & Villa Borghese

From the days of the Caesars until
the building boom of the late 1800s,
the area to the north and north-
east of the ancient settlement by
the Tiber was one of gardens,
villas and monasteries. From the
Renaissance, noble Roman families
such as the Borghese embellished
their sprawling estates here.

When Rome became the
capital of Italy in 1871, most

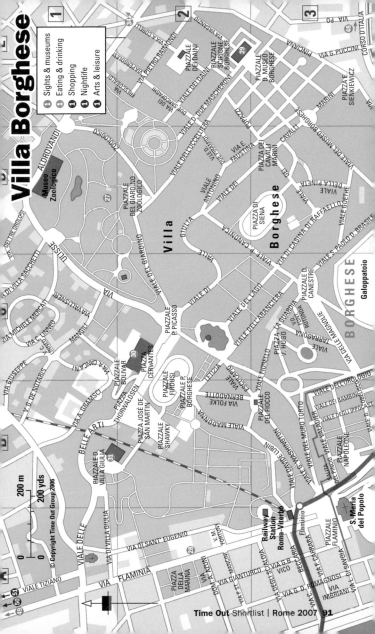

Villa Borghese

Legend:
- Sights & museums
- Eating & drinking
- Shopping
- Nightlife
- Arts & leisure

Museo Zoologico

Villa Borghese

BORGHESE

Galoppatoio

PIAZZALE SCIPIONE BORGHESE 29
PIAZZALE D. MUSEO BORGHESE
PIAZZALE DEI DAINI
PIAZZA DEI CAVALLI MARINI
PIAZZA E. SIENKIEWICZ
PIAZZA DI SIENA
PIAZZALE D. CANESTRE

PIAZZALE P. PICASSO
PIAZZA CERVANTES 30
PIAZZALE BOLIVAR
PIAZZA THORWALDSEN
PIAZZALE FIRDUSI
PIAZZALE R. BORGHESE
PIAZZA JOSÉ DE SAN MARTIN
PIAZZALE SHAWKY
PIAZZALE D. VILLA GIULIA 31
PIAZZALE DEL GIARDINO ZOOLOGICO 27
PIAZZALE NAPOLEONE

Railway Station
Roma-Viterbo

S. Maria del Popolo

PIAZZALE FLAMINIO

200 m
200 yds

© Copyright Time Out Group 2006

49 50 51

of the greenery was carved up to build pompous *palazzi*. Only the Villa Borghese was saved from post-Unification property speculators. It is now the city's most central public park, with one of Rome's great art repositories – the **Galleria Borghese** – at its heart, and one of Rome's greatest views – from the Pincio, over piazza del Popolo to the dome of St Peter's – from its western flank.

Descending south from the park, the via Vittorio Veneto (known simply as via Veneto) was the haunt of the famous and glamorous in the *dolce vita* years of the 1950s and '60s. These days, it's home to insurance companies, luxury business hotels and visitors wondering where that sweet life went.

At the southern end of via Veneto is piazza Barberini. In ancient times, erotic dances were performed here to mark the coming of spring. The square's magnificent centrepiece, Bernini's Fontana del Tritone, was once in open countryside. Now he sits – his two fish-tail legs tucked beneath him on a shell supported by four dolphins, blowing on a conch shell – amid thundering traffic. The bees around him are the Barberini family emblem.

Sights & museums

Bioparco-Zoo

Piazzale del Giardino Zoologico 1 (06 360 8211/www.bioparco.it). **Open** *Nov-Mar* 9.30am-5pm daily. *Apr-Oct* 9.30am-6pm daily. **Admission** €8.50; €6.50 reductions. **Map** p91 D1 ㉗

Slightly more sprightly since its makeover from 'zoo' to 'Biopark', this will keep your kids happy for an afternoon. Next door – and accessible through the zoo – is the Museo Civico di Zoologia di Roma (via U Aldrovandi 18) with sections on biodiversity and extreme habitats.

Explora – Museo dei Bambini di Roma

Via Flaminia 82 (06 361 3776/ www.mdbr.it). **Open** sessions at 9.30am, 11.30am, 3pm, 5pm Tue-Fri; 10am, noon, 3pm, 5pm Sat, Sun. **Admission** €7 3-12 years; €6 adults. **Map** p91 A2 ㉘

This children's museum is good educational fun for under-12s. The 3pm and 5pm sessions on Thursday afternoon cost €5 for all. Booking essential.

Galleria Borghese

Piazzale Scipione Borghese 5 (06 32 810/www.galleriaborghese.it). **Open** 9am-7.30pm Tue-Sun. **Admission** €8.50; €5.25 reductions. **Map** p91 E2 ㉙ **Note:** Booking is essential.

Begun in 1608, the Casino Borghese was designed to house the art collection of Cardinal Scipione Borghese, Bernini's greatest patron. The interior decoration (1775-90) was fully restored in the 1990s. A curved double staircase leads to the imposing entrance salon, with fourth-century AD floor mosaics showing gladiators fighting wild animals. In Room 1 is Antonio Canova's 1808 waxed marble figure of Pauline, sister of Napoleon and wife of Prince Camillo Borghese, as a topless Venus; Prince Camillo thought the work so provocative that he forbade even the artist from seeing it after completion. Rooms 2-4 contain some spectacular sculptures by Gian Lorenzo Bernini: the *David* (1624) in Room 2 is a self-portrait of the artist; Room 3 houses his *Apollo and Daphne* (1625); Room 4 his *Rape of Proserpine* (1622). Room 5 contains important pieces of classical sculpture, including a Roman copy of a Greek dancing faun and a sleeping hermaphrodite. Bernini's *Aeneas and Anchises* (1620) dominates Room 6, while Room 7 is Egyptian-themed: the classical statues include a second-century Isis. The six Caravaggios in Room 8 include the *Boy with a Basket of Fruit* (c1594) and the *Sick Bacchus* (c1593), believed to be a self-portrait.

Villa Borghese

FORTY 47 SEVEN
ALBERGO IN ROMA

Fortysevenhotel
Via Petroselli 47, 00186 – Rome
Tel +39.06.6787816; Fax +39.06.69190726
contact@fortysevenhotel.com
www.fortysevenhotel.com - www.circusbar.it

Year of Canova

Sculptor Antonio Canova (1757-1822) arrived in Rome aged 24, returning to his native Possagno, near Treviso, only when he decided it was time to build himself a mausoleum. During his years in the Eternal City, this extraordinarily prolific artist built tombs for popes, made portrait busts for the rich and famous, and filled the palaces and stately homes of Europe with neo-classical masterpieces.

To mark the 250th anniversary of the sculptor's birth, the **Galleria Borghese** has declared 2007 the Year of Canova. (Correggio will follow in 2008, then Caravaggio in 2009, Dosso Dossi in 2010, Titian in 2011, Cranach in 2012, Bernini in 2013 and Domenichino in 2014.) At the centre of the celebrations will be the gallery's best-known Canova: Pauline Bonaparte-Borghese as Venus.

Pauline is 200 years old now, but as striking as ever. Famously beautiful, and famously haughty, Napoleon's sister reclines topless on a well-upholstered divan, her white Carrara marble fingers holding an apple. Sibling rivalry led Pauline to engage the greatest sculptor of the neo-classical age to portray her: after all, he'd already carved Napoleon as a larger-than-life naked god of war. Pauline's husband Prince Camillo Borghese was so embarrassed that he gloated over the cold, silky statue by candlelight, alone in his rooms: no one else was permitted to observe his wife's beauty... except of course that they did, and the statue became the talk of Rome.

Their marriage did not survive Napoleon's downfall and exile, and the statue returned to the motley collection of sculpture left in the Borghese family's palazzo in the park after Prince Camillo's death (the best of it had been carted off to the Louvre years before). Pauline went back to France, along with the other rumbustious Corsican siblings foisted on to various European thrones after Napolean had persuaded Pope Pius VII to crown him emperor.

■ For information, consult www.galleriaborghese.it.

ROME BY AREA

Upstairs, the picture gallery holds a surfeit of masterpieces. Look out in particular for: Raphael's *Deposition* and Pinturicchio's *Crucifixion with Saints Jerome and Christopher* (Room 9); Lucas Cranach's *Venus and Cupid with Honeycomb* (Room 10); and Rubens's spectacular *Pietà and Susanna and the Elders* (Room 18). Titian's *Venus Blindfolding Cupid* and *Sacred and Profane Love*, recently restored but still difficult to interpret, are the centrepieces of Room 20, which also contains a stunning *Portrait of a Man* by Antonello da Messina.

Event highlights The gallery's artist of the year is Antonio Canova (see box p95). A major new exhibition of the sculptor's works is expected to be held in spring-summer.

Galleria Nazionale d'Arte Moderna e Contemporanea

Viale delle Belle Arti 131 (06 322 981/06 3229 8221/www.gnam.arti. beniculturali.it). **Open** 8.30am-7.30pm Tue-Sun. **Admission** €6.50; €3.25 reductions. No credit cards. **Map** p91 C2 ⑳

The collection housed in this neo-classical palace, purpose-built in 1911, begins with the 19th century: an enormous statue of *Hercules* by Canova dominates Room 4 of the left wing; in the Palizzi room are some interesting views of Rome before the sudden changes to the urban landscape in the late 19th century. The 20th-century component includes works by De Chirico, Modigliani, Morandi and Marini. International stars include *The Three Ages* by Klimt and *The Gardener* and *Madame Ginoux* by Van Gogh. Cézanne, Braque, Rodin and Henry Moore are also represented.

Museo Nazionale di Villa Giulia

Piazzale di Villa Giulia 9 (06 322 6571). **Open** 8.30am-7.30pm Tue-Sun. **Admission** €4; €2 reductions. No credit cards. **Map** p91 B1 ㉛

This collection records the pre-Roman peoples of central Italy, and the sophis-ticated, mysterious Etruscans in par-ticular. The villa was originally designed by Vignola and Michelangelo in the mid 16th century for Pope Julius III. The Etruscans went well prepared to their graves, and most of the collec-tion comes from excavations of tombs: the museum houses hundreds of vases, pieces of furniture and models of build-ings made to accompany the dead. In the courtyard, stairs descend to the nymphaeum; in an adjacent room is the sixth-century BC terracotta *Apollo of Veio*. In the garden there is a reconstruction of an Etruscan temple and a pleasant café.

Santa Maria della Concezione

Via Vittorio Veneto 27 (06 487 1185). **Open** *Church* 7am-noon, 3-7pm daily. *Crypt* 9am-noon, 3-6pm Mon-Wed, Fri-Sun. **Admission** *Crypt* donation expected. **Map** p83 E3 ㉜

Commonly known more simply as *i cappuccini* (the Capuchins) after the long-bearded, brown-clad Franciscan sub-order to which it belongs, this baroque church's attraction lies in the crypt. This is Rome's most macabre sight: the skeletons of over 4,000 monks have been dismantled and arranged in swirls and curlicues through four chapels. Ribs hang from the ceiling in the form of chandeliers, and inverted pelvic bones make the shape of hour-glasses – a reminder (as a notice states) that 'you will be what we now are'.

Eating & drinking

Cantina Cantarini

Piazza Sallustio 12 (06 485 528/ 06 474 3341). **Meals served** 12.30-3pm, 7.30-10.30pm Mon-Sat. Closed 3wks Aug; 2wks Dec-Jan. €€. **Map** p83 F2 ㉝

This high-quality trattoria is meat-based for the first part of the week, then turns fishy thereafter. The atmos-phere is as *allegro* as seating is tight – though outside tables take off some of the pressure in summer.

Galleria Nazionale d'Arte Moderna
e Contemporanea

Galleria Sordi

See, be seen, shop

Alberto Sordi was Italy's best-loved comedy actor, and a Roman. When he died in 2003, a massive refurbishment of the early 20th-century Galleria off via del Corso – once elegant, then sadly shabby – had just been completed. So what could have been more natural, in this country with an endearing habit of naming places after illustrious personages, than to name the arcade after him?

A glitzy novelty at first, the Galleria Sordi has swiftly become a packed, buzzing, crucial part of Rome's downtown scene. It's the sort of place the actor would have adored: there's often a pianist playing jazz on a grand piano in the air-conditioned foyer; sharply dressed teens, their *telefonini* stuck to their ears, use it as a rendezvous point; and chic shoppers – having plundered the bookshops, confectioners', jewellers' and yet another branch of the clothing retailer Zara – perch on cane chairs in the central aisle sipping American cocktails. Beyond the glass doors and across via del Corso, stretches Rome's political heart: the prime minister's office at Palazzo Chigi, and Palazzo Montecitorio, the seat of the lower house of parliament.

Indeed, the Galleria Sordi itself has become a satellite of this power centre. Politicians in ice-cream-coloured suits do deals in offices and hold court in the elegant cafés. A secret underpass beneath via del Corso discreetly conceals their comings and goings.

If politicians' wives and ladies who shop continue to wield credit cards in the designer boutiques closer to the Spanish Steps, and bright (but less well-heeled) young things deck themselves out in the high street fashion outlets along via del Corso, the Galleria Sordi is where the twain meet. In no time at all, the revamped arcade has become that all important Roman institution: a place to see and be seen.

Osteria del Rione

Via Basento 20 (06 855 1057). **Open**
12.30-2.30pm, 7.30-10.30pm Mon-Fri;
7.30-10.30pm Sat. Closed Aug; 1wk Dec.
€€. No credit cards. **Map** p91 E2 ③④
A short walk from Villa Borghese, the
Osteria del Rione is ideal for those sick
of *nouvelle cuisine* who want to eat like
a horse and drink like a fish for a total
of €16 per head (the price of the *menù
fisso*), which includes all the wine you
can drink.

Nightlife

Gregory's

*Via Gregoriana 54 (06 679 6386/
www.gregorysjazzclub.com).* **Open**
8pm-3.30am Tue-Sun. Closed Aug.
Admission €5. **Map** p82 C2 ③⑤
This cosy little venue oozes jazz culture
from every pore: top live acts from
Tuesday to Saturday.

Trevi Fountain & Quirinale

The high walls of the Quirinal
palace – once home to popes, today
to Italy's president – loom over a
tangle of medieval streets, all of
which seem in the end to lead to
the Trevi Fountain. This is said to
be the best water in Rome: Grand
Tourists used it to brew their tea.
Today's tourists hurl coins into it.

In ancient times, when water
was a luxury, Roman emperors
made a political statement when
they had monumentally expensive
aqueducts engineered to supply
enough – including the *acqua
vergine* that still supplies the
Trevi Fountain – to meet the city's
drinking and bathing requirements;
so too did Renaissance popes when
they repaired the ancient aqueducts
and commissioned famous sculptors
to create extravagant fountains
where they ended.

The whole of the Trevi district
acted as a service area for the

Quirinal palace: here were
the printing presses, bureaucratic
departments and service industries
that oiled the complex machinery
of the Papal States. Aristocratic
families, such as the Barberinis
and Colonnas, built their palaces
close by; their art collections are
now on view to the public.

Sharing the Quirinale hill with
the president's palace are two of
Rome's finest small baroque
churches – **San Carlino** and
San Andrea – and a crossroads
(between *vie* del Quirinale and
Quattro Fontane) adorned with
four fountains (1593) representing
river gods.

Sights & museums

Galleria Colonna

*Via della Pilotta 17 (06 678 4350/
www.galleriacolonna.it).* **Open** 9am-
1pm Sat. Closed Aug. **Admission**
€7; €5.50 reductions. No credit cards.
Map p83 D5 ③⑥
This little gallery was completed in
1703 for the Colonna family, whose
descendants still live here today. The
immense frescoed ceiling of the Great
Hall pays tribute to family hero
Marcantonio Colonna, who led the
papal fleet to victory against the
Turks in the battle of Lepanto in 1571.
The gallery's most famous picture
is Annibale Caracci's earthy peasant
Bean Eater, but make sure you don't
miss Bronzino's wonderfully sensuous
Venus and Cupid.

Museo Nazionale delle Paste Alimentari

*Piazza Scanderbeg 117 (06 699
1120/www.pastainmuseum.it).*
Open 9.30am-5.30pm daily.
Admission €10; €7 reductions.
No credit cards. **Map** p83 D4 ③⑦
This museum is dedicated to pasta-
making: rolling and cutting techniques,
the equipment, and the selection of
ingredients. There's a gift shop with all
kinds of pasta-related items.

Trevi Fountain p102

Palazzo Barberini – Galleria Nazionale d'Arte Antica

Via delle Quattro Fontane 13 (06 4200 3669/bookings 06 32 810/www.galleria borghese.it). **Open** 9am-7.30pm Tue-Sun. **Admission** €5; €2.50 reductions. No credit cards. **Map** p83 E3 ⑱

This vast baroque palace, built by the Barberini pope Urban VIII, houses one of Rome's most important art collections. Top architects like Maderno, Bernini and Borromini queued up to work on this pile, which was completed in just five years (1627-33). Highlights of the collection (which move around as interminable restoration work 'progresses') include Filippo Lippi's *Madonna* (with possibly the ugliest Christ-child ever painted); a recently restored, enigmatic portrait by Raphael of a courtesan who is traditionally believed to be his mistress; a *Nativity and Baptism of Christ* by El Greco; Tintoretto's dramatic *Christ and the Woman taken in Adultery*; Titian's *Venus and Adonis*; two Caravaggios, one of them showing Judith rather gingerly cutting off Holofernes' head; a Holbein portrait, *Henry VIII Dressed for his Wedding to Anne of Cleves*; a Bernini bust and painted portrait of Pope Urban VIII; and a self-assured self-portrait by Artemisia Gentileschi.

Palazzo del Quirinale

Piazza del Quirinale (06 46 991/ www.quirinale.it). **Open** 8.30am-noon Sun. Closed July-mid Sept. **Admission** €5. No credit cards. **Map** p83 D4 ⑲

The popes still had not finished the new St Peter's when (in 1574) they started building a summer palace on the highest of Rome's seven hills. In case an elderly pope died on his hols and had to be replaced, the Quirinale's Cappella Paolina was built as a faithful replica of the Vatican's Sistine Chapel, minus the Michelangelos. On Sunday mornings (though not always: it pays to ring ahead), when parts of the presidential palace open to the public, you may be lucky enough to catch one of the midday concerts held in this chapel.

San Carlino alle Quattro Fontane

Via del Quirinale 23 (06 488 3261/ www.sancarlino-borromini.it). **Open** 10am-1pm, 3-6pm Mon-Fri, Sun; 10am-1pm Sat. **Map** p83 E4 ㊵

This was Carlo Borromini's first solo composition (1631-41), and also the one he was most proud of. The most remarkable feature is the dizzying oval dome: its geometrical coffers decrease in size towards the lantern to give the illusion of additional height; hidden windows make the dome appear to float in mid-air.

Sant'Andrea al Quirinale
Via del Quirinale 29 (06 474 4872).
Open 8am-noon, 4-7pm daily. **Map** p83 E4 ④

Pope Alexander VII (1655-67) was so pleased with Bernini's design for this dazzling little church, built out of pale pink marble, that it became in effect the palace chapel. It is cunningly designed to create a sense of grandeur in a tiny space. The star turn is a plaster St Andrew floating through a broken pediment on his way to heaven.

Scuderie Papali al Quirinale
Via XXIV Maggio 16 (06 696 270/ bookings 06 3007 7500/www.scuderie quirinale.it). **Open** varies with exhibitions. **Admission** varies with exhibitions. **Map** p83 D5 ④

The former stables of the Quirinal palace, this large exhibition space was magnificently reworked by architect Gae Aulenti who took care to preserve original features like the brickwork ramp to the upper floors. There is a breathtaking view of Rome's skyline glimpsed from the rear staircase as you leave. Credit cards accepted for phone bookings only.

Trevi Fountain
Piazza di Trevi. **Map** p82 C4 ④

Anita Ekberg made this fountain famous when she plunged in wearing that strapless black evening dress (and a pair of waders... but you don't notice those) in Federico Fellini's classic *La dolce vita*. Now, wading in the fountain is strictly forbidden. Moreover, the sparkling water is full of chlorine (there's a chlorine-free spout hidden at the back of the fountain to the right). The *acqua vergine* was the finest water

in the city, brought by Emperor Agrippa's 25km (15.5-mile) aqueduct to the foot of the Quirinal hill. The fountain as we know it (the name Trevi comes from *tre vie* – 'three roads' – though more than that meet here now) was designed by Nicolo Salvi in 1762. It's a rococo extravaganza of sea horses, conch-blowing tritons, craggy rocks and flimsy trees erupting in front of the Palazzo Poli. Nobody can quite remember when the custom started of tossing coins in to ensure one's return to the Eternal City. The money goes to the Red Cross.

Eating & drinking

Al Presidente
Via in Arcione 94-95 (06 679 7342).
Meals served 1-3.30pm, 8-11pm Tue-Sun. Closed 2wks Aug; 2wks Jan. €€€€. **Map** p83 D4 ④

This restaurant under the walls of the Quirinal palace is one of the few really reliable addresses in the *menu turistico*-dominated Trevi Fountain area. The creative Italian menu is strong on fish: *primi* include a deliciously creamy asparagus and squid soup, while one of the highlights of the *secondi* is the fish and vegetable mille-feuille. Outside tables.

Antica Birreria Peroni
Via di San Marcello 19 (06 679 5310).
Meals served noon-midnight Mon-Sat. Closed 3wks Aug. €.
Map p82 C5 ④

This long-running, classic *birreria* is the perfect place for a quick lunch or dinner. Service is rough-and-Roman but friendly, and the food is good and relatively cheap. Sausage is the main act, with three types of German-style wurstel on offer.

Da Michele
Via dell'Umiltà 31 (349 252 5347).
Open 9am-8pm Mon-Thur, Sun; 9am-2pm Fri. Closed Jewish holidays; 10 days Pesach (usually April). No credit cards. **Map** p82 C5 ④

Recently relocated from the Ghetto, Da Michele (ex-Zi' Fenizia) does over 40 flavours of take-away pizza, all of them kosher, all of them dairy-free.

Il Gelato di San Crispino

Via della Panetteria 42 (06 679 3924). **Open** noon-12.30am Mon, Wed, Thur, Sun; noon-1.30am Fri, Sat. No credit cards. **Map** p83 D4 ⑰

Il Gelato di San Crispino serves what many consider to be the best ice-cream in the city – some say in the world. Flavours change according to what's in season – in summer the *lampone* (raspberry) and *susine* (yellow plum) arc fabulous. There are no cones here – only tubs are allowed.

Heading north

North from Villa Borghese well-heeled suburbs surround the Villa Ada public park. Down by the river, a vibrant sport and arts hub is springing to life: rugby is played in the **Stadio Flaminio** (viale Tiziano, 06 3685 7309, www.federugby.it) and football at the **Stadio Olimpico**; while the new **Auditorium** seethes with music-related activity.

Sights & museums

MACRO

Via Reggio Emilia 54 (06 6710 70400/ www.macro.roma.museum). **Open** 9am-7pm Tue-Sun. No credit cards. **Map** p91 E3 ㊽

Rome's contemporary art scene was given a shot in the arm in the 1990s with the opening of this municipal gallery in a converted brewery outside the walls west of Villa Borghese. This space will cover 10,000sq m (107,500sq ft), thanks to an extension designed by architect Odile Decq. As long as works continue, admission costs €1.

MAXXI

NEW *Ex-Caserma Montello, via Guido Reni 10 (06 321 0181/ www.maxximuseo.org).* **Open** (during exhibitions only) 11am-7pm Tue-Sun. No credit cards. **Map** p91 A1 ㊾

Financial hurdles have meant works to transform this enormous former army barracks into the Museo delle arti del XXI secolo (MAXXI), to a striking design by Zaha Hadid, have been very stop-go. For the time being, it hosts occasional temporary shows. Free guided tours 5pm Sat and 11.30am Sun.

Arts & leisure

Auditorium – Parco della Musica

Via P de Coubertin 15 (06 80 242/ bookings 199 109 783/fax 06 8024 1211/www.auditorium.com). **Map** p91 A1 ㊿

Rome's huge new performing arts centre is a buzzing success, thanks to an impressively eclectic programme and very approachable ticket prices. Guided tours cost €9 (€5 reductions; no credit cards): times change frequently so call ahead or check the website. Alternatively, wander in (open 10am-6pm daily, admission free) and have a look around for yourself. See box p104. **Event highlights** The first ever Rome Film Festival will be staged here and at other venues throughout the city from 13 21 Oct 2006; the second will bc held on dates to be announced in autumn 2007.

Foro Italico & Stadio Olimpico

Piazza de Bosis/via del Foro Italico. **Map** p91 A1 ㉛

A marble obelisk, 36m (120ft) high, with the words *Mussolini Dux* carved on it, greets visitors to the Foro Italico, a sports complex conceived in the late 1920s. The avenue leading west of the obelisk is paved with black-and-white mosaics of good Fascists doing sporty Fascist things. It's amazingly well preserved considering the tens of thousands of feet that trample the tiles every weekend on their way to the Stadio Olimpico beyond (built in the 1950s but modified for the 1990 World Cup), where AS Roma and SS Lazio both play. Tickets cost €15-€100 (no credit cards).

ROME BY AREA

Classical music reborn

Rome's recent musical renaissance centres on three scarab-shaped domes – futuristic concert halls designed by Genoese architect Renzo Piano – and on the recording studios, sound archives, specialist music shops and trendy eateries that make up the **Parco della Musica** (p103). The building of what Romans refer to simply as *l'auditorium* was visionary (nothing quite like it exists in London or Paris) and has shifted the fulcrum of Rome's cultural life to a leafy suburb along the via Flaminia.

Since its inauguration in 2002, the Auditorium has continued to go from strength to strength, enticing Romans of all tastes with a programme of extraordinary breadth. In 2005, around 1.3 million people visited the Music Park, and 720,000 tickets were issued – overtaking London's Barbican Centre (715,000) and South Bank complex (595,000), and Sydney's Opera House (534,000). Even more miraculous,

in a country where the arts are traditionally a financial black hole, the Auditorium is self-funding and firmly in the black.

Built with the materials of ancient Rome – the thin bricks, gleaming travertine stone and massive sheets of lead – the three concert halls (with 2,800, 1,200 and 700 seats) are miracles of acoustic science. They are also one of the smartest places in Rome. Well dressed Romans drift along here to take in a piano recital or a jazz concert, purchase a CD or two then linger over an alfresco post-concert supper.

In winter, show-offs can hire skates and attempt a couple of triple salchows (to a suitably stirring musical accompaniment) on an impromptu ice rink near the 3000-seat open-air seat *cavea*; on summer nights, concert-goers loll on the steps listening to Mozart, or watching a movie.

The music is world class. Which makes it all the more remarkable that that place is so unstuffy. There is something for everyone: jazz mornings for kids, recherché chamber operas, blockbuster evenings with international stars, open rehearsals, full symphony concerts and master classes.

If nothing on the programme attracts, the Auditorium is worth a visit just for the guided tour: every last rehearsal room is presented with enthusiasm, and technical explanations are given of the acoustics and of the traditional (Genoese) ship-building techniques used in the design.
■ Check the programme and buy tickets online at www.auditorium.com.

Michelangelo's *Moses* p111

The Esquiline & Celio

Monti & the Esquiline

When Italy was unified and Rome became its capital in the 1870s, this was an area of gardens, vineyards and ruins. But not for long: the country's new administrators were in need of offices and homes. By 1890 a district of solid, soulless *palazzi* had sprung up, in imitation of Turin, home town of Italy's new king, Vittorio Emanuele II. These anonymous, pompous buildings now look as if they have seen better days. A single *rione* until 1874, Monti and Esquilino encompassed some of the ancient city's most exclusive residential areas on its higher ground and its worst slum: swampy, smelly Suburra, down the hill.

That part of present-day Monti that was the Suburra – north-east of the Forum, between *vie* Nazionale and Cavour – is just as noisy, cosmopolitan and full of life today as it was 2,000 years ago. Via Nazionale, on the other hand, is a traffic artery lined by carbon-copy high street shops; half way down, the huge Palazzo delle Esposizioni showcase is still undergoing lengthy restoration; the pretty Villa Aldbrandini park, up a flight of steps at the south-western end, is a green haven with wonderful views over the city.

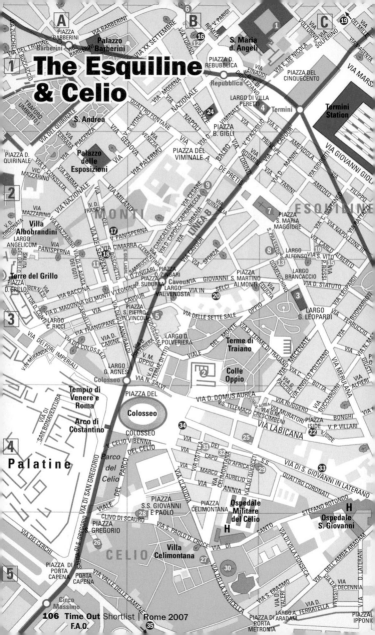

The Esquiline & Celio

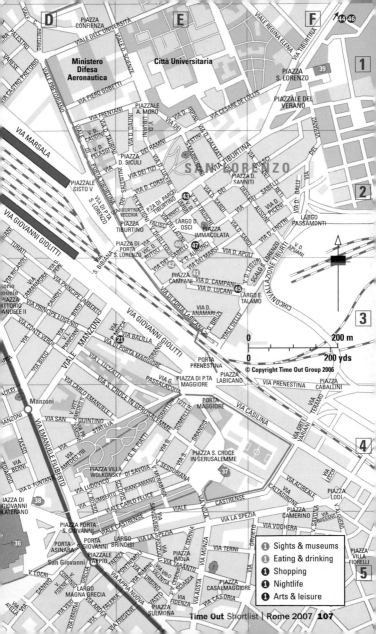

If you've come to Rome on a budget package or picked up a last-minute deal, the chances are you'll end up in a hotel on the Esquiline, around Termini railway station. It may come as a shock. For despite heroic efforts by the municipal authorities to convince us that a 'renaissance' is under way here, the Esquiline's grimy *palazzi* and questionable after-dark denizens may not be what you expected of the Eternal City. Don't despair: there are charms and attractions. Piazza Vittorio Emanuele II – the city's biggest square and known simply as piazza Vittorio – was given a new lease of life in the 1980s by a revamp of the central gardens and the arrival of a multi-ethnic community that injected life and colour; the food market, which recently moved from the piazza into a nearby ex-barracks, bursts with exuberant life. Then there are the vast basilicas (**Santa Maria Maggiore**), the intimate mosaic-crusted churches (**Santa Prassede**), the Roman artefacts of **Palazzo Massimo**, and a magnificent post-war station building at Termini.

To the south, on Colle Oppio, Nero fiddled in his **Domus Aurea**, entertaining guests with Imperial twanging on the lyre – not, as popular myth would have it, scraping at the violin. Nowadays this stretch of green is peopled by Roman mums and their offspring during the day, and some very dubious characters after dark.

Sights & museums

Baths of Diocletian

Via Enrico De Nicola 79 (06 3996 7700). **Open** 9am-7.45pm Tue-Sun. **Admission** €7; €3.50 reductions. No credit cards. **Map** p106 C1 ❶ **Note**: There's an extra charge of €2 during special exhibitions.

Now officially called the Museo Nazionale Romano – Terme di Diocleziano, Diocletian's baths were the largest in Rome when they were built in AD 298-306, covering over a hectare (2.5 acres) and able to accommodate 3,000 people. (Round the corner in via Romita, the Aula Ottagona, with its tasteful sprinkling of large classical sculptures, was part of the structure.) A convent complex was built around the largest surviving chunk of the baths by Michelangelo in the 1560s. It now contains a collection of stone inscriptions which is sufficiently low-key to allow you to focus on the massive bath buildings themselves and on Michelangelo's 16th-century restoration of the place, including its magnificent central cloister.

Domus Aurea

Via della Domus Aurea (06 3996 7700). **Open** 9am-7.45pm Mon, Wed-Sun. **Admission** €5; €2.50 reductions; plus €1.50 booking fee. No credit cards. **Map** p106 B3 ❷ **Note**: Crumbling masonry meant the Domus had to shut down in 2005; it is due to reopen in 2008.

In the summer of AD 64, fire devastated a large part of central Rome. Afterwards, anything unsinged east of the Forum was knocked down to make way for Emperor Nero's Domus Aurea (Golden House). A three-storey structure, its main façade faced south and was entirely clad in gold; inside, every inch not faced with mother-of-pearl or inlaid with gems was frescoed by Nero's pet aesthete Fabullus. The moment Nero died in AD 68, however, work was begun to eradicate every vestige of the hated tyrant. So thorough was the cover-up job that for decades after its frescoes were rediscovered in 1480, no one realised it was the Domus Aurea that they had stumbled across.

Museo Nazionale d'Arte Orientale

Via Merulana 248 (06 487 4415). **Open** 8.30am-2pm Mon, Wed, Fri, Sat; 8.30am-7.30pm Tue, Thur, Sun.

City of dreams

Rome is a wonderful town – or about to become one.

Rome is mainland Europe's biggest city. It's home to little more than 2.6 million souls, but nowhere else matches its metropolitan area of 1,290sq km (500sq miles). It's Europe's greenest city too, with 37sq km (14sq miles) of public parks and a further 42sq km (16sq miles) earmarked to become park… an average of 23sq m (250sq ft) per resident. In economic terms, Rome is Italy's healthiest city, with a growth rate in 2004 of 4.1 per cent, three times the national average. In 2005 it generated 6.7 per cent of Italy's gross domestic product, had an unemployment rate of 6.5 per cent against a national average of 7.7 per cent, and was visited by 16 million income-generating tourists.

Why, then, is it so difficult to cross a road amid the thundering traffic, or to get around on fine-when-it-works public transport? Why are the roads so full of potholes?

The past 13 years of efficient city government have made a difference, but they follow decades of administration that ranged from the negligent to the criminal. Moreover, imposing 21st-century standards and infrastructure on an ancient/medieval/renaissance/baroque framework was never going to be easy.

A new zoning masterplan approved by City Hall in 2006 aims to inject life into Rome's outer suburbs (in the hope that residents stop piling into the tiny *centro storico*) and to address the city's transport problems. *Cura del ferro* – iron treatment – is the buzzword, with the emphasis on subways, trams and local railways.

In a recent poll 79 per cent of Romans said they were 'pleased' or 'very pleased' with mayor Walter Veltroni's first four-year term. Will he deliver on his dream-city masterplan? *Staremo a vedere* (we'll see), as *romani* say.

Closed 1st & 3rd Mon of mth.
Admission €4; €2 reductions.
No credit cards. **Map** p106 C3 ❸
Despite its setting in a gloomy palazzo, this collection of oriental art is impressive. It is arranged geographically and roughly chronologically: first come the ancient artefacts from the Near East – pottery, gold, votive offerings – some dating from the third millennium BC, then 11th- to 18th-century painted fans from Tibet, sacred sculptures, and some Chinese pottery from the 15th century. There are even artefacts from the Swat culture in modern Pakistan.

Palazzo Massimo alle Terme

Largo di Villa Peretti 1 (06 480 201/ bookings 06 3996 7700). **Open** 9am-7.45pm Tue-Sun. **Admission** €7; €3.50 reductions. No credit cards. **Map** p106 C1 ❹
Note: There's an extra charge of €2 during special exhibitions.

In the basement of Palazzo Massimo – home to a large chunk of the Museo Nazionale Romano collection – is an extensive collection of coins, Roman luxuries, descriptions of trade routes and audio-visual displays. On the ground and first floors are busts of emperors and lesser mortals. On the ground floor, in Room 5, is a magnificent statue of Augustus as pontifex maximus. The first floor begins with the age of Vespasian (AD 69-79): his pugilistic portrait bust is in Room 1; Room 5 has a gracefully crouching *Aphrodite* from Hadrian's Villa at Tivoli; in Room 7 is a peacefully sleeping hermaphrodite, a second-century AD copy of a Greek original. On the second floor, rare wall paintings from assorted villas have been reassembled. Room 10 contains Botero-like, larger-than-life (megalographic) paintings, and Room 11 has dazzlingly bright marble intarsia works.

San Pietro in Vincoli

Piazza di San Pietro in Vincoli 4A (06 488 2865). **Open** 8am-noon, 3.30-6pm daily. **Map** p106 B3 ❺

Built in the fifth century but reworked many times since, this church is dominated by the monument to Pope Julius II and Michelangelo's imposing *Moses* (1515). Julius wanted a much grander tomb but died too soon to oversee it; his successors were less ambitious. As a result, the mighty Moses (in a bad translation of the Old Testament, the Hebrew word for 'radiant' was mistaken for 'horned') is wildly out of proportion, and infinitely better than the rest, by Michelangelo's students. Pilgrims come here for the chains. Eudoxia, wife of Emperor Valentinian III (445-55), was given a set of chains said to have been used to shackle St Peter in Jerusalem; with others used on the saint in the Mamertine prison, they are now conserved in a reliquary on the main altar.

Santa Maria Della Vittoria

Via XX Settembre 17 (06 4274 0571). **Open** 8.30am-noon, 3.30-6pm Mon-Sat; 3.30-6pm Sun. **Map** p106 B1 ❻
This modest-looking baroque church holds one of Bernini's most famous works. *The Ecstasy of St Teresa*, in the Cornaro chapel (fourth on the left), shows the Spanish mystic floating on a cloud in a supposedly spiritual trance after an androgynous angel has pierced her with a burning arrow. The result is more than a little ambiguous.

Santa Maria Maggiore

Piazza Santa Maria Maggiore (06 483 195/museum 06 483 058). **Open** *Church* 7am-7pm daily. *Museum* 9.30am-6.30pm daily. *Loggia* (guided tours only) Mar-Oct 9am-6.30pm daily; Nov-Feb 9am-1pm daily. **Admission** *Church* free. *Museum* €4. *Loggia* €3. No credit cards. **Map** p106 C2 ❼
One of the most striking basilica-form churches in Rome hides behind this blowsy baroque façade. Local tradition says a church was built on this spot in c366; documents place it almost 100 years later. The church was extended in the 13th and 18th centuries. Inside, above the columns of the nave, heavily restored fifth-century mosaics show scenes from the Old Testament. In the

ROME BY AREA

apse, mosaics from the 13th century show Christ crowning Mary Queen of Heaven. The Virgin theme continues in fifth-century mosaics on the triumphal arch. The ceiling in the main nave is said to have been made from the first shipment of gold from the Americas. In the 16th and 17th centuries two incredibly flamboyant chapels were added: the first was the Cappella Sistina (last chapel on the right of the nave), designed by Domenico Fontana for Sixtus V (1585-90); directly opposite is the Cappella Paolina, an even gaudier Greek-cross chapel, designed in 1611 by Flaminio Ponzio for Paul V to house a ninth (or possibly 12th) century icon of the Madonna on its altar. To the right of the main altar, a plaque marks the burial place of baroque genius Gian Lorenzo Bernini. In the loggia, high up on the front of the church (tours leave the baptistry about every ten minutes), are glorious 13th-century mosaics that decorated the façade of the old basilica, showing the legend of the foundation of Santa Maria Maggiore.

Santa Prassede

Via Santa Prassede 9A (06 488 2456). **Open** 7.30am-noon, 4-6.30pm daily. **Map** p106 C2 ❽
This church is a ninth-century scale copy of the original St Peter's. Artists from Byzantium made the rich, exotic mosaics. In the apse, Christ is being introduced to St Praxedes by St Paul on the right, while St Peter is doing the honours on the left for her sister St Pudenziana. The mosaic on the triumphal arch shows the heavenly Jerusalem, with palm-toting martyrs heading for glory. Off the right-hand side of the nave is the chapel of San Zeno, a dazzling swirl of blue and gold mosaics, punctuated with saints, animals and depictions of Christ and his mother. The wall and ceiling mosaics are ninth-century; the jolly Mary in the niche above the altar is 13th century. In a room to the right is a portion of column said to be the one that Jesus was tied to for scourging. Opens afternoons only in August.

Santa Pudenziana

Via Urbana 160 (06 481 4622). **Open** 8am-noon, 3-6pm Mon-Sat; 9am-noon, 3-6pm Sun. **Map** p106 B2 ❾
The mosaic in the apse of Santa Pudenziana dates from the fourth century (although it was hacked about in a brutal restoration in the 16th), and is a remarkable example of the continuity between pagan and Christian art, depicting Christ and the apostles as wealthy Roman citizens wearing togas, against an ancient Roman cityscape.

Eating & drinking

Agata e Romeo

Via Carlo Alberto 45 (06 446 6115/ www.agataeromeo.it). **Meals served** 12.30-2.30pm, 7.30-10pm Mon-Fri. Closed 2wks Aug; 2wks Jan. €€€€. **Map** p106 C2 ❿
Agata Parisella was the first chef to demonstrate that Roman cuisine could be refined without sacrificing its wholesome essence. Among the primi, the terrine of *coda alla vaccinara* is an affectionate tribute to a legendary Roman dish. Agata's husband, Romeo Caraccio, presides over the dining room and extensive wine list. The service is friendly but professional; the decor elegant but welcoming; the bill is steep.

Antico Caffè del Brasile

Via dei Serpenti 23 (06 488 2319). **Open** 5.30am-8.30pm Mon-Sat; 7am-8pm Sun. Closed 2wks Aug. No credit cards. **Map** p106 A3 ⓫
Its giant coffee-roaster no longer functions, but this café on the main street of Monti retains its traditional atmosphere. The place closes on Sundays from June to August.

Dagnino

Galleria Esedra, via VE Orlando 75 (06 481 8660). **Open** 7am-10.30pm daily. **Map** p106 B1 ⓬
Stunning 1950s decor sets the scene for this café-*pasticceria*, which is a corner of Sicily in Rome. If it's Sicilian and edible, it's here: ice-cream in buns, crisp *cannoli siciliani* filled with ricotta cheese, and shiny green-iced cassata.

San Giovanni in Laterano p119

Hang Zhou

*Via San Martino ai Monti 33C (06
487 2732).* **Meals served** noon-3pm,
7-11.30pm daily. Closed 3wks Aug. **€€.**
Map p106 C3 ⑬

Hang Zhou rises above most of Rome's
dull Chinese eateries not so much for
the food – which is quite acceptable –
but because it's colourful, friendly, theatrical and incredibly good value. Book
for dinner, or be prepared to queue.

Indian Fast Food

Via Mamiani 11 (06 446 0792).
Open 11am-4pm, 5-10.30pm Mon-Sat;
noon-4pm, 5-10.30pm Sun. **€.** No credit
cards. **Map** p107 D3 ⑭

This Indian takeaway is just off
piazza Vittorio. You can eat in too,
accompanied by Indian music videos.

Trattoria Monti

Via di San Vito 13A (06 446 6573).
Meals served 12.30-3pm, 7.30-11pm
Tue-Sat; 12.30-3pm Sun. Closed 3wks
Aug; 1wk Sept. **€€€.** **Map** p106 C3 ⑮

The cuisine, like the family that runs
the place, is from the Marches – so
meat, fish and game all feature on the
menu. Vegetarians are well served by
a range of *tortini* (pastry-less pies).
Make sure you book in the evening.

Shopping

The morning food market
once known simply as 'piazza
Vittorio' has now moved into
more salubrious premises in a
former barracks in via Lamarmora.
From Monday to Saturday stalls
here stock the usual Italian fresh
produce, cheese and meats,
supplemented by pulses, halal
meat, and spices. You'll also
find various exotic fabrics and
household goods.

Feltrinelli International

Via VE Orlando 84 (06 482 7878).
Open 9am-8pm Mon-Sat; 10.30am-
1.30pm, 4-8pm Sun. **Map** p106 B1 ⑯
Stocks an excellent range of fiction,
non-fiction, magazines and guidebooks
in English and other languages.

Le Gallinelle

*Via del Boschetto 76, Monti
(06 488 1017).* **Open** 4-8pm
Mon; 10am-1.30pm, 4-8pm Tue-Sat.
Closed 3wks Aug. **Map** p106 A2 ⑰

Vintage and ethnic garments are
reworked by Wilma Silvestri and her
daughter Giorgia in their funky shop.
There are also classic linen suits for
men and women.

Pulp

*Via del Boschetto 140, Monti (06
485 511).* **Open** 4-8pm Mon; 10am-
1pm, 4-8pm Tue-Sat. Closed 3wks
Aug. **Map** p106 A2 ⑱

This colourful store stocks selected
second-hand clothing; it's a good spot
for a rummage – and you just might
find a gem.

Trimani

Via Goito 20, Esquiline (06 446 9661).
Open 9am-1.30pm, 3.30-8pm Mon-Sat.
Closed 1wk Aug. **Map** p106 C1 ⑲
Trimani is Rome's oldest and best-
stocked wine shop. Purchases can be
shipped anywhere.

Nightlife

Hangar

*Via in Selci 69A (06 488 1397/
www.hangaronline.it).* **Open** 10.30pm-
2.30am Mon, Wed-Sun. Closed 2wks
Aug. No credit cards. **Map** p106 B3 ⑳
American John Moss has been at the
helm of Rome's oldest gay bar since it
opened over two decades ago. Hangar
maintains its friendly but sexy atmosphere whether half full (occasionally
midweek) or packed (at weekends and
for porn-video Monday and striptease
Thursday). The venue also boasts a
small dark area.

Micca Club

NEW *Via Pietro Micca 7A (06
8744 0079/www.miccaclub.com).*
Open 10pm-3am Thur-Sat; 6pm-
3am Sun. Closed last May to Aug.
Map p107 E3 ㉑

A huge spiral staircase leads down
to this cavernous new underground
venue with one of Rome's most eclec-

tic nightlife programmes, ranging from themed and fancy dress nights (toga parties, Hammond organ nights) to live acts (on Sundays) and international DJ sets. There's a music-fuelled Sunday vintage market from 6pm. Admission is free but you'll need to sign on to the guest list on the website.

Side

Via Labicana 50A (348 692 9472). **Open** 9.30pm-3.30am daily. No credit cards. **Map** p106 C4 **㉒**

Side is an unpretentious gay bar – an eco-savvy one to boot – that doesn't hide behind reinforced doors and a window-less façade. Warm evenings see the mainly young crowd spill out on to the pavement.

Arts & leisure

Fitness First

Via Giolitti 44, Esquiline (06 4782 6300/fax 06 487 0100/www.fitness first.it). **Open** 8am-11pm Mon-Fri; 9am-8pm Sat, Sun. **Rates** €16 per day. **Map** p106 C2 **㉓**

This gym is so pristine you'd think it was a showroom for fitness equipment rather than a place to work up a sweat. Classes in spinning, Latin dance, yoga and Thai kickboxing.

Teatro dell'Opera di Roma-Teatro Costanzi

Piazza B Gigli 1 (06 4816 0255/ www.opera.roma.it). **Map** p106 B1 **㉔**

The lavish late 19th-century *teatro all' italiana* interior is quite a surprise after the Mussolini-era angular grey façade and its esplanade with tacky potted palms. The acoustics vary greatly: the higher (cheaper) seats are unsatisfactory, so splash out on a box… it's all part of the experience.

Celio

If you're seeking a glimpse of what ancient, early Christian and medieval Rome were like, the Celio is the neighbourhood in which to do it. Here, what's underground is as

important as what's above. From the remains of ancient aqueducts near the verdant and lovely Villa Celimontana park (open daily, dawn to dusk), to frescoes of stretched and boiled martyrs in the church of **Santo Stefano Rotondo**, this area has a bit of everything.

In ancient times, the Celio was for an elite of a bucolic bent. After the city was sacked by Alaric the Goth in AD 410, the area was largely abandoned; today, much of it remains lush and unkempt. Around Villa Celimontana is a slew of ancient churches, including **Santi Giovanni e Paolo** with its excavated Roman houses beneath. Descending northwards towards the Colosseum, past **Santi Quattro Coronati** with its extraordinary frescoes, a neat grid of apartment blocks conceals the fascinating church of **San Clemente** and a lively neighbourhood community.

Sights & museums

San Clemente

Via San Giovanni in Laterano (06 774 0021). **Open** 9am-12.30pm, 3-6pm Mon-Sat; 10am-12.30pm, 3-6pm Sun. **Admission** *Church* free. *Excavations* €5; €3 reductions. No credit cards. **Map** p106 B4 **㉕**

This 12th-century basilica is a 3D time line. In the main church, the *schola cantorum* (choir), with its exquisite carving and mosaic decorations, survives from the fourth-century structure. The apse mosaic is 12th century: from the drops of Christ's blood springs the vine representing the Church, which swirls around peasants in their daily tasks, Doctors of the Church and a host of animals. In the chapel of St Catherine of Alexandria, frescoes by Masolino (c1430) show the saint praying as her torturers prepare the wheel on which she was stretched to death (later giving her name to a firework). From the sacristy, steps lead down into the

Termini railway station p109

fourth-century basilica. From there, a stairway descends to an ancient Roman alley. On one side is a second-century Roman *insula* (apartment building) containing a site where the Persian god Mithras was worshipped. On the other side of the lane are rooms of a Roman house used for meetings by early Christians.

San Gregorio Magno

Piazza di San Gregorio Magno 1 (06 700 8227). **Open** *Church* 9am-1pm, 3.30-6.30pm daily. *Chapels* 9.30am-12.30pm Tue, Thur, Sat, Sun. **Map** p106 A5 ㉖

This baroque church stands on the site of the home of one of the most remarkable popes, Gregory I (the Great; 590-604), who spent his 14-year pontificate vigorously reorganising the Church. In a chapel on the right is a marble chair dating from the first century BC, said to have been used by Gregory as his papal throne. Also here is the tomb of Tudor diplomat Sir Edward Carne, who visited Rome several times to persuade the pope to annul the marriage of Henry VIII and Catherine of Aragon, so that the king could marry Anne Boleyn. Outside stand three small chapels (closed Aug), behind which are the remains of shops that lined this ancient road, the Clivus Scauri.

Santa Maria in Domnica

Via della Navicella 10 (06 7720 2685). **Open** 8.30am-12.30pm, 4.30-7pm daily. **Map** p106 B5 ㉗

The carved wood ceiling and porticoed façade date from the 16th century but Santa Maria in Domnica – known as the Navicella (little ship), after the Roman statue that stands outside – is a ninth-century structure containing one of Rome's most charming apse mosaics. What sets this lovely design in rich colours apart is that Mary and Jesus look cheerful: the cherry-red daubs of blush on their cheeks give them a healthy glow.

Santi Giovanni e Paolo

Piazza Santi Giovanni e Paolo 13 (church 06 700 5745/excavations 06 7045 4544/www.caseromane.it). **Open** *Church* 8.30am-noon, 3-6pm daily. *Excavations* 10am-1pm, 3-6pm Mon, Thur-Sun. **Admission** *Church* free. *Excavations* €6; €4 reductions. No credit cards. **Map** p106 B5 ㉘

Traces of the original fourth-century church can be seen in the 12th-century façade on piazza Santi Giovanni e Paolo, which is overlooked by a 12th-century bell tower. An 18th-century revamp left the church's interior looking like a luxury banqueting hall. Outside and round the corner in Clivio Scauro is a door leading to labyrinthine excavations: from four different buildings (including a house that belonged to fourth-century martyrs John and Paul) and dating from the first century AD on, the 20-odd excavated rooms include some evidently used for secret Christian worship. Call ahead for tours in English.

Santi Quattro Coronati

Via dei Santi Quattro 20 (06 7047 5427). **Open** *Church* 6.30am noon, 3.30-7.30pm daily. *Oratory & cloister* 10am-noon, 4.30-6pm Mon-Sat; 4.30-6pm Sun. **Map** p106 C4 ㉙

A fourth-century church here was rebuilt as a fortified monastery in the 11th century; the outsize apse is from the original church. The church has an upper-level matronium, where women sat during religious functions. There is a beautiful cloister (c1220). In the oratory next to the church (ring the bell and ask for the key) are frescoes, painted in the 13th century as a defence of the popes' temporal power. They show a pox-ridden Constantine being healed by Pope Sylvester, crowning him with a tiara and giving him a cap to symbolise the pope's spiritual and earthly authority.

Santo Stefano Rotondo

Via di Santo Stefano Rotondo 7 (06 421 191). **Map** p106 B5 ㉚

Note: Closed as we went to press, but due to reopen in summer 2006. One of the very few round churches in Rome, Santo Stefano dates from the fifth century. The church must have been exceptionally beautiful, with its Byzantine-inspired simplicity. The atmosphere changed definitively in the 16th century when 34 horrifically graphic frescoes of martyrs being boiled and stretched were added.

Eating & drinking

Café Café
NEW *Via dei Santi Quattro 44 (06 700 8743).* **Open** 11am-1am Mon, Tue, Thur-Sun. Closed 2wks Aug. €€. **Map** p106 B4 ③

A café, yes, but it's also a perfect spot for lunch – there are soups, salads and pasta dishes – after a romp around the Colosseum. A €14 brunch buffet is available on Sundays from noon to 4pm. Café Café opens daily in summer.

Luzzi
Via Celimontana 1 (06 709 6332). **Meals served** noon-3pm, 7pm-midnight Mon, Tue, Thur-Sun. Closed 2wks Aug. €€. **Map** p106 B4 ③

On busy nights (and most are) this neighbourhood trat is the loudest and most crowded 40 square metres in Rome. Perfectly decent pizzas, pasta dishes and *secondi*, which, on our last visit, included an excellent baked *orata* (bream) with potatoes. The outside tables operate all year round.

Shopping

Soul Food
Via San Giovanni in Laterano 192-194, San Giovanni (06 7045 2025). **Open** 10.30am-1.30pm, 3.30-8pm Tue-Sat. Closed 2wks Aug. **Map** p106 C4 ③

This vintage music shop is a record collector's heaven: indie, punk, beat, exotica, lounge, rockabilly and more.

Nightlife

Coming Out
Via San Giovanni in Laterano 8 (06 700 9871/www.comingout.it). **Open** 5pm-2am daily. No credit cards. **Map** p106 B4 ③

This unassuming pub offers beers, cocktails and a fair range of snacks to a predominantly youthful crowd of gay men and women. A good place to meet before heading off in search of something a bit more frantic.

Gay Village
Parco San Sebastiano, piazza Numa Pompilio (www.gayvillage.it). **Open** *late June-early Sept* 7pm-3am daily. No credit cards. **Map** p106 B5 ③

A ten-week open-air bonanza that makes summer the pinkest season of the year: bars, restaurants, live acts, discos, cinema – a great place for boys and girls. From the 2006 season, the village moved from its traditional home in Testaccio to this park near the Terme di Caracalla.

San Giovanni

Amid the traffic, smog and drab post-Unification apartment buildings in this area are some of Christianity's most important churches and a host of fascinating minor ancient remains.

Emperor Constantine was clearly hedging his bets when he chose to build **San Giovanni in Laterano**, the first Christian basilica, in this (then) far-from-central spot. To the south of the basilica are the sunken brick remains of the Porta Asinaria, an ancient gate in the third-century AD Aurelian Wall. A park follows the ancient wall north to **Santa Croce in Gerusalemme** which is surrounded by a panoply of easily visible Roman ruins: through the opening in the Aurelian Walls to the right of the church is the Amphitheatrum Castrum, and part of the Circus Varianus; the Baths of Helena, of which you can see only the cistern; and the monumental travertine archway built by Emperor Claudius in the first century AD to mark the triumphal entrance of the aqueducts into the city. The well-preserved oven-shaped Tomb of Eurysaces, an ancient Roman baker, is to the east.

San Giovanni in Laterano

Piazza San Giovanni in Laterano 4 (06 6988 6433). **Open** *Church* 7am-6.30pm daily. *Baptistry* 9am-noon, 4-7pm daily. *Cloister & museum* 9am-noon, 4-6pm daily. **Admission** *Church* free. *Cloister & museum* €2 (free with Vatican museum ticket). No credit cards. **Map** p107 D5 ㉟

San Giovanni and the Lateran palace were the original papal headquarters until they were moved across the river to the Vatican in the 14th century. Constantine gave the plot of land to Pope Melchiades to build the church in 313. Little remains of the original basilica. The interior was revamped by Borromini in 1646. The façade, with its huge statues of Christ, the two Johns (Baptist and Evangelist) and Doctors of the Church, was added in 1735. A few treasures from earlier times survive: a 13th-century mosaic in the apse, a fragment of a fresco attributed to Giotto (behind the first column on the right) showing Pope Boniface VIII announcing the first Holy Year in 1300, and the Gothic *baldacchino* over the main altar. Off the left aisle is the 13th-century cloister; a small museum off the cloister contains vestments and some original manuscripts of music by Palestrina. The north façade was designed in 1586 by Domenico Fontana, who also placed Rome's tallest Egyptian obelisk outside. Also on this side is the octagonal baptistry that Constantine had built. The four chapels surrounding the font have mosaics from the fifth and seventh centuries; the bronze doors come from the Baths of Caracalla.

Santa Croce in Gerusalemme

Piazza Santa Croce in Gerusalemme 12 (06 701 4769/www.basilicasantacroce. it). **Open** 7am-1pm, 2-7pm daily. **Map** p107 E4 ㊲

Roma Pass

Negotiating Rome's discount ticket system for museums and archaeological sites was a headache for visitors long after other Italian cities launched special sights-and-transport offers. But in 2006 the capital finally caught up.

The **Roma Pass** is available from city-run information offices, hotels, *tabacchi* (tobacconists), anywhere selling bus tickets, museums and galleries involved in the scheme, and online at www.romapass.it. Costing €18 (€15 for 18-25s), it gives free entrance to the first two sights visited, then heavily discounted entrance to those visited thereafter during the three days for which it's valid.

Obviously, it pays to do your homework: opting to make the Colosseum (regular price €9), for example, one of the free first sights means you have already recouped half your expenditure.

But what makes the Roma Pass particularly advantageous is that it includes all public transport, making the €11 three-day ticket offered by the municipal bus company all but redundant.

The venues involved in the scheme include all city-run and most state-run museums, galleries and ancient sites. As the project got going, more and more establishments – from shops and restaurants to various theatres and the Rome opera house – began offering discounts to Roma Pass holders. A full list can be found on the website under 'news'.
■ www.romapass.it

ROME BY AREA

Founded in 320 by St Helena, mother of Emperor Constantine (who converted to and legalised Christianity in 313), this church was rebuilt in the 12th century, and again in 1743-44. Helena had her church constructed to house relics she brought back from the Holy Land: three chunks of Christ's cross, a nail, two thorns from his crown and the finger of St Thomas – allegedly the very one the doubter stuck into Christ's wound. All of these are displayed in a chapel at the end of a Fascist-era hall at the left side of the nave. The gorgeous vegetable garden, kept by the monks of the adjoining monastery, can be visited by appointment.

Scala Santa & Sancta Sanctorum

Piazza di San Giovanni in Laterano (06 772 6641). **Open** *Scala Santa* 6.30am-noon, 3-6pm daily. Closed July & Aug. *Sancta Sanctorum* by appointment only. **Admission** *Scala Santa* free. *Sancta Sanctorum* €3.50. No credit cards. **Map** p107 D4 ③⑧

Tradition says that these are the stairs that Jesus climbed in Pontius Pilate's house before being sent to his crucifixion. They were brought to Rome in the fourth century by St Helena, mother of the Emperor Constantine. A crawl up the Scala Santa has been a fixture on every serious pilgrim's list ever since. At the top of the Holy Stairs (but also accessible by non-holy stairs to the left) is the pope's private chapel, the Sancta Sanctorum. In a glass case on the left wall is a fragment of the table on which the Last Supper was supposedly served. The exquisite 13th-century frescoes in the lunettes and on the ceiling are attributed to Cimabue.

Shopping

Immediately outside the Roman walls by the basilica of San Giovanni, via Sannio is home each morning weekdays and all day Saturday to three long corridors of stalls piled high with new and second-hand low-priced clothes.

San Lorenzo

Badly built, densely populated and still showing the wounds it suffered during World War II, San Lorenzo is one of Rome's liveliest districts, full of restaurants, artists, graffiti and cultural diversity.

The area has a history of rebellion. It was designed in the 1880s as a working-class ghetto, with few public services or amenities, and soon developed into Rome's most radical district. The street battles between *squadracce fasciste* and the *sanlorenzini* are part of Italian left-wing legend. Along the north-east side is the vast Verano cemetery, with the basilica of San Lorenzo fuori le Mura by its entrance.

To the north-west is the Città universitaria, which is the main campus of La Sapienza, Europe's biggest university. The university buildings were designed in the 1930s by Piacentini and Foschini, and show the Fascist take on the architecture of higher education.

Sights & museums

San Lorenzo fuori le Mura

Piazzale del Verano 3 (06 491 511). **Open** 7.30am-12.30pm, 3-7pm daily. **Map** p107 F1 ③⑨

Donated by Constantine, this basilica was built to house the remains of St Lawrence after the saint met his fiery end on a griddle. Rebuilt in the sixth century, it was later united with a neighbouring church. Bombs plunged through the roof in 1943, making San Lorenzo the only Roman church to suffer war damage, but it had been painstakingly reconstructed by 1949. On the right side of the 13th-century portico are frescoes from the same period, showing scenes from the life of St Lawrence. Inside the triumphal arch are sixth-century mosaics.

Eating & drinking

Arancia Blu
Via dei Latini 55-65, East (06 445 4105). **Meals served** 8.30-11.45pm daily. **€€€**. No credit cards. **Map** p107 E2 ㊵

This vegetarian restaurant has shaken off its rather earnest macrobiotic origins and become a stylish urban bistro with a great wine list; good-value meat-free fare in a space with a jazzy, alternative feel. The potato-filled ravioli topped with pecorino cheese and mint was excellent; the large cheese selection and well-priced wine list are pluses.

Marcello
Via dei Campani 12, East (06 446 3311). **Meals served** 7.30-11.30pm Mon-Fri. Closed Aug. **€€**. No credit cards. **Map** p107 E3 ㊶

There's no name outside this restaurant, just a sign that says '*Cucina*'. Inside, hordes of hungry students from the nearby university occupy the old wooden tables. Alongside Roman offal specialities like tripe and *pajata* are lighter and more creative dishes such as *straccetti ai carciofi* (strips of veal with artichokes).

Uno e Bino
Via degli Equi 58, East (06 446 0702). **Meals served** 8.30-11.30pm Tue-Sun. Closed 3wks Aug. **€€€**. **Map** p107 E3 ㊷

An elegantly minimalist, creative Italian restaurant with one of the best quality-price ratios in Rome. With such pared-back decor the place needs to be full to really work. Sicilian chef Andrea Buscema betrays his origins in audacious combinations of vegetables and herbs with fish, meat and game. Book well in advance.

Shopping

Disfunzioni Musicali
Via degli Etruschi 4-14 (06 446 1984/ www.disfu.com). **Open** 3-8pm Mon; 10.30am-8pm Tue-Sat. Closed 1wk Aug. **Map** p107 E2 ㊸

One of Rome's best sources of underground records, new and second-hand. Music and film DVDs are also in stock.

Nightlife

La Palma
Via G Mirri 35 (06 4359 9029/www. lapalmaclub.it). **Open** 10pm-2am Mon-Thur, Sun; 10pm-4am Fri, Sat. Closed Aug. **Admission** varies (with annual membership, €2). **Map** p107 F1 ㊹

Beyond San Lorenzo, La Palma is an oasis in a post-industrial landscape, offering good concerts and quality DJ sets. The schedule is eclectic, though very jazz-focused. In the summer, it hosts the Fandango Jazz Festival in a spacious outside courtyard complete with restaurant.

Locanda Atlantide
Via dei Lucani 22B (06 4470 4540). **Open** 7pm-4am Tue-Sun. Closed mid June-Sept. **Admission** €5-€10. No credit cards. **Map** p107 E3 ㊺

An unpretentious venue hosting an array of events ranging from concerts and DJ acts to theatrical performances. It pulls an alternative crowd. Extra charge for concerts.

Qube
Via di Portonaccio 212 (06 438 5445). **Open** 11pm-5am Thur-Sat. Closed mid June-Sept. **Admission** €2 Thur; €15 Fri; €8 Sat. No credit cards. **Map** p107 F1 ㊻

One of Rome's biggest clubs, Qube has a week as eclectic as its patrons: there's rock on Thursdays (live) and Saturdays, while Fridays see the Muccassassina ('KillerCow') drag queens offering light-hearted transgression.

Skyline
Via degli Aurunci 26-28 (06 444 1417/ www.skylineclub.it). **Open** 10.30pm-3am Tue-Thur, Sun; 10.30pm-4am Fri, Sat. No credit cards. **Map** p107 E2 ㊼

The decor of this compact gay club is a strange hybrid, but the crowd is relaxed and mixed, with constant movement between the bar and the cruisy balcony and mini dark areas.

ROME BY AREA

The Aventine & Testaccio

Aventine & Caracalla

Though first inhabited by King Ancius Marcius in the seventh century BC, the Aventine was later colonised by foreigners, sailors, merchants and other undesirables who crept up the hill from the rough-and-tumble river port. In the fifth century BC, the plebs forced ruling patricians to grant them a say in the running of the Republic, and in 456 BC the whole of the Aventine hill was earmarked for plebeians. There they remained, organising guilds and building temples. As they became more successful, so their villas became gentrified. By the time the Republic gave way to the Empire, this was an exclusive neighbourhood.

It still is, and is lovely for a walk: the Parco Savello, surrounded by the crenellated walls of a 12th-century fortress, has dozens of orange trees and a spectacular view; peek through the keyhole of the priory of the Knights of Malta at nearby piazza Cavalieri di Malta 3 to enjoy the surrealistic surprise designed by Gian Battista Piranesi – a telescopic view of St Peter's dome.

Across busy viale Aventino is the similarly well-heeled San Saba district and, beyond, the giant Baths of Caracalla.

Sights & museums

Baths of Caracalla
Viale delle Terme di Caracalla 52 (06 574 5748). **Open** 9am-1pm Mon; 9am-sunset Tue-Sun. **Admission** €6; €3.50

Goa p130

The Aventine & Testaccio

Santa Sabina
Piazza Pietro d'Illiria 1 (06 5794 0600).
Open 7am-12.30pm, 3.30-7pm daily.
Map p124 B1 ❷

Santa Sabina was built in the fifth century over an early Christian place of worship; the bit of mosaic floor visible through a grate at the entrance is all that remains. Restored mercilessly in the 1930s, the church is now arguably the closest thing to an unadulterated ancient basilica in Rome. The fifth-century cypress doors are carved with biblical scenes. The nave's Corinthian columns support an arcade decorated with ninth-century marble inlay work, and the choir dates from the same period. Selenite has been placed in the windows, just as it would have been in the ninth century. A window in the entrance porch looks out on to the place where St Dominic is said to have planted an orange tree brought from Spain in 1220.

reductions. No credit cards.
Map p124 E2 ❶

The high-vaulted ruins of the Terme di Caracalla are pleasantly peaceful today, but were anything but tranquil in their heyday, when up to 1,600 Romans could sweat it out in the baths and gyms. You can get some idea of the original splendour of the baths from the fragments of mosaic and statuary littering the grounds, although the more impressive finds are in the Vatican Museums.

The baths were built between AD 213 and 216. The two cavernous rooms down the sides were the gymnasia, where Romans engaged in such strenuous sports as toss-the-beanbag. There was also a large open-air *natatio* (pool). There were saunas and baths of varying temperatures, as well as a library, a garden, shops and stalls. Underneath it all was a network of tunnels, totalling 9.5km (six miles) in length, where slaves trod giant wheels that pumped clean water up to bathers. Caracalla's baths were in use until 537 when the Visigoths sacked Rome and severed the city's aqueducts.

Testaccio & Ostiense

Tucked below the quiet heights of the Aventine is bustling, noisy Testaccio, where residents are stridently – even brusquely – salt-of-the-earth *romani*. Few people here support any football team other than AS Roma; elderly ladies still traipse to the market in their slippers of a morning; yelling children reign supreme.

There are no wondrous monuments here, just sites that tell of Testaccio's industrious past: an ancient river port and warehouse (*emporio*), a rubbish tip of discarded potsherds (Monte Testaccio) and an abandoned slaughterhouse (Mattatoio), now destined to become a cultural centre (see box p127). And, incongruously, Rome's most exciting nightlife hub.

Further south, via Ostiense slices through once run-down suburbs into which Testaccio's vibrant after-hours activity is seeping.

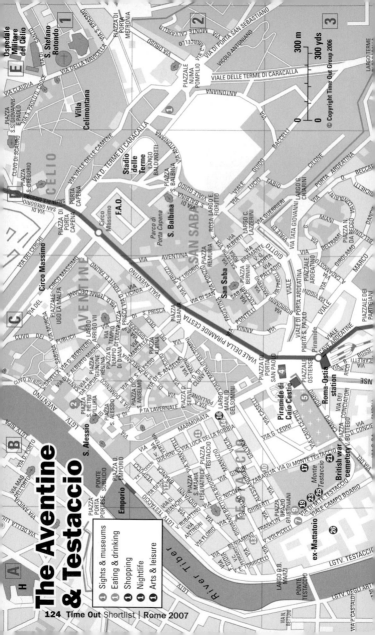

The Aventine & Testaccio

- ① Sights & museums
- ① Eating & drinking
- ① Shopping
- ① Nightlife
- ① Arts & leisure

© Copyright Time Out Group 2006

Protestant Cemetery

Sights & museums

Centrale Montemartini

Via Ostiense 106 (06 574 8030/
www.museicapitolini.org). **Open**
9.30am-7pm Tue-Sun. **Admission**
Museum €4.50; €2.50 reductions.
Special exhibitions €6; €4 reductions.
No credit cards. Map p125 B5 ❸

It may be true that the Centrale
Montemartini contains merely the left-
over ancient statuary from the
Capitoline Museums but, this being
Rome, the dregs are pretty impressive;
moreover, the setting itself is worth a
visit. Fauns and Minervas, bacchic revellers and Apollos are all starkly white
but oddly at home against the gleaming machinery of this decommissioned
generating station.

Museum of Via Ostiense

Via R Persichetti 3 (06 574 3193).
Open 9.30am-1.30pm, 2.30-4.30pm Tue,
Thur; 9.30am-1.30pm Wed, Fri, Sat, 1st
& 3rd Sun of mth. **Admission** free.
Map p124 C3 ❹

A third-century AD gatehouse, called
Porta Ostiensis in antiquity and Porta
San Paolo today, contains artefacts and
prints describing the history of via
Ostiense – the Ostian Way, built in the
third century BC to join Rome to its
port. There's also a large-scale model
of the ancient port. Upstairs are copies

of ancient inscriptions and decorations
dealing with the life of St Paul. Best of
all, you can cross the crenellated walkway for a bird's-eye view of the true
finesse of the modern Roman driver.

Protestant Cemetery

Via Caio Cestio 6 (06 574 1900/
www.protestantcemetery.it). **Open**
9am-4.30pm Mon-Sat. **Admission**
free (donation expected). **Map** p124
B3 ❺

This heavenly oasis of calm in the
midst of a ruckus of traffic has been the
resting place for foreigners who have
passed on to a better world since 1784.
Officially the 'acatholic' cemetery, this
charmingly old-world corner of the
city provides a final resting place
for Buddhists, Russian Orthodox
Christians and atheists. In the older
sector is the grave of John Keats, who
coughed his last at the age of 26. Close
by is the tomb of Shelley, who died a
year after Keats in a boating accident.

San Paolo fuori le Mura

Via Ostiense 184 (06 541 0341). **Open**
Basilica 7am-6.30pm Mon-Fri; 7am-7pm
Sat, Sun. *Cloister* 9am-1pm, 3-6.30pm
daily. **Map** p125 B6 ❻

Constantine founded this basilica to
commemorate the martyrdom of St
Paul nearby. The church has been
destroyed and rebuilt several times;

most of the present church is only 150 years old. Features that have survived include 11th-century doors; a strange 12th-century Easter candlestick that features human-, lion- and goat-headed beasts spewing the vine of life from their mouths; and a 13th-century ciborium (canopy) above the altar, by Arnolfo di Cambio. In the nave are mosaic portraits of all the popes from Peter to the present incumbent. There are only seven spaces left; once they are filled, the world, apparently, will end. In the confessio beneath the altar is the tomb of St Paul, topped by a stone slab pierced with two holes through which devotees stuff bits of cloth to imbue them with the apostle's holiness. The cloister's twisted columns support an elaborate arcade of sculpted reliefs.

Eating & drinking

Bar del Mattatoio

Piazza O Giustiniani 3 (06 574 6017). **Open** 6am-8.30pm Mon-Sat. Closed 2wks Aug. **No credit cards**. **Map** p124 A3 **7**

This brick-built doll's house is one of the earliest-opening bars in Rome, once catering to early-bird workers from the slaughterhouse opposite but now to dawn revellers limping home from Testaccio's high-density clubs.

Bishoku Kobo

Via Ostiense 110B (06 574 4190). **Meals served** 7.30-11pm Mon-Sat. Closed 1wk Aug. **€€**. **No credit cards**. **Map** p125 B5 **8**

This Japanese restaurant on via Ostiense is well placed for visitors to the collection of antique statues in the adjacent Centrale Montemartini. The food is classic Japanese, the ambience pure neighbourhood trattoria.

Checchino dal 1887

Via di Monte Testaccio 30 (06 574 6318/www.checchino-dal-1887.com). **Meals served** 12.30-3pm, 8pm-midnight Tue-Sat. Closed Aug; 1wk Dec. **€€€€**. **Map** p124 A3 **9**

Imagine a pie shop becoming a top-class restaurant, and the odd mix of

Young & fair, Part 1

The kids get their culture fix among former markets.

Over the past decade, a pulsating nightlife zone has spread, inexorably, from the area around Monte Testaccio, out along the western side of via Ostiense, and then across to the eastern side around what used to be the wholesale fruit and veg *mercati generali*. The spread took place amid the general indifference of all but dedicated clubbers: by day, these areas looked desolate, punctuated by huge abandoned buildings and linked by pot-holed roads.

But with property prices soaring, and an adminstration looking to give parts of its city a 'swinging' veneer, the desolation seems destined to end.

The Mattatoio, Testaccio's magnificent former municipal slaughterhouse, was decommissioned in 1975; for decades, opposing political forces wrangled over what to do with 24 acres of abattoir and holding pens. Some squatters took matters into their own hands, setting up the **Villaggio Globale** (p131) in the holding pens, staging concerts and cultural events... lately in a newly scrubbed venue and with City Hall's blessing. Already housing a music school, a university architecture department and **MACRO** (p103), the structure has since early 2006 enjoyed a low-key facelift. The *Città dell'altra economia* – a kind of fair-trade mall – should be one result.

humble decor, elegant service, hearty food and huge cellar falls into place. Vegetarians should give this place a wide berth: offal is the speciality. Pasta dishes including the traditional bucatini all'amatriciana are delicious.

Il Seme e la Foglia

Via Galvani 18 (06 574 3008). **Open** 8am-1.30am Mon-Sat; 6.30pm-1.30am Sun. Closed 3wks Aug. **No credit cards. Map** p124 B3 ⑩

This lively daytime snack bar and evening pre-club stop is always packed with students from the music school opposite. At midday there's generally a pasta dish, plus large salads (around €6) and creative filled rolls.

L'Oasi della Birra

Piazza Testaccio 38 (06 574 6122). **Meals served** 7.30pm-midnight daily. Closed 2wks Aug. **Map** p124 B2 ⑪

The 'Oasis of Beer' has over 500 brews on offer, including beers from award-winning Italian micro-breweries. The selection of wines by the bottle is almost as impressive. Food ranges from snacks (crostini, bruschette, a well-stocked cheese board) to full-scale meals with a Teutonic slant.

Remo

Piazza Santa Maria Liberatrice 44 (06 574 6270). **Meals served** 7pm-12.30am Mon-Sat. Closed 3wks Aug. €. **No credit cards. Map** p124 B2 ⑫

This pizzeria is a Testaccio institution. You can sit at wonky tables balanced on the pavement, or in the cavernous interior. The thin-crust Roman pizzas are excellent, as are bruschette al pomodoro.

Tallusa

Via Beniamino Franklin 11 (333 752 3506). **Open** 11.30am-3pm, 6.30-11pm Mon-Fri; 6.30-11pm Sat, Sun. €. **Map** p124 A2 ⑬

Always packed, this tiny eat-in or take-away joint specialises in southern and eastern Mediterranean cuisine – ranging from Sicilian specialities to felafel and a full range of Lebanese-style mezzes, served with pitta bread. Very friendly, and very cheap.

Tuttifrutti

Via Luca della Robbia 3A (06 575 7902). **Meals served** 8-11pm daily. Closed 2wks Aug. €€€. **Map** p124 B2 ⑭

Behind an anonymous frosted-glass door, this trattoria is Testaccio's best-value dining experience. Michele guides you through a changing menu of creative pan-Italian fare, which might include fusilli with sun-dried tomatoes, pecorino, bacon and pine nuts and then baked lamb with potatoes and rosemary. There are always a few veggie

Tuttifrutti

Zampagna

options and the wine is excellently priced. Beware: Tuttifrutti sometimes closes on a Monday.

Zampagna

Via Ostiense 179 (06 574 2306).
Meals served 12.30-2.30pm Mon-Sat.
Closed Aug. €€. **No credit cards**.
Map p125 B6 ⑮
This is basic Roman cooking as it once was, with filling dishes for the confirmed carnivore. Primi include *spaghetti alla carbonara* or *tagliatelle alla gricia* (with bacon and pecorino cheese), while most of the second courses are served swimming in the thick house *sugo* (tomato sauce). Service is brisk.

Shopping

The produce market in piazza Testaccio is arguably Rome's best. Surrounding streets, and the north-western aisle of the market itself, have been colonised by vendors of shoes of every description and price, including some astounding bargains on last season's models.

Volpetti

Via Marmorata 47 (06 574 2352/ www.volpetti.com/www.fooditaly.com).
Open 8am-2pm, 5-8.15pm Mon-Sat.
Map p124 B2 ⑯
One of the best delis in Rome. It's hard to get away without one of the jolly assistants loading you with goodies – pleasant, but painful on the wallet.

Nightlife

Akab

Via di Monte Testaccio 68-69 (06 5725 0585/www.akabcave.it). **Open** 11pm-4am Tue-Sat. Closed July & Aug. **Admission** (incl 1 drink) €10-€20. Map p124 B3 ⑰
This busy club has an underground cellar and a street-level room, plus a garden for warmer months. Featuring occasional cool concerts, this long-term fixture of the Testaccio scene has survived passing fads. Its Tuesday night electronic sessions are popular.

Alpheus

Via del Commercio 36 (06 574 7826/ www.alpheus.it). **Open** 10pm-4am Fri-Sun; other days vary. Closed July & Aug. **Admission** €5-€20. Map p125 B4 ⑱
An eclectic club with a varied crowd, the Alpheus has four big halls for live gigs, music festivals, theatre and cabaret, all followed by a disco. The music changes every night and from room to room: rock, chart R&B, Latin, world music, revival and happy trash.

ROME BY AREA

Young & fair, Part 2

Rome's Covent Garden.

The first faint glimmer of a renaissance along via Ostiense came in 1997 when some of the extraordinary contents of the Capitoline Museum storerooms were moved to a decommissioned generating station, the **Centrale Montemartini** (p126), to create one of Rome's most striking sights – a meeting of classical and industrial archaeology. Ever since, the area has been the object of enthusiastic planning.

From generating plants and gasworks, a *Città della scienza* would arise. So far, it hasn't; a timeline on the project's website (www2.comune.roma.it/citta scienza) grinds to a halt in 2002. On the other side of via Ostiense, the HQ of Rome's third university Roma Tre has, however, been shaking up the whole area with its student hordes demanding entertainment and services.

The rather down-at-heel streets round the now-deserted fruit market now bristle with bars and clubs, and the western part of the Garbatella suburb has restaurants galore and the beautifully restored, excitingly active 1920s **Teatro Palladium**.

In the markets, work was due to start in summer 2006 on a design by Dutch architectural whizzkid Rem Koolhaas: culture, shopping, sport… you name it, it will, by perhaps 2009, be here in the unimaginatively named *Città dei giovani* – city of youth – or what authorities like to call 'Rome's Covent Garden'.

Caruso-Caffè de Oriente

Via di Monte Testaccio 36 (06 574 5019). **Open** 10.30pm-3.30am Tue-Thur, Sun; 11pm-4.30am Fri, Sat. Closed mid June-mid Sept. **Admission** (incl 1 drink) €8-€15; free Sun. **No credit cards. Map** p124 B3 ⑲

A must for lovers of salsa, this club offers Latin American tunes every night apart from Saturdays, and live acts almost daily. There's a roof terrace.

Classico Village

Via Libetta 3 (06 5728 8857/www. classico.it). **Open** 9pm-1.30am Mon-Thur; 9pm-4am Fri, Sat. **Admission** €5-€15. **Map** p125 C5 ⑳

This former factory has a live music menu focused on jazz. At the weekends, concerts are followed by a DJ. The outside space is a heavenly spot to chill on warmer evenings.

Fake

NEW *Via di Monte Testaccio 64 (06 4544 7627/www.faketheclub. blogspot.com).* **Open** 11.30pm-4am Wed, Thur; midnight-4am Fri, Sat; 7pm-2am Sun. Closed June-Sept. **Admission** free (€10 compulsory drink Fri & Sat). **Map** p124 B3 ㉑

This new arrival is a stunning mix of white, 1960s space-age design, pop-art motifs and ancient brick. The music on offer centres on electronica but stretches to hip hop, R&B and beat. There's a garden, and international DJs calling the tunes.

Goa

Via Libetta 13 (06 574 8277). **Open** 11pm-5am Tue-Sun. Closed mid May-Sept. **Admission** (incl 1 drink) €20-€25. **Map** p125 C5 ㉒

One of the best of Rome's fashionable clubs, Goa is a techno-ethno fantasy, marrying iron and steel with oriental-style statues and colours. The quality of its Italian and international DJs is generally above the competition, but don't expect to find anything alternative. Not open every Sunday.

L'Alibi

Via di Monte Testaccio 40-44 (06 574 3448). **Open** midnight-5am Wed-Sun.

Teatro Palladium

Admission free with compulsory drink Wed, Thur; €15 (incl 1 drink) Fri-Sun. **Map** p124 B3 ㉓

Rome's original gay club, the Alibi is still, in theory, a great place to bop the night away, with a well-oiled sound system covering two floors in winter and three in summer, when the roof garden opens. But it is showing its age.

La Saponeria

Via degli Argonauti 20 (06 574 6999/ www.lasaponeria.com). **Open** 11.30pm-3am Thur-Sat. Closed mid May-mid Sept. **Admission** €5-€15. **No credit cards. Map** p125 C5 ㉔

One of the liveliest clubs in the via Libetta area, La Saponeria is a stylish white and curvy space with a large bar in the middle. Very mainstream music.

Metaverso

Via di Monte Testaccio 38A (06 574 4712/www.metaverso.com). **Open** 10.30pm-4am Wed-Sat. Closed mid June-Sept. **Admission** free or €5, depending on event; extra for concerts. **No credit cards. Map** p124 B3 ㉕

Metaverso is an inexpensive, friendly little club that hosts international DJs, plus some of Rome's home-grown best,

and pulls in an alternative crowd. Wednesdays are for fans of reggae; other nights are mostly dedicated to different kinds of electronica.

Spazio Boario/Villaggio Globale

Ex-Mattatoio, lungotevere Testaccio (06 575 7233/www.vglobale.org). **Open** times & days vary. Closed Aug. **Admission** €6. **No credit cards. Map** p124 A3 ㉖

Villaggio Globale survived frequent eviction threats, and for the time being operates out of a circus tent in the Spazio Boario (cattleyard) of the old slaughterhouse. It's a hot location if you're looking for top-quality concerts at bargain prices.

Arts & leisure

Teatro Palladium

Piazza Bartolomeo Romano 8 (06 5706 7768/www.teatro-palladium.it). **Admission** varies. **Map** p125 C6 ㉗

This beautiful 1920s theatre offers a mixture of top-quality electronic music acts, cutting-edge theatre, art performances and, oddly, university seminars on diverse topics.

Ponte Sisto

Trastevere & the Gianicolo

Trastevere

Trastevere – a corruption of *trans tiberim*, across the Tiber – looks very like the idyllic image of 'typical Rome' you had in mind before you came to the Eternal City: peeling *palazzi*, dark wine cellars and unspoilt trattorias that serve whatever is simmering in *mamma*'s saucepan. Many foreigners develop a passionate love affair with the quarter – the wealthier ones to the point of acquiring a little *pied-à-terre*, but this has pushed prices up and locals out of what is now, under the veneer, a very high-rent area of town.

Yet for all that, Trastevere still retains much of its slightly louche charm. The locals who have hung in there have a particular kind of charm, although other Romans would say that since ancient times the *trasteverini* have had a bit of an attitude problem.

Trasteverini claim descent from slave stock. Through the Imperial period, much of the *trans Tiberim* area was agricultural, with farms, vineyards, country villas and gardens laid out for the pleasure of the Caesars. Trastevere was a working-class district in papal Rome and remained so until well after Unification.

Viale Trastevere cuts the district in two. At the hub of the much-visited western part is piazza **Santa Maria in Trastevere** with its eponymous church. Fewer tourists make it to the warren of cobbled alleys in the eastern half,

where craftsmen still ply their trades around the lovely church of **Santa Cecilia**.

Sights & museums

Museo di Roma in Trastevere

Piazza Sant'Egidio 1B (06 589 7123/ www.comune.roma.it/museodiroma. trastevere). **Open** 10am-8pm Tue-Sun. **Admission** €2.60; €1.60 reductions. No credit cards. **Map** p134 C3 ❶

Rome's folklore museum, housed in a 17th-century convent, has a few faded watercolours of a long-vanished Rome and some whiskery waxwork tableaux that evoke the life, work, pastimes and superstitions of 18th-century and 19th-century *trasteverini*. The pretty courtyard occasionally plays host to good photo exhibits.

Orto botanico (Botanical Gardens)

Largo Cristina di Svezia 24 (06 4991 7107). **Open** *Nov-Mar* 9.30am-5.30pm Mon-Sat. *Apr-Oct* 9.30am-6.30pm Tue-Sat. **Admission** €4; €2 reductions. No credit cards. **Map** p134 B2 ❷

Established in 1883, Botanical Gardens are a welcome haven from the rigours of a dusty city: plants tumble over steps and into fountains and fish ponds, creating luxuriant hidden corners disturbed only by frolicking children.

Palazzo Corsini – Galleria Nazionale d'Arte Antica

Via della Lungara 10 (06 687 4845/ www.galleriaborghese.it). **Open** 8.30am-1.30pm Tue-Sun. **Admission** €4; €2 reductions. No credit cards. **Map** p134 C2 ❸

A 17th-century convert to Catholicism, Sweden's cultured Queen Christina established her glittering court here in 1662. The stout monarch smoked a pipe, wore trousers and entertained female and (ordained) male lovers here. Today her home houses part of the national art collection, with scores of Madonnas and Children (the most memorable, a Madonna by Van Dyck). Other works include two St Sebastians (one by Rubens, the other by Annibale Carracci); a pair of Annunciations by Guercino; Caravaggio's unadorned *Narcissus*; and a triptych by Fra Angelico. There's also Guido Reni's melancholy *Salome*.

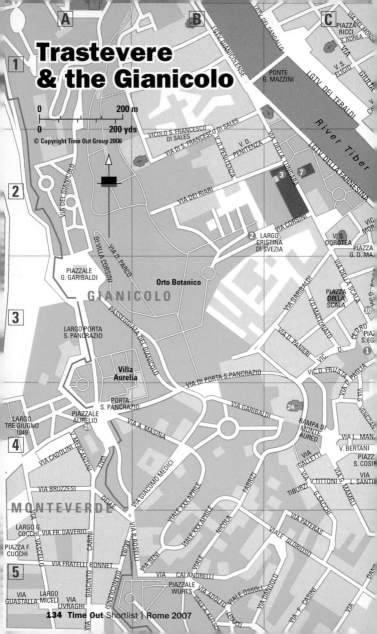

Trastevere
& the Gianicolo

0   200 m
0   200 yds

© Copyright Time Out Group 2006

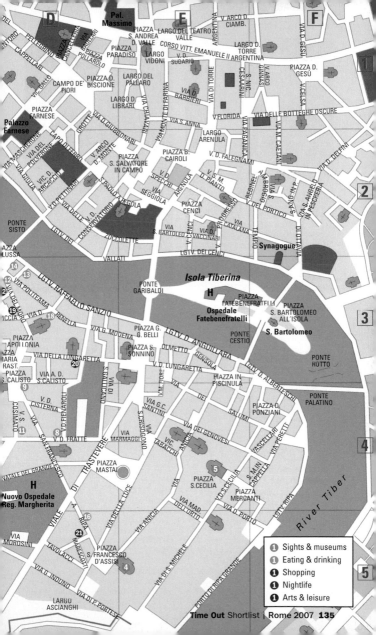

D Pal. Massimo
E
F

V. DEL TORO
CAPPELLARI
PELLEGRINO
PIAZZA CANCELLERIA
VIA BAULLARI
PIAZZA POLLAROLO
PIAZZA PARADISO
LARGO VIDONI
PIAZZA S. ANDREA D. VALLE
LARGO DEL TEATRO VALLE
CORSO VITT. EMANUELE II
ARGENTINA
V. ARCO D. CIAMB.
V.D. GESÙ

V. DEL GALLO
VIC. SUGHELLI
CAMPO DE' FIORI
PIAZZA D. BISCIONE
LARGO DEL PALLARO
V.D. SUDARIO
LARGO D. TORRE ARGENTINA
S. NIC. CESARINI
LARGO D. TORRE
V. ARCO GINNASI
PIAZZA D. GESÙ

PIAZZA FARNESE
Palazzo Farnese
VIA D. GIUBBONARI
LARGO D. LIBRARI
GROTTE
V. MONTE DI FARINA
VIA CHIAVARI
VIA S. ANNA
V. DI TORRE
VIA BARBIERI
V. FLORIDA
VIA DELLE BOTTEGHE OSCURE
V. CELSA
PIAZZA D. MONTEVECCHIO

VIA MASCHERONE
VIA DEL POLVERONE
CAPO DI FERRO
VIA GIULIA
VIC. D. ARCACCIO
V. ARCO D. MONTE
PIAZZA S. SALVATORE IN CAMPO
V. D. PETTINARI
S. PAOLO A REGOLA
PIAZZA B. CAIROLI
V.D. SPECCHI
ARENULA
LARGO ARENULA
V. PAGANICA
V.D. FALEGNAMI
V. S. M. DEL PIANTO
VIA M. CAETANI
V.D. DELFINI

PONTE SISTO
LGTV. DEI CONSERVATORIO
VIA DELLE ZOCCOLETTE
SEGGIOLA
PIAZZA CENCI
VIA S. BARTOLEO
VIA DEL PROGRESSO
VIA CATALANA
TEMPIO
VIA DEL PORTICO
D'OTTAVIA
S. ANG. IN P.
V. S. ANGELO IN PESCHERIA
AMB. PESCHERIA

PIAZZA LUSSA
14
13
12
19
18
VIA POLITEAMA
VALLATI
LGTV. DEI CENCI
VIC. VACCINARI
VIC. CENCI
Synagogue

VIA DEL MORO
RENELLA
VIA G. MODENA
LGTV. RAFFAELLO SANZIO
PONTE GARIBALDI
Isola Tiberina
PIAZZA FATEBENEFRATELLI
H
Ospedale Fatebenefratelli
PIAZZA S. BARTOLOMEO ALL'ISOLA
3

CCIA
VIA D.
PIAZZA G. G. BELLI
LGTV. D'ANGUILLARA
PONTE CESTIO
S. Bartolomeo
PONTE ROTTO

PIAZZA APOLLONIA
MARIA RAST.
VIA DELLA LUNGARETTA
PIAZZA S. SONNINO
OLMETTO
GENSOLA
V.D. LUNGARETTA
VIA FIORE
PIAZZA IN PISCINULA
LGTV. D. ALBERTESCHI
PONTE PALATINO

PIAZZA S. CALISTO
9
VIA A. D. S. CALISTO
V. DI STATULANO
PIAZZA IN PISCINULA
VIA D. SALUMI
PIAZZA D. PONZIANI

V.S. COSIMATO
11
V.D. CISTERNA
VIA FIENAROLI
VIA G.C. SANTINI
VIA CRISOSTOMO
VIA DEI GENOVESI
VIA D. VASCELLARI
VIA PERETTI

8
V.D. FRATTE
VIA S. FRANCESCO
VIA MARMAGGI
VIC. TABACCHI
VIC. ANICIA
S. MIN CAPPELLA
VIA S. ELIGIO

H Nuovo Ospedale Reg. Margherita
PIAZZA MASTAI
VIA DELLA LUCE
5
PIAZZA S. CECILIA
V.D.S. CECILIA
PIAZZA MERCANTI
VIA D. PORTO
LGTV. RIPA
River Tiber
4

16
VIALE DI TRASTEVERE
VIA ANICIA
VIA MAD. DELL'ORTO
21
VIA MOROSINI
TAVOLACCI
VIA RIPA
MARMORCCI
PIAZZA S. FRANCESCO D'ASSISI
4
VIA DI S. MICHELE
PORTO DI RIPA GRANDE
5

VIA G. INDUNO
LARGO ASCIANGHI
VIA DI P. PORTESE

1	Sights & museums
1	Eating & drinking
1	Shopping
1	Nightlife
1	Arts & leisure

Santa Cecilia

Orto botanico p133

San Francesco a Ripa

Piazza San Francesco d'Assisi 88 (06 581 9020). **Open** 7.30am-noon, 4-7pm daily. **Map** p135 E5

This 17th-century church stands on the site of the hospice where St Francis of Assisi stayed when he visited Rome in 1219; a near-contemporary portrait hangs in the cell where he stayed. The original 13th-century church was rebuilt in the 1680s, and contains Bernini's Beata Ludovica Albertoni (1674), which shows the aristocratic Franciscan nun dying in an agonised, sexually ambiguous baroque ecstasy.

Santa Cecilia in Trastevere

Piazza Santa Cecilia (06 581 2140). **Open** *Church, excavations & crypt* 9.30am-12.30pm, 4-6.30pm daily. *Cavallini frescoes* 10.15am-12.15pm Mon-Sat; 11am-12.30pm Sun. **Admission** *Excavations & crypt* €2.50. *Cavallini frescoes* €2.50. No credit cards. **Map** p135 E4 ❺

This church stands on the site of a fifth-century building that was itself built over an older Roman house, part of which can be visited. According to legend it was the home of the martyr Cecilia: after an attempt to suffocate her in her bath, her persecutors tried to behead her with three strokes of an axe (the maximum permitted). She sang for the several days it took her to die, and so became the patron saint of music. Her tomb was opened in 1599, revealing her undecayed body. It disintegrated, but not before a sketch was made, on which Stefano Maderno based the sculpture below the high altar. Her sarcophagus is in the crypt. In the upstairs gallery is a small fragment of what must have been one of the world's greatest frescoes. In this 13th-century *Last Judgement*, Pietro Cavallini flooded the apostles with a totally new kind of light – the same that was to reappear in Giotto's work.

Santa Maria in Trastevere

Piazza Santa Maria in Trastevere (06 581 4802). **Open** 7.30am-8pm daily. **Map** p134 C3 ❻

Legend has it that a miraculous well of oil sprang from the ground where

Statue of Garibaldi p141

Santa Maria now stands the moment that Christ was born, and flowed to the Tiber all day. The first church on this site was begun in 337; the present building was erected in the 12th century, and has wonderful mosaics. Those on the façade – from the 12th and 13th centuries – show Mary breast-feeding Christ, and ten women with crowns and lanterns; they may represent the parable of the wise and foolish virgins. Inside, the apse has a 12th-century mosaic of Jesus and his mother. Lower down, between the windows, there are beautiful 13th-century mosaics showing scenes from the life of the Virgin by Pietro Cavallini. The Madonna and child with rainbow overhead is also by Cavallini. In the chapel immediately to the left of the high altar is a very rare sixth-century painting on wood of the Madonna.

Villa Farnesina

Via della Lungara 230 (06 6802 7268/ www.lincei.it). **Open** *Jan-mid Mar, July-mid Sept, Nov* 9am-1pm Mon-Sat. *Mid Mar-June, mid Sept-Oct, Dec* 9am-4pm Mon, Sat; 9am-1pm Tue-Fri & 1st Sun

of mth. **Admission** €5; €4 reductions. No credit cards. **Map** p134 C2 **7**
Built between 1508 and 1511 for the rich papal banker Agostino Chigi, this palazzo became the property of the powerful Farnese family in 1577. Chigi was one of Raphael's principal patrons. The stunning frescoes in the ground-floor Loggia of Psyche were designed by Raphael but executed by his followers while the master dallied with his mistress. The Grace with her back turned, to the right of the door, is attributed to him. In the Loggia of Galatea, Raphael himself created the victorious goddess in her seashell chariot.

Eating & drinking

Alle Fratte di Trastevere

Via delle Fratte di Trastevere 49-50 (06 583 5775). **Meals served** 6.30-11.30pm Mon, Tue, Thur-Sat; 12.30-3pm, 6.30-11.30pm Sun. Closed 3wks Aug. **€€**. **Map** p135 D4 **8**
The cheap and cheerful Alle Fratte does honest Roman trattoria fare with Neapolitan influences. First courses,

Santa Maria in Trastevere p136

such as *pennette alla sorrentina* (pasta with tomatoes and mozzarella), come in generous portions. *Secondi* include roast sea bream and veal escalopes in marsala. Post-prandial *digestivi* flow freely, and service is friendly, attentive and bilingual.

Bar San Calisto
Piazza San Calisto (no phone). **Open** 5.30am-2am Mon-Sat. No credit cards. **Map** p135 D4 ⑨
Harsh lighting in a dingy space mean this bar is no picture postcard. But arty and fringe types flock here, to down a beer or an *affogato* (ice-cream swamped with liqueur), or savour some of the best chocolate in Rome: hot and thick with whipped cream in winter, and as creamy *gelato* in warmer months.

Dar Poeta
Vicolo del Bologna 45 (06 588 0516). **Meals served** 7.30pm-midnight daily. **€€**. **Map** p134 C3 ⑩
Dar Poeta does good-quality pizza with creative toppings, such as the house pizza (courgettes, sausage and spicy pepper) and the bodrilla (apples and

Grand Marnier). The varied *bruschette* are first-rate, and healthy salads offer a break from pastry. Be prepared to queue, as they don't take bookings.

Da Vittorio
Via di San Cosimato 14A (06 580 0353). **Meals served** 7.30pm-midnight Mon-Sat. Closed 1wk Aug. **€€**. **Map** p135 D4 ⑪
Vittorio is as expansively *napoletano* as they come and so are his succulent pizzas, which include the self-celebratory Vittorio (mozzarella, parmesan, fresh tomato and basil). Kids will delight in his heart-shaped junior specials.

Enoteca Ferrara
Piazza Trilussa 41A (06 5833 3920). **Open** *Wine bar & shop* 10am-3pm, 6pm-2am daily. **Meals served** 7.30-11.30pm daily. **Map** p135 D3 ⑫
This warren of a place is also a restaurant (**€€€€**) but we recommend sticking to the comfortable, dimly lit wine bar with its good choice of wines by the glass, and perhaps indulging in the wholesome dishes available at the bar.

Freni e Frizione

NEW *Via del Politeama 4-6 (06 5833 4210).* **Open** 6pm-2am daily. **Map** p135 D3 ⑬

Bar of the moment, 'Brakes and Clutch' is a shabby-chic temple to the Turinese *aperitivo* cult that has now set down serious roots in Rome. It occupies a former car mechanic's workshop in a small square just downriver from piazza Trilussa, but most nights uncontainable crowds spill across the square outside.

Friends Art Café

Piazza Trilussa 34 (06 581 6111). **Open** 7.30am 2am Mon-Sat; 5.30pm-2am Sun. Closed 1wk Aug. **Map** p135 D3 ⑭

Habitués meet in this lively bar for everything from breakfast to after-dinner cocktails. The chrome detailing and brightly coloured plastic chairs, plus the constant din of fashion TV, lend the place a retro-'80s funhouse feel. Lunch and dinner menus offer *bruschette*, salads and pastas at reasonable prices.

Aperitivo time

The after-work *aperitivo* is associated much more with the north of Italy, where hours are more regular and income more disposable, than it is with Rome. But over the last five years, the city's wine bar boom has gone exponential. The form of the evening *aperitivo* ritual is evolving too. It's goodbye to tiny dishes of peanuts and crisps, hello to huge spreads of couscous, barbecued peppers, smoked salmon, tomato and basil bruschetta, and myriad other delights.

Leaders of the revolution are Turinese gallery owners Riccardo Ronchi and Luca Conzato, who realised around the turn of the millennium that a formula that worked so well in their native town – where they already have three artsy bars – could also be applied to the capital.

The first of their Roman outposts to open, at the end of 2003, was **Société Lutèce** (p79), followed in July 2005 by **Freni e Frizione** (p139). With their recycled furniture, contemporary artworks and laid-back vibe, both venues were hits from day one. But what most excited Romans was the very Turinese habit of fuelling up before dinner – or even, in some cases, instead of dinner – from a table of free gourmet nibbles alongside one's cocktail or glass of wine.

Whether by copycat influence or pure zeitgeist, the Roman *aperitivo* craze is spreading like wildfire. The only difference is that it tends to happen a good hour later than in Milan or Turin: in Rome, nobody really starts drinking before 7.30pm.

ROME BY AREA

Glass Hostaria

NEW *Vicolo del Cinque 58 (06 5833 5903)*. **Meals served** 8pm-midnight Tue-Sat. €€. **Map** p134 C3 ⑮
Don't be put off by the ultra-modern design: though Glass Hostaria kicks against the trad Trastevere dining scene, the service is surprisingly warm, the wine list interesting, and the pan-Italian food a lot less pretentious than you might expect (outside of a couple of kooky numbers such as ice lasagne with cool mousse). It's also unexpectedly good value for money, given the setting and location.

Jaipur

Via di San Francesco a Ripa 56 (06 580 3992/www.ristorantejaipur.it). **Meals served** 7pm-midnight Mon; noon-3pm, 7pm-midnight Tue-Sun. €€. **Map** p135 D5 ⑯
Jaipur does some of Rome's best Indian food (not that there's much competition), and it's good value too – which helps make up for the garish lighting and colour scheme. The menu ranges from basic starters to a large selection of tandoori specials, curries and murghs, plus a range of vegetarian dishes.

Ombre Rosse

Piazza Sant'Egidio 12 (06 588 4155). **Open** 8am-2am Mon-Sat; 6pm-2am Sun. Closed 1wk Aug. **Map** p134 C3 ⑰
In the heart of Trastevere, this café is a meeting spot day and night: perfect for morning coffee, a late lunch or a light dinner (try the chicken salad or fresh soups). It fills to bursting after dark, when snagging an outside table is a coup.

Vizi Capitali

Vicolo della Renella 94 (06 581 8840/www.vizicapitali.com). **Open** 7pm-midnight Mon-Sat. Closed 2wks Aug. €€. **Map** p135 D3 ⑱
This recent opening shoots for a sophisticated clientele with an interesting mix of dishes and flavours. The shellfish and crustacean soup with cherry tomatoes and grilled bread is a tasty starter. Pastas – like the *tonnarelli* with scampi, pears and parmesan –

are flavoursome. Stick with straightforward *secondi*. Service is a bit slow, but gracious.

Shopping

Piazza San Cosimato is home to a produce market (early to about 2pm Mon-Sat) which manages to retain a local feel in this heavily touristed area. On Sunday mornings, the Porta Portese flea market engulfs via Portuense and surrounding streets: watch out for pickpockets as you root through bootleg CDs, furniture, clothes, bags and fake designer gear.

Almost Corner Bookshop

Via del Moro 45 (06 583 6942). **Open** 10am-1.30pm, 3.30-8pm Mon-Sat; 11am-1.30pm, 3.30-8pm Sun. **Map** p135 D3 ⑲
This English-language bookshop has a good selection of fiction, as well as history, art, archaeology and more. Check the noticeboard if you're seeking work, lodgings or Italian lessons.

Roma – Store

Via della Lungaretta 63 (06 581 8789). **Open** 10.30am-8pm daily. **Map** p135 D3 ⑳
This blissful sanctuary of lotions and potions stocks an array of gorgeous scents: old-school Floris, Creed and Penhaligon's rub shoulders with modern classics such as home-grown Acqua di Parma and Lorenzo Villoresi.

Nightlife

Big Mama

Vicolo San Francesco a Ripa 18 (06 581 2551/www.bigmama.it). **Open** 9pm-1.30am Tue-Sat. Closed early June-Sept. **Admission** free with membership (annual €13, monthly €8); extra for big acts. **Map** p135 D5 ㉑
Rome's temple of blues, where an array of respected Italian and international artists play regularly, guaranteeing a quality night out for live-music aficionados. There's jazz too. Food is served: book to ensure you get a table.

Stardust

Vicolo de' Renzi 4 (06 5832 0875).
Open 7pm-2am Mon-Sat; noon-2am
Sun. No credit cards. **Map** p135 D3 ㉒
This tiny space is an institution for
local night owls. After 11pm, the
Stardust becomes a raucous bar/pub in
which the bartenders blast out any
kind of music from Lenny Kravitz to
Cuban jazz, from Euro-rap to owner
Anna's favourite, Italian opera, to a
mixed clientele of locals, out-of-work
actors and expats.

Arts & leisure

L'Albero e la Mano

*Via della Pelliccia 3, Trastevere (06
581 2871/www.lalberoelamano.it).*
Open depends on course schedule.
Closed Sun & mid July-mid Sept.
Rates €12-€13 per class. No credit
cards. **Map** p135 D3 ㉓
This incense-scented studio offers
Shiatsu, Ayurvedic and Thai massages
at a cost of €40 per hour. There are also
daily classes in Ashtanga and Hatha
yoga, as well as several classes each
week in stretching, t'ai chi chuan and
belly-dancing.

The Gianicolo & Monteverde

Every day at noon a cannon is
fired from beneath the terrace on
the Gianicolo where an equestrian
statue of Unification hero Giuseppe
Garibaldi stands. The view over the
city from this terrace is superb. To
the south, tortuous via Garibaldi
passes by the baroque Fontana
Paola, an extravagant fountain
that was constructed in 1612 to
celebrate the reopening of an
ancient aqueduct; the columns
come from the original St Peter's.

West of here stretches the
leafy and well-heeled suburb of
Monteverde, home to vast, green
expanses of the Villa Pamphili
park. Nearby, to the south-east,
is the smaller but equally lovely

Villa Sciarra garden, with rose
arbours, children's play area and
miniature big dipper.

Sights & museums

Tempietto di Bramante & San Pietro in Montorio

*Piazza San Pietro in Montorio 2
(06 581 7377).* **Open** *Tempietto*
Nov-Apr 9.30am-12.30pm, 2-4pm
Tue-Sun; May-Oct 9.30am-12.30pm,
4-6pm Tue-Sun. *Church* 9am-noon,
4-6pm daily. **Map** p134 C4 ㉔
High up on the Gianicolo, on one of the
spots where St Peter was said to have
been crucified (St Peter's is another), San
Pietro in Montorio conceals in its courtyard one of Rome's architectural gems:
the Tempietto, designed by Bramante in
1508. This much-copied round construction was the first modern building
to follow exactly the proportions of one
of the classical orders (in this case,
Doric). In 1628, Bernini added the staircase that leads down to the crypt. The
15th-century church has a chapel by
Bernini (it's the second one on the left).
Paintings here include Sebastiano del
Piombo's *Flagellation* and a *Crucifixion
of St Peter* by Guido Reni.

Eating & drinking

Antico Arco

Piazzale Aurelio 7 (06 581 5274).
Meals served 7.30-11.30pm Mon-
Sat. Closed 1wk Aug. €€€€. **Map**
p134 A4 ㉕
The menu at this warm and modern
restaurant is strong on all fronts from
the *antipasti*, which include a quite out-
standing onion flan with *grana* cheese
sauce, to the *primi*, where classics like
risotto with *castelmagno* cheese are
flanked by new favourites such as chick-
pea soup with salt cod risotto and black
truffle. The *secondi* cover the board from
meat to fish to game, and the choreo-
graphic desserts are simply fantastic.
Sommelier Maurizio will you steer a
course through an extensive, well-priced
wine list. Be sure to book at least a
couple of days in advance.

Castel Sant'Angelo

The Vatican & Prati

The Vatican & Borgo

In the first century BC, the *Campus vaticanus* was just marshland by the Tiber, across the river from the city centre and known mainly for its poor-quality wine.

Emperor Nero built a circus here in AD 54 and added a bridge to the other bank. In the summer of AD 64, a fire destroyed two-thirds of Rome. When Romans blamed Nero, he blamed the Christians and the persecution of this troublesome new cult began in earnest. Nero's circus was the main venue for Christian-baiting. Top apostle Peter is traditionally believed to have been crucified here and buried close by on the spot where, in AD 326, Emperor Constantine built the first church of St Peter.

Not all of the following popes resided here but throughout the Christian era, pilgrims have flocked to the tomb of the founder of the Roman Church. All around, the Borgo grew up to service the burgeoning Dark Age tourist industry. Pope Leo IV (847-55) enclosed Borgo with the 12-metre-high (40 feet) Leonine Wall. Pope Nicholas III (1277-80) extended the walls and provided a papal escape route, linking the Vatican to the impregnable Castel Sant'Angelo by means of a long *passetto* (covered walkway).

After the Sack of Rome in 1527, Pope Paul III got Michelangelo to build bigger, better walls but the popes moved to the Lateran, then the Quirinale palaces. Only in 1870, with the Unification of Italy, were they forced back across the Tiber once more. Until 1929 the pope pronounced the Italian state to be sacrilegious. But on 11 February 1929 Pius XII and Mussolini signed the Lateran Pacts, awarding the Church a huge cash payment, tax-free status and a constitutional role that led to an important continuing moral influence over legislation on social issues.

The Vatican City occupies an area of less than half a square kilometre, making it the smallest state in the world. Despite having fewer than 800 residents, it has its own diplomatic service, postal service, army (the Swiss Guard), heliport, supermarket, railway station, and radio and TV stations. It has observer status at the UN, and issues its own stamps and currency. Outside in Borgo, salt-of-the-earth Romans mingle with off-duty Swiss Guards and immaculately robed priests from the Vatican Curia (administration).

Vatican tips

Dress code: the Vatican enforces its dress code strictly, both in St Peter's and in the Vatican Museums. Anyone wearing shorts or a short skirt, or with bare shoulders or midriff, will be turned away.
Papal audiences: when in Rome, the Pope addresses crowds in St Peter's square at noon on Sunday. On Wednesday mornings he holds a general audience in St Peter's square, if the weather is fine, otherwise in the modern Sala Nervi audience hall. Apply to the Prefettura della Casa Pontificia for tickets (06 6988 4857, fax 06 6988 5863, open 9am-1.30pm Mon-Sat), which are free and can be picked up on the morning of the audience.
Vatican Gardens: the Vatican walls surround splendid formal gardens, which can be visited – weather permitting – on guided

tours (€12, €8 reductions) on Tuesday and Thursday, and on Saturday too from November to March. Phone 06 6988 4676 at least one week in advance to book.

Sights & museums

Castel Sant'Angelo

Lungotevere Castello 50 (06 681 9111). **Open** 9am-7pm Tue-Sun. **Admission** €5; €2.50 reductions. No credit cards. **Map** p145 D4 ❶
Begun by Emperor Hadrian as his own mausoleum in AD 135, Castel Sant' Angelo has been a fortress, prison and papal residence. It now plays host to temporary art shows, although the real pleasure of a visit lies in wandering from Hadrian's original spiralling ramp entrance to the upper terraces, with their superb views over the city. Between, there is much to see: lavish Renaissance salons, decorated with spectacular frescoes and trompe l'oeils; the glorious chapel in the *Cortile d'Onore* designed by Michelangelo; and, halfway up an easily missed staircase, Clement VII's tiny bathroom, painted by Giulio Romano.
Event highlights 'Baroque Rome: Bernini, Borromini and Pietro da Cortona', until 29 Oct 2006.

Museo Storico Nazionale dell'Arte Sanitaria

Lungotevere in Sassia 3 (06 689 3051). **Open** 10am-noon Mon, Wed, Fri. Closed Aug. **Admission** €3. No credit cards. **Map** p144 C5 ❷
A hostel and church was established here around 726 by King Ine of Wessex to cater for weary pilgrims from the north. Known as the *burgus saxonum* or in Sassia, this became the nucleus of the world's first purpose-built hospital. British funds for the hostel were cut off with the Norman invasion of England in 1066, after which it passed into papal hands and thence to the Templar knight Guy de Montpellier, who founded the Order of the Holy Spirit. A few rooms of the modern hospital house a gruesome collection of medical artefacts.

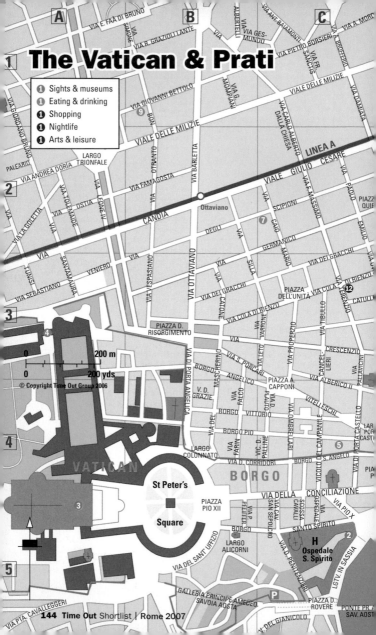

The Vatican & Prati

- **1** Sights & museums
- **1** Eating & drinking
- **1** Shopping
- **1** Nightlife
- **1** Arts & leisure

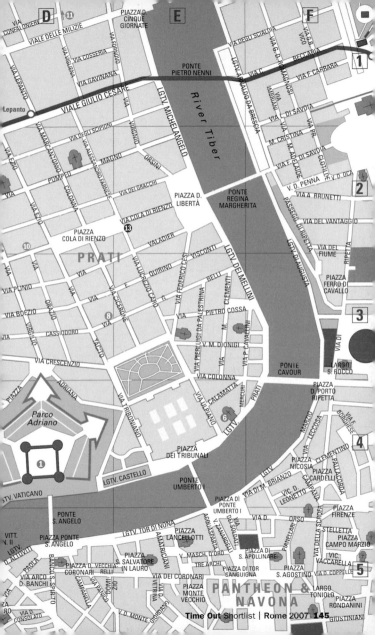

Strait is the gate

Pope Benedict reopens Porta Santa Rosa.

Pope Benedict XVI doesn't give the impression of being a particularly welcoming chap, but his first public work, unveiled in 2006, is a grand new entrance to his Vatican stronghold.

In fact, the narrow Porta Santa Rosa was made in the early 20th century then bricked up again. But recent works have graced the opening with a pair of imposing bronze doors by sculptor Gino Giannetti. For the foreseeable future, however, this breech in the medieval fortifications will remain mostly shut.

Security has been paramount at the Holy See since 850 when Leo IV built the Leonine Walls after an attack by Saracen pirates. Later, Michelangelo – who might have been better employed painting more ceilings – designed impregnable bastions.

The new doors, on piazza del Risorgimento, are inscribed *Benedictus XVI Pont. Max. Anno Domini MMV Pont. I'* ('Benedict XVI, Pontifex Maximus, in the year of our Lord 2005, the first year of his reign'). They are emblazoned with the arms of Vatican City, and with *Papa* Ratzinger's personal papal arms, which incorporate the bear, moor and scallop shell of his diocese of Munich and Freising, beneath the crossed gold and silver keys of St Peter and – in a break with tradition – a silver bishop's mitre rather than the usual gold papal tiara.

Only on the busiest days will the new gate swing open: vehicles will enter by the old Porta Sant'Anna and exit here, thus doing away with the traditional red-letter-day logjam in the alleys of the world's smallest state. But most of the time it will remain shut, its undulating brushed-bronze panels dazzling tourists in the interminable queue for the Vatican Museums.

For however early you set off on your pilgrimage to the Sistine Chapel, you will spend at least an hour in blazing sun or pouring rain, inching your way along beneath the towering Vatican walls. It's a problem that planners have failed to solve over the years, but salvation may be at hand. A glass-covered Louvre-style underground entrance is now on the drawing board, linking the museums to piazza Risorgimento and the under-construction third metro line. Naturally it will be a retail opportunity as well as a convenience: toilets and seating areas will be flanked by souvenir shops and cafés. But it won't happen overnight: the Vatican tends to think in the long term... and that can mean centuries.

Two massive 15th-century frescoed wards were emptied not all that long ago of their beds to provide space for itinerant exhibitions.

St Peter's (Basilica di San Pietro)

Piazza San Pietro (06 6988 1662/ www.vatican.va). No credit cards. **Map** p144 A5 ❸

Basilica Open *Oct-early Mar* 7am-6pm daily. *Early Mar-Sept* 7am-7pm daily. **Admission** free. Audio guide €5.
Dome Open *Oct-Mar* 8am-4.45pm daily. *Apr-Sept* 8am-5.45pm daily. **Admission** €4. *With lift* €7.
Grottoes Open *Oct-Mar* 7am-5pm daily. *Apr-Sept* 7am-6pm daily. **Admission** free.
Necropolis Apply at the Uffizio degli Scavi (06 6988 5318/fax 06 6988 5518 or 06 6987 3017/scavi@fsp.va). **Open** *Guided tours* 9am-5pm Mon-Sat. **Admission** €10.
Treasury Museum Open *Oct-Mar* 9am-5pm daily. *Apr-Sept* 9am-6pm daily. **Admission** €5; €3 children.

The current St Peter's was consecrated on 18 November 1626 by Urban VIII, exactly 1,300 years after the consecration of the first basilica on the site. By the mid 15th century, the south wall of the original basilica was collapsing. Pope Nicholas V had 2,500 wagonloads of masonry from the Colosseum carted here, just to make running repairs. It took the arrogance of Pope Julius II and his pet architect Donato Bramante to knock the 1,000-year-old basilica down, which was done in 1506.

Following Bramante's death in 1514, Raphael took over the work. In 1547 he was replaced by Michelangelo; he died in 1564, aged 87, after coming up with a plan for a massive dome. This was completed in 1590, the largest brick dome ever constructed, and still the tallest building in Rome. In 1607 Carlo Maderno designed a new façade, crowned by enormous statues of Christ and the apostles.

After Maderno's death Bernini took over and became the hero of the hour with his sumptuous *baldacchino* and elliptical piazza. This latter was built between 1656 and 1667; the oval measures 340 by 240 metres (1,115 by 787 feet), and is punctuated by the central Egyptian obelisk and two symmetrical fountains by Maderno and Bernini. The 284-column, 88-pillar colonnade is topped by 140 statues of saints.

In the portico (1612), opposite the main portal, is a mosaic by Giotto (c1298), from the original basilica. Five doors lead into the basilica: the central ones come from the earlier church, while the others are all 20th century. The last door on the right is opened

Raphael's *School of Athens* p152

Monday, Monday

How to make the most of your last day in town.

It's Monday, the last day of your long weekend in Rome, and you're still raring to go. Off to the Vatican Museums: *lunedì chiuso* (closed Monday). Some last-minute boutique browsing? *Lunedì mattina chiuso* (closed Monday morning). Monday can be a frustrating experience in Rome, so be sure to plan ahead.

Some major sights, including the **Colosseum** (p53), **Palatine** (p57) and **Roman Forum** (p58), open seven days a week. If you've already done these, stick with churches. Almost all of them – including **St Peter's** (p147) – open Monday mornings and many contain splendours: this is a good time to catch the Caravaggios at **Santa Maria del Popolo** (p87) or **Sant'Agostino** (p73), for example.

If you're planning to take something edible home, Monday morning is great for produce markets. You'll find **piazza Testaccio** (p129) positively humming with housewives refilling their fridges. For something a little more recherché, add **Volpetti** (p129) to your itinerary.

But if the sun is shining and all this sounds too much like hard work, take a well-earned rest at a pavement café table in any of the city's spectacular squares. You'll pay way over the odds, but just think of the extra charge as a theatre ticket and soak in the drama of everyday life in Rome.

ROME BY AREA

only in Holy Years by the pope himself. Inside, a series of brass lines in the floor show the lengths of other churches around the world that aren't as big. But Bernini's vast *baldacchino*, cast from bronze purloined from the Pantheon (1633), hovering over the high altar, is the real focal point. Below the altar, two flights of stairs lead to the confessio, where a niche contains a ninth-century mosaic of Christ, the only thing from old St Peter's that stayed in the same place. Far below lies the site of what is believed to be St Peter's tomb, discovered during excavations in 1951.

Pilgrims head straight for the last pilaster on the right before the main altar, to kiss the big toe of Arnolfo da Cambio's brass statue of St Peter (c1296), or to say a prayer before the crystal casket containing the mummified remains of Pope John XXIII, who was beatified in 2002. Tourists make a beeline for the first chapel on the right, where Michelangelo's Pietà (1499), is found. Proceeding around the basilica in an anti-clockwise direction, the third chapel has a tabernacle and two angels by Bernini, plus St Peter's only remaining painting: a Trinity by Pietro da Cortona (the others have been replaced by mosaic copies). Bernini's Throne of St Peter (1665) stands at the far end of the nave. Encased within Bernini's creation is a wood and ivory chair, probably dating from the ninth century but for many years believed to have belonged to Peter himself. To the right of the throne is Bernini's 1644 monument to his patron Urban VIII. On the pillars supporting the main dome are much-venerated relics, including a chip off the True Cross. In the left aisle, beyond the pilaster with St Veronica holding the cloth with which she wiped Christ's face, Bernini's tomb for Pope Alexander VIII shows the pope seated above a doorway shrouded with a cloth of reddish marble, from beneath which struggles a skeleton clutching an hourglass. Near the portico end is a group of monuments to the Old Pretender James Edward Stuart and family.

Beneath the basilica are the Vatican Grottoes – Renaissance crypts containing papal tombs. The Necropolis, where St Peter is said to be buried, lies under the grottoes. The small treasury museum off the left nave of the basilica contains some stunning liturgical relics. The dome, reached via hundreds of stairs (there's a cramped lift as far as the basilica roof), offers fabulous views.

Vatican Museums

Viale del Vaticano (06 6988 3333/ www.vatican.va/mv.vatican.va). **Open** *Early Mar-Oct* 8.45am-3.20pm Mon-Fri; 8.45am-12.20pm Sat. *Early Nov-early Mar* 8.45am-12.20pm Mon-Sat. *Year-round* last Sun of each month 8.45am-12.20pm. Closed Catholic holidays. **Admission** €12; €8 reductions; free last Sun of month. No credit cards. **Map** p144 A3 ❹

Begun by Pope Julius II in 1503, this immense collection represents the accumulated fancies and obsessions of a long line of strong, often contradictory personalities. One-way routes cater for anything from a dash to the Sistine Chapel to a five-hour plod around the lot. There are also itineraries for wheelchair users. Wheelchairs can be borrowed at the museum: you can't book them, but you can call ahead (06 6988 3860) to check there's one free.

Borgia Rooms

This six-room suite was adapted for the Borgia Pope Alexander VI (1492-1503) and decorated by Pinturicchio with a series of frescoes.

Galleria Chiaramonte

Founded by Pius VII in the early 19th, this is an eclectic collection of Roman statues, reliefs and busts.

Gallerie dei Candelabri & degli Arazzi

The long gallery studded with candelabra contains Roman statues, while the next gallery has ten huge tapestries (*arazzi*), woven by Flemish master Pieter van Aelst from cartoons by Raphael.

Galleria delle Carte Geografiche

A 120m-long (394ft) gallery, with the Tower of the Winds observation point at the north end. Ignazio Danti drew the extraordinarily precise maps of Italian regions and cities.

Egyptian Museum

Founded in 1839, this selection of ancient Egyptian art from 3000 BC to 600 BC includes statues of a baboon god, painted mummy cases, real mummies and a marble statue of Antinous, Emperor Hadrian's lover.

Etruscan Museum

This collection contains Greek and Roman art as well as Etruscan masterpieces, including the contents of the Regolini-Galassi Tomb (c650 BC).

Museo Paolino

Highlights of this collection of Roman and neo-Attic sculpture include a beautifully draped statue of Sophocles and a trompe l'oeil mosaic of an unswept floor.

Museo Pio-Clementino

The world's largest collection of classical statues fills 16 rooms. Don't miss the first-century BC *Belvedere Torso* by Apollonius of Athens, the Roman copy of the bronze *Lizard Killer* by Praxiteles and, in the octagonal Belvedere Courtyard, the exquisite *Laocoön* and *Belvedere Apollo*.

Pinacoteca

The Pinacoteca ('picture gallery') holds many of the pictures that the Vatican managed to recover from France after Napoleon whipped them in the early 19th century. The collection ranges from Byzantine school works and Italian primitives to 18th-century Dutch and French old masters, and includes Giotto's *Stefaneschi Triptych*; a *Pietà* by Lucas Cranach the Elder; several delicate Madonnas by Fra Filippo Lippi, Fra Angelico, Raphael and Titian; Raphael's last work, *The Transfiguration*; *Entombment*, which is a Caravaggio; and a chiaroscuro *St Jerome* by Leonardo.

Sistine Chapel

The world's most famous frescoes cover the ceiling and one immense wall of the Cappella Sistina, built by Sixtus IV in 1473-84. For centuries it has been used for popes' private prayers and papal elections. In the 1980s and '90s, the 930 sq m (10,000 sq ft) of *Creation*

Nuova Trattoria Paradiso

A new kind of old restaurant makes itself at home.

L'Arcangelo p154

Though Rome has not been immune to the designer restaurant virus, it was only ever infected in a mild way. Modish, architect-styled restaurants like 'Gusto, Reef or Experanto saved locals the price of a plane ticket to London or Paris. But the design-for-design's-sake fad was short lived: by the early years of the millennium, any restaurant – design or otherwise – that didn't offer either decent value for money or a really special dining experience was struggling, or on the way out (*ciao ciao* Reef, *ciao ciao* Experanto).

But a different sort of restaurant has risen to fill the breach: the *Nuova Trattoria* (the coinage is our own). Based partly on the growing demand for value, partly on the influence of the French bistrot renaissance, partly on the sheer passion of a varied group of Roman wine and food enthusiasts, these places take one of the most successful Italian inventions of all time, the neighbourhood trattoria, and give it a modern twist. And

they do this without losing sight of what makes a trattoria great: a warm atmosphere, and tasty food based on genuine raw ingredients.

What changes, in restaurants like Settembrini or Uno e Bino (one of the forerunners of this return to basics) is the desire to work creative variations on the over-traditional trattoria menu without going to the fusion excesses of many more refined and expensive chef-dominated joints. There's also a new attention to wine, as Romans, traditionally wine drinkers rather than wine experts, become more choosy about what's in their glass.

The following are our top five picks for the best of these New Trattorias, not in order of merit (they're all good) but on a sliding scale that runs from most traditional to most creative.

- L'Arcangelo (p154)
- Settembrini (p154)
- Trattoria Monti (p114)
- Tuttifrutti (p128)
- Uno e Bino (p121)

ROME BY AREA

(on the ceiling) and the *Last Judgement* (on the wall behind the altar) were subjected to a controversial restoration.

In 1508 Michelangelo was commissioned to paint something undemanding on the ceiling. He offered to do far more than that, and embarked upon his massive venture alone, spending the next four and a half years standing (only Charlton Heston lay down) on 18m-high (60ft) scaffolding. A sequence of biblical scenes, from the Creation to the Flood, begins at the *Last Judgement* end; they are framed by monumental Old Testament prophets and classical sibyls.

In 1535, aged 60, Michelangelo returned. Between the completion of the ceiling and the beginning of the wall, Rome had suffered. From 1517, the Protestant Reformation threatened the power of the popes, and the sacking of the city in 1527 was seen by Michelangelo as the wrath of God. The *Last Judgement* dramatically reflects this gloomy atmosphere. Hidden among the larger-than-life figures, Michelangelo painted his own miserable face on the human skin held by St Bartholomew, below and to the right of the powerful figure of Christ.

Before Michelangelo even set foot in the chapel, the stars of the 1480s – Cosimo Roselli, Chirlandaio, Botticelli, Perugino – had created the paintings along the walls.

Raphael Rooms

Pope Julius II gave 26-year-old Raphael carte blanche to redesign four rooms of the Papal Suite. The Study (Stanza della Segnatura; 1508-11) covers philosophical and spiritual themes. The star-packed *School of Athens* fresco has contemporary artists as classical figures: Plato is Leonardo; the glum thinker on the steps at the front – Heraclitus – is Michelangelo; Euclid is Bramante; and Raphael himself is on the far right-hand side behind a man in white. Raphael next turned to the Stanza di Eliodoro (1512-14), where the portrayal of God saving the temple in Jerusalem from the thieving Heliodorus was intended to highlight the divine protection enjoyed by Pope Julius. The Dining Room (Stanza dell'Incendio; 1514-17) is dedicated to Pope Leo X (the most obese of the Popes, he died from gout aged 38). The room is named for the *Fire in the Borgo*, which Leo IV apparently stopped with the sign of the

St Peter's p147

also available by the glass, to be savoured with a selection of hot and cold gastronomic delights. No pasta here: instead, choose from cold platters that include salamis, and cheeses matured in interesting ways. Hot dishes might include polenta served with porcini mushrooms, truffles, wild boar or hare sauce.

Prati

After Rome became capital of the newly unified Italian state in 1871, the meadows (*prati*) around the ramparts north of Borgo were required for housing for the staff of the ministries and parliament across the Tiber. The largest of the *piazze* by the Vatican walls was provocatively named after the Risorgimento, the movement that destroyed the papacy's hold on Italy. Broad avenues were laid out and named after freedom fighters.

A solidly bourgeois district, Prati has a main drag, via Cola di Rienzo, that provides ample opportunities for retail therapy. Imposing military barracks line viale delle Milizie and the bombastic Palazzo di Giustizia (popularly known as il *palazzaccio*, 'the big ugly building') sits between piazza Cavour and the Tiber. On the riverbank is one of Catholic Rome's truly weird experiences: the Museo delle Anime dei Defunti.

Sights & museums

Museo delle Anime dei Defunti

Lungotevere Prati 12 (06 6880 6517). **Open** *mid Sept-June* 7.30-11am, 4.30-7pm daily. *July-mid Sept* 7.30-10am, 5.30-7.30pm daily. **Map** p145 E4 ❻
This macabre collection, attached to the neo-Gothic church of Sacro Cuore di Gesù in Prati, contains hand- and fingerprints left on the prayer books and clothes of the living by dead loved ones, to request masses to release their souls from purgatory.

cross. The Reception Room (Sala di Constantino; 1517-24) was completed by Giulio Romano after Raphael's death in 1520, and tells the legend of Emperor Constantine's miraculous conversion. The Loggia di Raffaello (usually closed) has a beautiful view over Rome; started by Bramante in 1513, and finished by Raphael, it has 52 small paintings on biblical themes, and leads into the Sala dei Chiaroscuri. The adjacent Chapel of Nicholas V has scenes by Fra Angelico (1448-50) from the lives of Saint Lawrence and Saint Stephen.
Event highlights 'Laocoön, the origins of the Vatican Museums', marking the 500th anniversary of the founding of the Vatican Museums, begins on 16 Nov 2006.

Eating & drinking

Borgo Antico

Borgo Pio 21 (06 686 5967). **Meals served** 7-10.30pm Mon; noon-3pm, 7-10.30pm Tue-Sat; 12.30-3pm Sun. Closed 3wks Aug. €€. **Map** p144 C4 ❺
This tiny wood-beamed hostelry offers an extensive selection of wines, many

ROME BY AREA

Eating & drinking

Del Frate

Via degli Scipioni 118 (06 323 6437).
Meals served 1-3pm, 7.30pm-1am
Mon-Sat; 7.30pm-1am Sun. Closed
2wks Aug. **€€**. **Map** p144 C2 ❼
Del Frate, an historic Prati bottle shop,
expanded a few years back and opened
a wine-bar annexe. Of an evening, the
tables spill over into the *enoteca* itself,
amid tall shelves crammed with bot-
tles. The oven-baked ravioli with
salmon and courgette sauce is a good
demonstration of the place's modern
approach; main courses might include
an escalope of sea bass with pan-fried
cicoria. The only off-note is the steep
mark-up on wines.

L'Arcangelo

NEW *Via GG Belli 59-61 (06 321
0992).* **Meals served** 1-2.30pm,
8-11.30pm Mon-Fri; 8-11.30pm Sat.
Closed Aug. **€€€**. **Map** p145 D3 ❽
Elegant L'Arcangelo has wood pan-
elling below tobacco-sponged walls,
linen tablecloths and a soft jazz soundtrack. But it's what's on the plate that
really impresses. A tartlet of octopus
and potato with olive oil is simple but
delicious, and fresh pasta *chitarrini*
with marinated anchovies and fried
artichokes a worthy follow-up. *Secondi*,
such as steamed *baccalà* (cod) with
puréed broccoli and warm ricotta with
cocoa beans, are clever variations on
the Roman tradition. The wine list
includes some real discoveries from
small-scale Italian producers.

Osteria dell'Angelo

Via G Bettolo 32 (06 372 9470).
Meals served 8-11pm Mon, Sat;
12.30-2.30pm, 8-11pm Tue-Fri. Closed
2wks Aug. **€€**. No credit cards. **Map**
p144 B1 ❾
The decor at this neighbourhood trat
consists of photos of boxers and rugby
players – the two sporting passions of
host Angelo Croce. The menu – which,
in the evening, comes at a fixed price
(€25), rough-and-ready house wine
included – celebrates the Roman tradition in dishes such as *tonnarelli cacio e*

pepe (pasta with cheese and pepper)
and meatballs flavoured with nutmeg,
pine nuts and sultanas.

Pellaccia

*Via Cola di Rienzo 103 (06 321
0807).* **Open** 6.30am-1am Tue-Sun.
Closed 1wk Aug. No credit cards.
Map p145 D2 ❿
This bar on Prati's busiest street pro-
duces some of the best ice-cream north
of the river. It's perfect for recovering
after a slog around the Vatican.

Settembrini

NEW *Via Luigi Settembrini 25 (06 323
2617).* **Meals served** 11am-12.30am
Mon-Sat. **€€€**. Closed 2wks Aug.
Map p145 D1 ⓫
One of the most interesting new kids
on the block, Settembrini mixes design
and tradition both in its warmly
minimalist decor and in its menu. In
chef Marco Poddi's Italo fusion
approach, the flavours of his native
Sardinia are prominent – as in the
spaghetti with Cabras sea urchins –
and all ingredients are sourced with an
obssessive regard for quality. It's open
all day from 11am on, segue-ing from
morning panini to buffet lunch to
afternoon tea to *aperitivi* to the full-on
dinner experience.

Shopping

Castroni

*Via Cola di Rienzo 196, Prati (06 687
4383/www.castroni.com).* **Open** 8am-
8pm Mon-Sat. **Map** p144 C3 ⓬
This wonderful shop sells all sorts of
Italian regional specialities and a wide
range of imported foodstuffs: anything
from Chinese noodles to HP Sauce.
Online shopping available.

Iron G

Via Cola di Rienzo 50 (06 321 6798).
Open 10.30am-7.30pm Mon-Sat. Closed
2wks Aug. **Map** p145 E2 ⓭
This warehousey boutique supplies
clubwear to the fashion victims of
this well-heeled neighbourhood. The
hippest labels mix with ethnic and
local accessories and some jewellery.

Out of Town

The Appian Way

The most picturesque of the ancient Roman *vie consolari* (consular roads), the via Appia Antica was Rome's first great military highway, stretching first to Capua in the south, and on to Brindisi to link *caput mundi* with the Adriatic.

Built in the fourth century BC by Appius Claudius Caecus, a statesman and censor, it was the first to bear the name of its builder rather than its destination. By the time it reached Brindisi in 121 BC, the Appia was the Romans' main route to the eastern Empire and was known as the *regina varium*, 'the Queen of Roads'. Well-to-do Roman families began building their mausoleums alongside, and

soon it was lined with tombs, vaults, sarcophagi and every imaginable kind of magnificent mortuary decoration.

Christians, too, started to bury their dead here (burial was always performed outside a sacred city boundary known as the *pomerium*), initially in necropoli and, later, underground, creating the estimated 300-kilometre (200-mile) network of tunnels known as the catacombs. This system wasn't used for secret worship as once thought: authorities were perfectly aware of the existence of the catacombs. A Jewish catacomb still exists at via Appia Antica 119.

The via Appia Antica suffered at the hands of marauding Goths and Normans; successive popes did as much damage, grabbing any good pieces of statuary or marble that remained and reducing the ancient monuments to unrecognisable stumps. Miraculously, there are still things to see: this is a wonderful place to spend a day, preferably a Sunday or holiday when all but local traffic is banned.

Explore more extensively by renting a bike at the **Centro Visite Parco Appia Antica Antica** (via Appia Antica 58-60, 06 513 5316, www.parcoappia antica.org, open 9.30am-1.30pm, 2-4.30pm daily). Buses 118 and 218 stop nearby.

Getting there

You can take the hop-on, hop-off **Archeobus** (information 06 4695 2252; tickets €8), which leaves from Termini railway station and stops by most major sights. Alternatively, the following regular bus services ply part of the way:

118 from viale Aventino (Circo Massimo metro) to the catacombs of San Callisto and San Sebastiano

660 from Colli Albani metro to the Circus of Maxentius and Tomb of Cecilia Metella.

Sights & museums

Catacombs of San Callisto

Via Appia Antica 78, 110 & 126 (06 513 0151/www.catacombe.roma.it). **Open** 9am-noon, 2.30-5pm Mon, Tue, Thur-Sun. Closed Feb. **Admission** €5; €3 reductions.

These are the largest of Rome's underground burial sites. Buried in the 29km (12.5 miles) of tunnels were nine popes, dozens of martyrs and thousands of Christians. They are stacked down, with the oldest on the top. Named after third-century Pope Callixtus, the area became the first official cemetery of the Church of Rome. The crypt of St Cecilia is the spot where this patron saint of music is believed to have been buried before she was moved to her eponymous church in Trastevere.

Catacombs of San Sebastiano

Via Appia Antica 136 (06 785 0350). **Open** 9am-noon, 2.30-5pm Mon-Sat. Closed mid Nov-mid Dec. **Admission** €5; €3 reductions. No credit cards.

The name 'catacomb' originated in this spot, where a complex of underground burial sites situated near a tufa quarry was described as being *kata kymbas* – 'near the quarry'. The guided tour will take you into the crypt of St Sebastian, the martyr always depicted nastily pierced by a hail of arrows (though these were just one of several unpleasant tortures), who was buried here in the late third century. Above, the fourth-century basilica of San Sebastiano (open 8.30am-6pm daily) was originally called basilica Apostolorum, because the remains of Saints Peter and Paul were hidden here. On display is the marble slab in which Christ left his footprints during his miraculous apparition at the spot where the Domine Quo Vadis? church (open 7am-7pm daily) now stands on the via Appia. (These are the real thing: the prints in Domino Quo Vadis? are just a copy.)

Circus of Maxentius

Via Appia Antica 153 (06 780 1324). **Open** 9am-1pm Tue-Sun. **Admission** €3. No credit cards.

One of the best preserved Roman circuses, this was built by the Emperor Maxentius for his private use in the early years of the fourth century AD. Remains of the Imperial palace are perched above the track, at its northern end. Earthenware jugs (amphorae) in the upper sections of the long walls helped lighten the load above the vaults. At the north end is the mausoleum Maxentius built for his beloved son Romulus.

Tomb of Cecilia Metella

Via Appia Antica 161 (06 780 0093). **Open** *Oct-mid Mar* 9am-4pm Tue-Sun. *Mid Mar-Sept* 9am-6.30pm Tue-Sun. **Admission** €6; €3 reductions. No credit cards. **Note**: Opening hours are erratic.

This colossal cylinder of travertine is the final resting place of a woman who married into the wealthy Metella family in the first century BC. During the 14th century the powerful Caetani family, relatives of Pope Boniface VIII, incorporated the tomb into a fortress, adding the crenellations to the top. High up on a wall, a plaque honours Cecilia, and the spot where she was buried is a fine example of brick dome-making. Inside, a roofless gallery holds funerary statues. Downstairs, pieces of the volcanic rock used in the construction of the via Appia Antica can be seen.

EUR

Italian Fascism managed to be simultaneously monstrous and absurd, but its delusions of grandeur nonetheless produced some of the most interesting European architecture and town planning of the 20th century.

In the early 1930s Giuseppe Bottai, governor of Rome and the leading arbiter of Fascist taste, had the idea of expanding landbound Rome along via Ostiense towards the sea, some 20km (12.5 miles) away. Using as an excuse the universal exhibition, pencilled in for 1942, he intended to combine cultural exhibition spaces with a monument to the regime.

Architect Marcello Piacentini was charged with coordinating the ambitious project but few of the original designs were ever built. The planning committee became so bogged down in argument that little had been achieved by the outbreak of World War II. After the war, work resumed with a different spirit. Still known as EUR (*Esposizione universale romana*), it's now a business district, where unrelieved planes of icy travertine and reinterpretations of classical monuments let you know you're not in Kansas any more.

A slew of appropriately didactic museums – the Museo dell'Alto Medioevo, **Museo della Civiltà Romana** (now containing a new astrology museum and planetarium), Museo delle Arti e Tradizioni Popolari, the Museo Preistorico ed Etnografico – allows a glimpse inside these grandiose monuments to Fascist grandeur.

Getting there

Take metro line B to EUR Fermi, or bus numbers 30, 170 or 714, are a better way to approach it.

ROME BY AREA

The Appian Way p155

Sights & museums

Abbazia delle Tre Fontane

Via Acque Salvie 1 (06 540 1655/shop 06 540 2309/tre.fontane@flashnet.it). **Open** *San Vincenzo Anastasio* 6.45am-12.30pm, 3-8pm daily. *Other churches* 8am-1pm, 3-6.30pm daily. *Shop* 9am-1pm, 3.30-6.30pm daily.

North-east of the centre of the EUR (and accessible on buses 671, 707, 716, 761 or 767) there lies a haven of ancient, eucalyptus-scented green, with three churches that commemorate the points where St Paul's head supposedly bounced after it was severed from his body in AD 67. (Being a citizen of Rome, Paul was eligible for the relatively quick and painless head-chop, as opposed to the considerably less appealing prospect of a long, drawn-out crucifixion.) These are the grounds of the Trappist monastery of Tre Fontane, where water has gurgled and birds have sung since the fifth century. The church of San Paolo delle Tre Fontane is said to be built on the spot where the apostle was executed; apart from a column to which Paul is supposed to have been tied, all traces of the fifth-century church were done away with in 1599 by architect Giacomo della Porta, who was also responsible for the two other churches. Monks planted the eucalyptus trees here in the 1860s, believing they would drive away the malarial mosquitoes; a liqueur is now brewed from the trees and sold in a little shop (no credit cards accepted) along with chocolate and various other remedies for all ills.

Museo dell'Alto Medioevo

Viale Lincoln 3 (06 5422 8199). **Open** 9am-8pm Tue-Sun. **Admission** €2; €1 reductions. No credit cards.

Focusing specifically on the decorative arts between the fall of the Roman Empire and the Renaissance, this museum has intricate gold- and silver-decorated swords, buckles and horse tackle, as well as more mundane objects: ceramic bead jewellery and the metal frames of what may well be Europe's earliest folding chairs.

Museo della Civiltà Romana

Piazza G Agnelli 10 (06 5422 0919). **Open** *Museum* 9am-2pm Tue-Sun. **Admission** *Museum* €6.50; €3 reductions. *Planetarium (booking obligatory 06 8205 9127) & museum* €8.50; €6.50 reductions. No credit cards.

This museum dates from 1937, when Mussolini mounted a massive celebration to mark the second millennium of Augustus becoming the first emperor. The fact that the celebration came about 35 years too early was, it would seem, overlooked by *il Duce*, who was obviously eager to draw parallels between Augustus' glory and his own.

With its blank white walls and lofty, echoing corridors, the building is Fascist-classical at its most startling and grandiloquent. Inside, there's a fascinating cutaway model of the Colosseum's maze of tunnels and lifts, as well as casts of the intricate reliefs on Trajan's column. The centrepiece is a giant model of Rome in the fourth century AD, which puts Rome's scattered fragments and artefacts into context very helpfully. The palazzo also contains the new Museo dell'Astrologia and a planetarium.

Museo delle Arti e Tradizioni Popolari

Piazza G Marconi 8 (06 592 6148/ 06 591 2669). **Open** 9am-6pm Tue-Fri; 9am-8pm Sat, Sun. **Admission** €4; €2 reductions. No credit cards.

Note: Staff shortages sometimes force this museum to close in the afternoon. This enormous collection is dedicated to Italian folk art and rural tradition. Exhibits include elaborately decorated carts and horse tackle, as well as craft-related implements and bizarre votive offerings left to local saints. Malevolent-looking puppets fill one room; another has *carnevale* artefacts.

ROME BY AREA

Museo Preistorico ed Etnografico L Pigorini

Piazza G Marconi 14 (06 549 521).
Open 9am-8pm daily. **Admission**
€4; €2 reductions. No credit cards.

This museum displays prehistoric Italian artefacts together with material from a range of world cultures. The lobby contains a reconstruction of the prehistoric Guattari cave near Monte Circeo, south of Rome, with a genuine Neanderthal skull. On the first floor you'll find hut-urns, arrowheads, jewellery, masks and a couple of shrunken heads. The second floor has archaeological finds from digs all over Italy, including mammoth tusks and teeth, and some human bones.

Ostia Antica

The ruins (*scavi*) of Ostia Antica convey the everyday life of a working Roman town as well as Pompeii does; rather than endure the punishing day-trip from Rome to Pompeii, do yourself a favour and come here instead.

Five minutes' walk from the entrance to the excavations, the medieval village of Ostia Antica has a castle (built in 1483-86 for the bishop of Ostia, the future Pope Julius II) and picturesque cottages, once inhabited by the people who worked in the nearby salt pans.

Getting there

Ostia Antica is a 20-minute train ride from Roma-Lido station, next to Piramide metro.

Sights & museums

Scavi di Ostia Antica

Viale dei Romagnoli 717, Ostia Antica (06 5635 8099/www.itnw.roma.it/ostia/ scavi). **Open** *Mar* 8.30am-6pm Tue-Sun. *Apr-Oct* 8.30am-7pm Tue-Sun. *Nov-Feb* 8.30am-5pm Tue-Sun. **Admission** €4; €2 reductions. No credit cards.

Legend has it that Ostia was founded by Ancus Martius, the fourth king of Rome, in the second half of the seventh century BC, although the very oldest

Ostia Antica

remains date 'only' from c330 BC. Ostia was Rome's main port for over 600 years.

Abandoned after having been sacked by barbarians in the fifth century, the town was gradually buried by river mud. Over the centuries, the coastline receded, leaving Ostia landlocked and obsolete. Visit on a sunny weekday and bring a picnic (not actually allowed but keep a low profile and you probably won't be ejected).

The *decumanus maximus* (high street) runs from the Porta Romana for almost a kilometre (half a mile), past the theatre and forum, before forking left to what used to be the seashore (now three kilometres/two miles away at Ostia). The right fork, via della Foce, leads to the Tiber. Either side of these main arteries lies a network of intersecting lanes where the best discoveries can be made.

Behind the theatre is one of Ostia's most interesting features: the Forum of the Corporations. Here the trade guilds had their offices, and mosaics on the floors of shops that ring the open square indicated the products that each guild dealt in – shipowners had ships on the floor, ivory dealers had elephants. Further along on the right is the old mill, where the grindstones and the circular furrows ploughed by the blindfolded donkeys that turned them are still visible today. In the tangle of streets between the decumanus and the museum, make sure you don't miss the thermopolium: an ancient Roman drinking hole, complete with a marble counter, a fresco advertising the house fare and a garden with a fountain. Located off the forum to the south-east are the forum baths – the preserved terracotta pipes that heated the walls are still visible. Nearby is the *forica*, or ancient public latrine. Off via della Foce, the House of Cupid and Psyche is an elegant fourth-century construction; the House of the Dioscuri has beautiful mosaics; the Insula of the Charioteers still has many of its frescoes.

Tivoli

Just 20km (12.5 miles) from Rome, Tivoli (ancient Tibur) is home to two UNESCO World Heritage Sites: **Villa d'Este** in Tivoli itself, and **Hadrian's Villa** five kilometres (three miles) down the hill. They're ideal for a day-trip from Rome.

Getting there

Take the COTRAL bus from Ponte Mammolo metro station; note that the bus marked *autostrada* is a quicker service. If travelling by bus, visit Tivoli town first (the regular service is marked 'via Tiburtina' and takes about 45mins to Tivoli) – get off at the main square (piazza Garibaldi) for Villa d'Este. From the bus stop in front of the tourist office in piazza Garibaldi, frequent orange (local) buses 4 and 4X serve Villa Adriana (10mins) down the hill. From Villa Adriana, both local and COTRAL buses go to Rome.

Local trains go to Tivoli from Tiburtina station; bus 4 goes from Tivoli station to the centre of town for the Villa d'Este.

Sights & museums

Hadrian's Villa

Via di Villa Adriana, Villa Adriana (0774 382 733). **Open** *Nov-Jan* 9am-5pm daily. *Feb* 9am-6pm daily. *Mar, Oct* 9am-6.30pm daily. *Apr, Sept* 9am-7pm daily. *May-Aug* 9am-7.30pm daily. **Admission** €6.50; €3.25 reductions. No credit cards.

Villa Adriana, the retreat of Emperor Hadrian, is strewn across a gentle slope. Built from AD 118 to 134, it has some fascinating architectural spaces and water features.

Hadrian was an amateur architect and is believed to have designed many of the unique elements in his villa himself. In the centuries after the fall of the Empire it became a luxury quarry for treasure-hunters. At least 500 pieces of statuary including a marble crocodile. At the far (southern) end of the pool is a structure called the *Serapeum*, used for lavish entertaining. Summer guests enjoyed an innovative form of air-conditioning – a sheet of water poured from the roof over the open face of the building, enclosing diners.

Villa d'Este

Piazza Trento 1, Tivoli (0774 335 850/villadestetivoli.info). **Open** *Feb* 9am-5.30pm Tue-Sun. *Mar* 9am-6.15pm Tue-Sun. *Apr* 9am-7.30pm Tue-Sun. *May-Aug* 8.30am-7.45pm Tue-Sun. *Sept* 9am-7.15pm Tue-Sun. *Oct* 9am-6.30pm Tue-Sun. *Nov-Jan* 9am-5pm Tue-Sun. **Admission** €6.50; €3.25 reductions. No credit cards.

Dominating the town of Tivoli is the Villa d'Este, a lavish pleasure palace built in 1550 for Cardinal Ippolito d'Este, son of Lucrezia Borgia, to a design by architect Pirro Ligorio. Inside the villa there are frescoes and paintings by Correggio, Da Volterra and Perin Del Vaga (including views of the villa shortly after its construction). The gardens are the main attraction. Ligorio developed a complex 'hydraulic machine' that channelled water from the River Aniene (still the source today) through a series of canals under the garden. Using know-how borrowed from the Romans, he created 51 fountains spread around the terraced gardens. Sybils (pagan high-priestesses) are a recurring theme – it was at Tivoli that the Tiburtine sybil foretold the birth of Christ – and the grottoes of the sybils behind the vast fountain of Neptune echo with thundering artificial waterfalls.

Technological gimmickry was also another big feature; the Owl Fountain imitated an owl's song using a hydraulic mechanism (sadly lost a long time ago), while the *Fontana dell'organo idraulico* (restored and now functioning) used water pressure to compress air and play tunes.

Electric carts enable disabled visitors to tour the gardens; booking is essential (0774 332 920, 0774 335 850).

Christ's footprints p156

in collections around the world have been identified as coming from here.

The restored remains lie amid olive groves and cypresses and are still impressive. The model in the pavilion just up the hill from the entrance gives an idea of the villa's original size.

Where the original entrance to the villa lay is uncertain; today, the first space you'll encounter after climbing the road from the ticket office is the *pecile* (or *poikile*), a large pool that was once surrounded by a portico with high walls, of which only one remains. Directly east of the *poikile*, the *Teatro marittimo* (Maritime Theatre) is one of the most delightful inventions in the whole villa. A circular brick wall, 45 metres (150 feet) in diameter, encloses a moat, at the centre of which is an island of columns and brickwork; today a cement bridge crosses the moat, but originally there were wooden bridges, which could be removed.

Beneath the building called the winter palace, visitors can walk along the perfectly preserved cryptoporticus (covered corridor).

In the valley below is the lovely Canopus: a long, narrow pool, framed on three sides by columns and statues,

Essentials

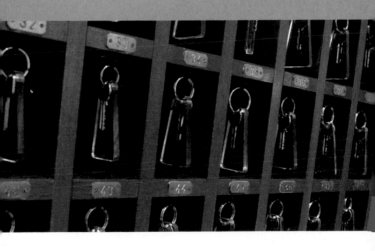

The Beehive p177

Hotels

Sixteen million tourists passed through Rome in 2005, making it one of the most-visited destinations on the planet. And the city is doing all it can to make its visitors comfortable, with the number of hotel beds rising from 83,000 in 2001 to 91,000 in 2005.

Where once there was little to bridge the gap between the extremely plush and the scuzzy-round-the-station, the Eternal City now offers everything from B&Bs and gorgeous guesthouses to boutique hotels and grand luxury institutions, as well as countless apartments set aside expressly for short-term stays. With the opening in May 2006 of Ferragamo's hotel (see box p168), the Italian capital caught up with other major Italian cities currently being colonised by fashion designers-turned-hoteliers.

Fierce competition has helped to drive standards up across the board, and the vast majority of hotels have had revamps and improved facilities over the past few years. But if choice and quality are on the up and up, so are prices. Rome is a more expensive place to stay than most other European capitals. Also, with the exception of nun-run hostels for visiting pilgrims, the city continues to offer slim pickings for budget travellers; unless they're lucky enough to squeeze into exceptions such as **The Beehive** or **Colors**, cash-strapped style-seekers will find the accommodation on offer decidedly unappetising.

In fact, a recent explosion at the top end of the accommodation market suggests a deliberate policy on the part of city luminaries to

ESSENTIALS

encourage big-bucks tourism. With three of these relatively new luxury pads – the **Exedra**, the **Radisson** and the long-running but totally refurbished **St Regis Grand** – within a stone's throw of Termini station, this is partly attributable to ongoing attempts to spruce up the down-at-heel Esquilino district. But the trend is not limited to there: work is forging ahead on other, huge, five-star hotels next door to the Ara Pacis in the *centro storico* and hard by the Vatican walls.

Location

Despite the presence of these luxury interlopers, the vast majority of hotels in the Esquilino quarter around Termini station area are cheap *pensioni* – some of dubious cleanliness – swarming with budget backpackers. It is definitely worth considering looking further afield, even if it costs you a bit more: Termini is extremely well connected, in terms of transport, but it's probably not what you dreamt of for your Roman holiday.

To find what you were expecting, you'll need to take a room in the *centro storico*. A shower between sightseeing and dinner, and a pleasant stroll (rather than a bus) back to the hotel afterwards, can make all the difference. The area around campo de' Fiori offers low- to medium-priced hotels with lots of character, and a central piazza that is a lively market by day and a colourful hangout for visiting students and alternative types by night.

The area around the Pantheon and piazza Navona is generally a bit pricier, although there are good-value places to be found.

Moving distinctly up the price range, Rome's top-end hotels have traditionally clustered around the

ESSENTIALS

once-chic via Veneto; though slowly undergoing a makeover, this famous street is currently more Hard Rock Café than *dolce vita*.

The Tridente, the area of designer shopping streets by the Spanish Steps, offers elegant hotels, mostly in the mid-to-upper price range.

If you're looking for some peace, the Celio – just by the Colosseum – offers a break from the frantic activity of the *centro storico*, as does another of Rome's seven hills: the Aventine, an exclusive residential outpost close to the headquarters of the Food and Agriculture Organization (a division of the UN that has its headquarters in Rome).

Heading across the river, the characteristic bar- and trattoria-packed quarter of Trastevere has recently acquired several accommodation options, after many anomalous decades when rooms simply didn't exist in this wildly popular area.

Just north of Trastevere, the medieval alleys around the Vatican give on to the busy retail thoroughfares of Prati: it's lively during the day but very hushed at night.

Standards & prices

Italian hotels are classified on a star system, from one to five. One star usually indicates *pensioni*, which are cheap but have very few facilities; you may have to share a bathroom. The more stars, the more facilities a hotel will have; but bear in mind the fact that a higher rating is not a guarantee of friendliness, cleanliness or decent service.

A double room in a one-star will set you back €40-€100; a two-star, €45-€150; a three-star, €70-€300; a four-star, €200-€600. Five-star prices start at around €500, and don't stop until your bank manager starts to weep.

Prices generally rise by a relentless ten per cent a year, so it's worth keeping an eye out for special deals, particularly in low season. Hotel websites are the place to look for latest details. If you're staying in a group or for a longish period, ask about discounts.

If you're visiting with children, most hotels will be happy to squeeze a cot or camp bed into a room, but will probably charge 30 to 50 per cent extra for the privilege. Some offer triple or quadruple rooms, which tend to have a bit more space.

Flat rents

If you're here for any length of time, or with children, renting an apartment could prove a more economical and flexible alternative. The Short Lets Assistance agency (www.shortletsassistance.com) has a wide choice of apartments all over central Rome, while the London-based A Place in Rome (www.aplaceinrome.com) offers delightful apartments in the heart of the *centro storico*.

Booking a room

Always reserve a room well in advance, especially at peak times, which now means most of the year, with lulls during winter (January to March) and in the dog days of August. If you're coming at the same time as a major Christian holiday (Christmas or Easter) it's wise to book weeks, or even months, ahead.

It is standard practice for hotels to ask you to fax confirmation of a booking, with a credit card number as deposit. In high season, smaller hotels may ask for a money order to secure rooms. The www.venere.com booking service offers many hotels in all price ranges. If you

Designer beds

The top names in Italian fashion design have moved into the hotel trade in a big way in several Italian cities: Bulgari's elegant Milan hostelry is now *the* place to be seen for the chic and the well-heeled, and Ferragamo has colonised large swathes of prime riverside real estate around the Ponte Vecchio in Florence. But no one saw fit to descend on Rome.

Then, in May 2006, Ferragamo pulled Rome out of its designer doldrums, opening the opulent Portrait Suites above the firm's showrooms on the corner of via Condotti and via Bocca di Leone. As Roman addresses go, there's none quite so chic in the whole city.

In Rome, as in Florence, the Ferragamo family has entrusted the decor to architect Michele Bonan. But Rome's heat and vitality has pushed Bonan beyond his usual pale, cool colour range and into flashes of intense hues. Inspired by London's gentlemen's clubs, and by the discreet pampering of a *haute couture* tailor's workshop, Bonan aimed to create a warm, welcoming feel.

Nine studios, four suites and one split-level penthouse all have lavish marble bathrooms and kitchen corners. But the greatest draw of this exclusive hostelry is its roof-terrace, with a 360-degree view across the rooftops of the *centro storico*.
■ Portrait Suites, via Bocca di Leone 23 (055 2726 4000, www.lungarnohotels.it)

arrive with nowhere to stay, try the APT tourist office (p187), which provides a list of hotels; you have to do the booking yourself. The Enjoy Rome tourist information agency (p187) will book a hotel for you at no extra charge. You can also try the Hotel Reservation service (www.hotel reservation.it) which has desks at both Fiumicino and Ciampino airports. Avoid the touts that hang around Termini station: you're likely to end up paying more than you should for a very grotty hotel.

Our choice

The hotels listed in this guide have been chosen for their location, because they offer value for money, or simply because they have true Roman character. In the Deluxe category (€€€€) the emphasis is on opulence and luxury. Those in mid- to upper-price ranges (€€-€€€) are smaller, many in old *palazzi*, with pretty, though often small, bedrooms. *Pensioni* (€-€€) are fairly basic, but those listed here are friendly and usually family-run. Few Roman hotels – with the exception of the grander ones – have access for the disabled. Though staff are generally very willing to help guests with mobility difficulties, the real problem is that most places have so many stairs that there's not much they can do. As hotels renovate, they do tend to add a room for the disabled when they can.

Unless stated, rates quoted are for rooms with bathrooms, and include breakfast.

Il Centro

Abruzzi
Piazza della Rotonda 69 (06 679 2021/fax 06 6978 8076/www.hotel abruzzi.it). €€.

Lancelot p174

by Latte e Miele

Sleep in Italy
apartments and b&b
in Rome – Florence – Venice

web site: www.sleepinitaly.com
tel/fax: +39 063211783
(from 10am to 6pm italian time)
Skype user: sleepinitaly

The splendid location is really this hotel's selling point, although recent renovations have upgraded what used to be a dingy establishment. Many rooms have breathtaking views of the Pantheon. Some rooms are very small. Breakfast is taken in a nearby café.

Albergo Della Lunetta

Piazza del Paradiso 68 (06 686 1080/ 06 687 7630/fax 06 689 2028/www. albergodellalunetta.it). €€.

The Lunetta is built on the foundations of the ancient Pompey's Theatre, but nowadays is altogether a quieter and significantly less impressive venue. Rooms are best described as functional. However, it's clean, slap-bang between campo de' Fiori and piazza Navona, has a roof terrace with a stunning view over surrounding rooftops and is about as cheap as it gets around here.

Due Torri

Vicolo del Leonetto 23-25 (06 6880 6956/fax 06 686 5442/www.hoteldue torriroma.com). €€.

In a labyrinth of cobbled streets, the Due Torri has a welcoming feel. The 26 rooms here are cosy rather than spacious, and are furnished with dark wooden furniture. If you're persistent, you might even get one of the rooms with a private terrace that overlooks the rooftops.

Mimosa

Via di Santa Chiara 61 (06 6880 1753/fax 06 683 3557/www.hotel mimosa.net). €€.

In medieval times this very central palazzo housed an order of crusading knights, and it's still a bit like barracks. Some rooms have been redecorated, others remain dingy. But it's clean and remarkably cheap for this central position. Breakfast is included only in high season.

Navona

Via dei Sediari 8 (06 686 4203/fax 06 6880 3802/www.hotelnavona.com). €€.

This hotel has a welcoming, community atmosphere: a good choice for lone travellers. It's on the second floor of a palazzo, built on the site of the ancient baths of Agrippa. The hotel's staff and Australian owners are friendly and helpful.

Ponte Sisto

Via dei Pettinari 64 (06 686 310/ fax 06 6830 1712/www.hotelponte sisto.it). €€€.

The Ponte Sisto combines a business hotel aesthetic with a tourist's prime location. Although the rooms are simple, the ample marble bathrooms give a taste of Roman luxury. The palm-lined courtyard provides a gorgeous backdrop to a breakfast or *aperitivo*.

Raphael

Largo Febo 2 (06 682 831/fax 06 687 8993/www.raphaelhotelrome.com). €€€€.

This ivy-draped palazzo in a delightful piazza is a gem. Rooms are enthusiastically decorated in rich colours and are well appointed. There's a roof terrace and a sauna.

Residenza Farnese

Via del Mascherone 59 (06 6821 0980/fax 06 8032 1049/www. residenzafarneseroma.it). €€.

This converted convent in a narrow ivy-lined alley has been refurbished without losing its charm, and the result is an inviting hotel in a great neighbourhood. Rooms run from basic updated cells with wood furnishings and small marble bathrooms to more eccentric pastel-hued rooms with hand-painted furniture.

Residenza Zanardelli

Via G Zanardelli 7 (06 6821 1392/ fax 06 6880 3802/www.residenza zanardelli.com). €€€.

Quiet and pleasant, the Zanardelli is around the corner from piazza Navona and not far from St Peter's. With only seven rooms, it's a bit more intimate and upmarket than sister hotel, the Navona (see above).

ESSENTIALS

Smeraldo

Vicolo dei Chiodaroli 9 (06 687 5929/ fax 06 6880 5495/www.smeraldoroma. com). €€.

Though recently refurbished, the decor isn't particularly adventurous, but the rooms are clean and all mod cons are provided. The hotel is next to campo de' Fiori, well connected with the whole city, and its terrace offers a pretty view across Rome's rooftops.

Sole al Pantheon

Piazza della Rotonda 63 (06 678 0441/fax 06 6994 0689/www.hotel solealpantheon.com). €€€.

Dating back to the 15th century, the Sole al Pantheon is one of Europe's oldest hotels. Rooms have a fresh feel though, with tiles and pretty frescoes. All bathrooms have jacuzzis. Ask for one of the rooms at the front for superb views over the Pantheon.

Tridente & Borghese

Aleph

Via di San Basilio 15 (06 422 901/fax 06 4229 0000/www.boscolohotels.com). €€€€.

This hotel is a welcome, playful addition to Rome's upscale accommodation, with a lobby, bar, reading room and seafood restaurant, all in various intensities of devil-red. A top-floor terrace bar and restaurant operate in warmer months; there's a subterranean spa in cool tones of white and icy blue. The rooms are modern and luxurious.

Barocco

Via della Purificazione 4 (06 487 2001/fax 06 485 994/www.hotel barocco.com). €€€.

The Barocco combines a central location with calmness, not least because its 41 rooms are well soundproofed. The rooms are stylish, with marble bathrooms, flouncy curtains and enormous mirrors; some have balconies.

Casa Howard

Via Capo le Case 18; via Sistina 149 (06 6992 4555/fax 06 6794 6444/ www.casahoward.com). €€.

Casa Howard started life as a beautiful residenza near piazza di Spagna; in January 2003, Casa Howard II opened with five more rooms just round the corner. All rooms have been individually designed with a strong emphasis on quality. The new (and slightly more expensive) rooms in via Sistina have en suite bathrooms; in via Capo le Case, your (private) bathroom may be along the hall. There's a Turkish bath, and massages can be arranged.

Daphne Inn

Via degli Avignonesi 20; via di San Basilio 55 (06 4782 3529/fax 06 2332 40967/www.daphne-rome.com). €€.

The Daphne Inn has two locations: one near the Trevi Fountain, the other off via Veneto. Each has seven rooms – some with en suite baths and some that share – all of which are fitted out in organic-modern style with terracotta floors, neutral tones and simple framed leaf prints on the walls.

De Russie

Via del Babuino 9 (06 328 881/fax 06 3288 8888/www.hotelderussie.it). €€€€.

The De Russie's modern elegance is a million miles away from the luxury-schmaltz hotels on via Veneto. Fabulous gardens and a state-of-the-art health centre make it a star-magnet.

Eden

Via Ludovisi 49 (06 478 121/fax 06 482 1584/www.hotel-eden.it). €€€€.

Beautifully understated, the Eden is stylish yet relaxed, offering the attentiveness and attention to detail of a top-notch hotel without the stuffiness. Elegant reception rooms, tastefully decorated bedrooms and a roof terrace with restaurant, piano bar, and truly spectacular views.

Fontanella Borghese

Largo Fontanella Borghese 84 (06 6880 9504/06 6880 9624/ fax 06 686 1295/www.fontanella borghese.com). €€€.

This hotel is elegantly done out in relaxing cream and muted colours, brightened by a generous array of potted plants. Shopping meccas via del Corso and via Condotti are just around the corner: it's an ideal bolthole when the credit cards start to melt.

Hassler Villa Medici

Piazza Trinità dei Monti 6 (06 699 340/fax 06 678 9991/www.hotel hasslerroma.com). €€€€.

This is one of Rome's classic hotels, with all the trimmings you might expect: chandeliers everywhere, polished wood and marble, plush fabrics and grand oil paintings, and a garden out back. Request the fifth floor for an art-deco 'black & white' room.

Hotel Art

Via Margutta 56 (06 328 711/fax 06 3600 3995/www.hotelart.it). €€€€.

On a street famed for its art studios, this new hotel's entryway and lobby area have white pods that serve as check-in and concierge desks. Hallways are in retina-burning shades, but bedrooms have creamy bed linens and dark wood furniture. There's also a small gym on the premises.

Marcus

Via del Clementino 94 (06 6830 0320/06 687 3679/fax 06 687 3679). €€.

Descend the Spanish Steps and keep on walking to get to the peaceful, family-operated Marcus, which is in the heart of Rome but doesn't charge top-of-the-range prices. It's a bit shabby, with an old-fashioned mix of bric-a-brac and ill-matched furniture.

Ostello della Gioventù Foro Italico

Via delle Olimpiadi 61 (06 323 6267/fax 06 324 2613/www.ostellionline.org). €. No credit cards.

There are more than 300 dormitory beds at this neo-brutalist building located handily near the football stadium but a long way north of the centre of the city. The IYHF's main hostel in Rome, it's open to members only, but it is possible for you to join on the spot.

Boutique chic

Maybe it was centuries of catering to pilgrims with thoughts focused more on salvation than designer-label sheets. Or maybe it was that the Eternal City was a seller's market, with visitors lining up for each drear room. But it's only now that *caput mundi* has finally found its chic boutiques.

Casa Howard (p172) led the way. There's an exotic Chinese room, a serious blue room, and some lovely furniture designed by Ilaria Miani (p69). And there's a Turkish bath. The one drawback was that some of the (private) bathrooms were not en suite, a problem ironed out in Casa Howard's second location.

The Beehive (p177) attracts a very different clientele. Americans Steve and Linda Brenner have put together very reasonable prices and basic amenities with design-icon furniture, a pretty garden and hotel services that include a free in-house guidebook and free internet access.

The **Daphne Inn** (p172) is another good-value boutique hotel run by an ebullient couple, Elyssa and Alessandro (who are American and Italian, respectively). The two locations have seven rooms each – some with en suite baths – all of which are organic-modern in style with terracotta floors, neutral tones and simple framed leaf prints on the walls. The emphasis here is on itinerary planning and personalised service.

Westin Excelsior

Via V Veneto 125 (06 47 081/fax 06 482 6205/www.starwood.com). €€€€.
The entrance is lavish; rooms – all with marble bathrooms – are a Hollywood-style fantasy. The mind-boggling Villa La Cupola suite is one of the biggest in Europe, and the priciest bed in Rome at just over €20,000 a night.

Esquiline & Celio

Bailey's

Via Flavia 39 (06 4202 0486/fax 06 4202 0170/www.hotelbailey.com). €€.
Bailey's opened in March 2001 in a charming 19th-century townhouse in the uninspiring area near via XX Settembre. But stucco ceilings and lashings of marble in its 29 rooms have made it very popular.

Exedra

Piazza della Repubblica 47 (06 489 381/fax 06 480 9800/www.boscolo hotels.com). €€€€.
The Exedra is every bit as glam as it looked on celluloid in *Ocean's Twelve.* The lobby is opulent; the rooms run from plush and utterly comfortable to outrageous. From May to September, the rooftop bar/restaurant and pool offer spectacular views. There's a spa too.

Lancelot

Via Capo d'Africa 47 (06 7045 0615/ fax 06 7045 0640/www.lancelothotel. com). €€.
This beautifully kept and attractive, family-run hotel has a delightfully cool Mediterranean feel, with elegant mixes of linen, wood and tiles in the bedrooms, some of which have terraces looking towards the Palatine and the Colosseum. The reception has been given a personal touch with tiled floors and antique furniture, along with some unusual *objets.*

Nerva

Via Tor de' Conti 3 (06 678 1835/ fax 06 6992 2204/www.hotelnerva. com). €€.
The family-run Nerva is well located, by the Forum, and the rooms have been refurbished without losing their original features. The staff and proprietors are a friendly bunch.

Radisson SAS Hotel

Via F Turati 171 (06 444 841/fax 06 4434 1396/www.rome.radisson sas.com). €€€€.
This relative newcomer is seriously minimalist. Beds are on a low platform with bathroom incorporated behind, divided from the rest of the room only by a glass screen. Plasma screen TVs have DVD and internet connections. The rooftop bar – which offers visitors tables beside the pool – does a great line in cocktails.

Residenza Cellini

Via Modena 5 (06 4782 5204/fax 06 4788 1806/www.residenzacellini.it). €€.
This spacious *residenza* has three double rooms and another three junior suites. The huge rooms are decorated in 'classic' style – with *faux*-antique wooden furniture and stripes. The bathrooms have jacuzzis or showers with hydro-massage.

St Regis Grand

Via VE Orlando 3 (06 47 091/ fax 06 474 7307/www.stregis. com/GrandRome). €€€€.
The hotel's original chandeliers dazzle in massive marbled reception rooms, decorated in opulent gold, beige and red. Rooms have been individually designed using rich fabrics, and are filled with silk-covered Empire and Regency-style furnishings. There is a gym and a sauna.

Tempio di Pallade

Via Giolitti 425-427 (06 7045 1521/ fax 06 7707 2040/www.hoteltempiodi pallade.it). €.
In a neighbourhood full of inexpensive hotels, this one stands out. Located near the old Roman gate of Porta Maggiore, its 50 rooms have been recently refurbished, and come complete with squeaky-clean private baths and all basic mod cons, in blue and gold.

Tempio di Pallade

HOTEL EDEN

ROMA

RESTAURANT
"LA TERRAZZA DELL'EDEN"

VIA LUDOVISI, 49 · 00187 ROMA · ITALIA
TEL. (39) 06 47812752 · 06 4814473
www.hotel-eden.it

The Beehive

*Via Marghera 8 (06 4470 4553/www.
the-beehive.com). €. No credit cards.*
The Beehive manages to create a
'youth hostel meets boutique hotel'
vibe. This comes from a combination
of very reasonable prices and basic
amenities with design-icon furniture,
bright decor, a cute garden and hotel
services that include a free in-house
guidebook, free internet access and a
lounge café for guests.

YWCA

*Via Cesare Balbo 4 (06 488 0460/
fax 06 487 1028/www.ywca-ucdg.it).
€. No credit cards.*
Bedrooms for women with one to
four beds in each, and a midnight cur-
few. Women travelling alone may feel
safer here than in mixed hostels. Lunch
costs €11.

Villa San Pio, Sant' Anselmo & Aventino

*Via di Santa Melania 19/piazza di
Sant'Anselmo 2 (06 574 5231/fax 06
578 3604/www.aventinohotels.com).
€€€.*
Within a stone's throw of each other,
the three hotels in this group are located in a leafy residential area. The Villa
San Pio consists of three separate
buildings that share the same pretty
gardens and airy breakfast room; it
has a light feel that makes it a very
pleasant place to stay. The more
ornate Sant'Anselmo has recently
reopened following refurbishment
work. The Aventino is the least man-
icured of the three. Some of the rooms
have a jacuzzi.

Sant'Anna p179

Hotel Santa Maria

Trastevere & Gianicolo

Hotel San Francesco

Via Jacopa de' Settesoli 7 (06 5830 0051/fax 06 5833 3413/www.hotel sanfrancesco.net). €€.

On the quieter eastern side of viale Trastevere, the San Francesco has an attractive marble-floored entrance hall and a lovely roof terrace where breakfast is served when the weather's warm. Rooms are well equipped and reasonably big, though they have a slightly corporate feel.

Hotel Santa Maria

Vicolo del Piede 2 (06 589 4626/ 06 589 5474/fax 06 589 4815/ www.htlsantamaria.com). €€.

Located on the site of a 16th-century convent, the Santa Maria has rooms with cool tiled floors, slightly anonymous peach decor and some spacious bathrooms. They all open on to a sunny central courtyard, planted with orange trees.

Hotel Trastevere House

Vicolo del Buco 7 (06 588 3774/ www.hoteltrasterehouse.it). €€

This inn is hidden down a tiny side street to the east of viale Trastevere, inside an 18th-century palazzo. Its bedrooms are small but they do have wood-beamed ceilings and all the basic amenities. The owners' other hotel, the Domus Tiberina (same contact details), is on a nearby piazza by the river and features a suite with a balcony.

Vatican & Prati

Bramante

Vicolo delle Palline 24 (06 6880 6426/ fax 06 6813 3339/www.hotelbramante. com). €€.

Home to 16th-century architect Domenico Fontana, this became an inn in 1873. It has a large, pleasant reception and a little patio for the summer. The 16 rooms of varying sizes are simple yet elegant; most have high beamed ceilings, some have wrought-iron beds.

Colors Hotel & Hostel

Via Boezio 31 (06 687 4030/fax 06 686 7947/www.colorshotel.com). €.

Colors has bright, clean dorm and hotel accommodation, plus self-catering kitchen and laundry facilities, and a terrace. A new floor opened in 2005; its superior rooms have air-conditioning, LCD satellite TVs and breakfast included. Credit cards are accepted for superior rooms only.

Franklin Hotel Rome

Via Rodi 29 (06 3903 0165/fax 06 3975 1652/www.franklinhotelrome.it). €€€.

Tucked somewhat out of the way beyond the Vatican, the Franklin is owned by and aimed at music lovers. It has a polished modern feel and the themed rooms – jazz, soul, rock and so on – are light and airy, if not particularly spacious. But each room has state-of-the-art sound equipment on which to enjoy the hotel's extensive collection of vinyl and CDs, and many have computers too. The Peter Pan suite also has electronic entertainments for kids.

Hotel dei Mellini

Via Muzio Clementi 81 (06 324 771/ fax 06 3247 7801/www.hotelmellini. com). €€€.

The Hotel dei Mellini has 80 spacious rooms and suites elegantly decorated with neutral colours and occasional knick-knacks. There's a sunny roof terrace. Children up to 12 years old sleep in their parents' room for free, and complimentary baby cribs are available.

Sant'Anna

Borgo Pio 133-134 (06 6880 1602/ fax 06 6830 8717/www.hotelsant anna.com). €€.

A stone's throw from the Vatican wall, the Sant'Anna is a quiet hotel with 20 fairly dated rooms decorated in pastel shades. There's a small courtyard at the back for warm-weather *aperitivi*.

ESSENTIALS

Getting Around

Arriving & leaving

Airports

Aeroporto Leonardo Da Vinci, Fiumicino

Via dell'Aeroporto di Fiumicino 320 (switchboard 06 65 951/information 06 6595 3640/www.adr.it).
There's an express rail service between Fiumicino airport and the main Termini railway station, which takes 31mins and runs every 30mins from around 6.30am until around 11.30pm daily (6am-11pm to Fiumicino). A one-way ticket costs €9.50.

The regular rail service from Fiumicino takes 25-40mins, and stops at Trastevere, Ostiense, Tuscolana and Tiburtina stations; to reach many parts of the city, it makes sense to opt for this service. Trains leave about every 20mins (less often on Sun) between around 6am and 11.20pm (5am-10.30pm to Fiumicino). A one-way ticket costs €5.

Terravision (06 6595 8646, www.terravision.it) runs a coach service from Fiumicino to Termini, stopping in the northern suburbs and at Lepanto metro station (journey time to Termini: 70mins). Departures are about every two hours between 8.30am and 8.30pm daily. Coaches from Termini to Fiumicino leave from opposite the Royal Santina Hotel (via Marsala 22) from 6.30am to 6.30pm. Tickets cost €9 one way, €15 return, and can either be booked online (all major credit cards), or paid for in cash at the Terravision desk in the arrivals hall or at the reception of the Royal Santina Hotel.

During the night, a bus service runs between Fiumicino's Terminal C and Tiburtina railway/metro station in Rome. Tickets cost €3.60 from machines or €5 on the bus.

Buses leave Tiburtina at 12.30am, 1.15am, 2.30am and 3.45am, stopping at Termini railway station 10mins later. Departures from Fiumicino are at 1.15am, 2.15am, 3.30am and 5am. Neither Termini nor Tiburtina are attractive places at night, so it's best to get a taxi from there to your final destination. Buses are infrequent; metro line B closes at around 11.30pm (12.30am Sat), A at 9.30pm.

Aeroporto GB Pastine, Ciampino

Via Appia Nuova 1650 (06 794 941/ www.adr.it). **Open** 24hrs daily.
The easiest way to get into town from Ciampino is to take the Terravision coach service (06 7949 4572, www. terravision.it) to Termini station (journey time: 40mins). Buses leave from outside the arrivals hall about every half hour from 8.40am to 12.20am daily. Buses from Termini to Ciampino leave from outside the Royal Santina Hotel (via Marsala 22) from 4.30am to 7.30pm. Tickets (€8.50 single, €13.50 return) can be booked online, or bought (cash only) in the arrivals hall at Ciampino or at the reception of the Royal Santina.

Alternatively, COTRAL buses (information 06 722 2153) run from Ciampino to Anagnina metro station, leaving from in front of the arrivals hall every 30-40mins, 6am-10.30pm daily (5.30am-11pm to Ciampino). Buy tickets (€1) from the automatic machine in the arrivals hall or at the newsstand in the departures hall.

After the last Terravision bus has departed, getting into the city is well-nigh impossible, as taxis don't bother to pass by.

By rail

Most long-distance trains arrive at Termini station, which is the hub of Rome's transport network.

Night trains arrive at Tiburtina or Ostiense, both some way from the *centro storico*. The metro, bus routes 492 and 649, and night bus 40N run from Tiburtina into the city centre, though you won't want to hang around for long in this seedy area waiting for a bus after dark; if you arrive at Ostiense after midnight, there are no buses and you will have to take a taxi.

Some daytime trains bypass Termini, while others stop at more than one station in Rome; it may be more convenient to get off at a smaller station rather than going all the way into Termini.

For bookings and general information on mainline rail services, phone the Trenitalia call centre (operates 7am-9pm daily) on 892 021 (199 166 177 from mobile phones) or consult the helpful website (www.tren italia.it) where you can also book tickets.

By bus

There is no central long-distance bus station in Rome. Most coach services terminate outside these metro stations: Cornelia, Ponte Mammolo and Tiburtina (routes north); Anagnina and EUR Fermi (routes south).

In town

Public transport

Rome's transport system is co-ordinated by ATAC. City-centre and inner-suburb destinations are served by the buses and trams of the Trambus transport authority. The system is relatively easy to use and as efficient as the traffic-choked streets allow.

Pickpocketing is an escalating problem on public transport, particularly on major tourist

routes, notoriously the 64 and 40 Express between Termini station and the Vatican.

The ATAC site, www.atac. roma.it, has a useful journey planner. Information (in Italian only) is dispensed on the toll-free number 800 431 784. ATAC's customer service office (via Ostiense 131L, 06 4695 2027) has free transport maps.

Tickets

The same tickets are valid on all city bus, tram and metro lines, whether operated by Trambus, MetRo or regional transport authority COTRAL. Though buses and trams are gradually being fitted out with on-board ticket dispensers (coins only), it's safer to purchase tickets before boarding; and they are also available from ATAC automatic ticket machines, information centres, some bars and newsstands, and all *tabacchi*.

Discounts for students, the disabled and pensioners are only available on monthly or annual passes, for residents.

BIT valid for 75mins, during which you can use an unlimited number of city buses, plus one metro trip; €1.

BIG valid for one day, until midnight, and covers the whole urban network; €4.

BTI a three-day pass, covering all bus and metro routes, and local mainline trains to Ostia; €11.

BIRG valid for one day on rail journeys within the Lazio region. The price varies from €2.50 to €10.50, depending on the zone of your destination. It can be used on buses and metro and local mainline trains, but not the Fiumicino airport lines.

CIS valid for seven days; it covers all bus routes and the whole metro system, including the lines to Ostia; €16.

ESSENTIALS

Abbonamento mensile valid for unlimited travel on the entire metropolitan transport system during the calendar month in which the ticket was bought; €30 (€18 for under-20s; theoretically for Rome residents only, but inspectors are unlikely to ask for proof).

When you board a bus, you must stamp tickets in the machines by the rear and/or front doors. Fare-dodging is common, but if you are caught without a validated ticket, you'll be fined €51 on the spot.

Travelling with children

Under-tens travel free; older kids have to pay the adult fare for single, daily and weekly tickets, as must pensioners.

Bus

Bus is the best way to move about in Rome, and though they may not come as regularly as you'd like, buses are easy to use once you've got the hang of them. A sign at each bus stop tells you the lines that stop there, and the stops on each line. Note that the 'Express' buses are so-called because they make fewer stops along their route: check before boarding so you don't get whisked past your destination.

Most bus services run 5.30am-midnight daily, every 10-45mins, depending on the route.

Trams

Tram routes mainly serve suburban areas. An express tram service – No.8 – links largo Argentina to Trastevere and the western suburbs. Due to interminable maintenance work, the scenic No.3 tram route was being plied by buses when this guide went to press.

Metro

MetRo is responsible for Rome's two metro lines, which cross beneath Termini mainline train station. Line A runs from south-east to north-west; line B from EUR to the north-eastern suburbs. Line B is open from 5.30am to 11.30pm (12.30am Sat). Line A also opens at 5.30am but closes at 9pm daily for work on the long-awaited line C (due for completion in 2008). Two shuttle bus services replace metro line A 9-11.30pm (12.30am Sat), running every 2-7mins.

Taxis

Licensed taxis are painted white and have a meter. Touts are rife at Termini and other major tourist magnets; ignore them if you don't want to risk an extortionate fare. Though drivers like to pretend otherwise, most taxi cooperatives, including those listed below, accept major credit cards.

When you pick up a taxi at a rank or hail one in the street, the meter should read zero. As you set off, it will indicate the minimum fare – at time of writing it is €2.33 (€3.36 on Sundays and public holidays; €4.91 if you board 10pm-7am). There's a €1.04 charge for each item of luggage placed in the boot. Tariffs outside the GRA, Rome's major ring road, are much higher.

If you phone for a taxi, you'll be given the taxi code-name (always a location followed by a number) and a time, as in *Bahama 69, in tre minuti* ('Bahamas 69, in three minutes'). Radio taxis start the meter from the moment your phone call is answered.

Most of Rome's taxi drivers are honest; if you do suspect you're being fleeced, take down the driver's name and serial number from the metal plaque inside the car's rear door; the more ostentatiously you do this, the more likely it is that the fare will return to a reasonable level. If it doesn't, report the driver to his/her cooperative, the phone number of which will be written on the outside of the car. You should also ask for a receipt (*una ricevuta*).

Unless you are very clearly a no-nonsense Rome habitué speaking excellent Italian, prepare to be ripped off on trips from both airports into town. A veritable 'mafia' of drivers has put a price-fixing operation in place. Trips that when metred, cost around €40 (Fiumicino) or €30 (Ciampino) may well cost much more. There is little you can do about this, if you ever want to reach the centre.

Cooperativa Samarcanda *06 5551, www.samarcanda.it.*
Cosmos Radio Taxi *06 88 177, 06 8822*
Società Cooperativa Autoradio Taxi Roma *06 3570, www.3570.it*
Società la Capitale Radio Taxi *06 49 94*

Driving

Much of the centre of Rome is off-limits for most of the day to anyone without a permit. Municipal police and video cameras guard these areas; any vehicle without the required pass will be fined €68.25 if it enters at restricted times. A strictly enforced no-car policy applies in the city centre on the first (and sometimes more) Sunday of most months. If your hotel is in the ZTL (*zona a traffico limitato*) and you need to drive in, ask hotel staff about allowed access hours to that part of the city.

Parking

A system in which residents park for free and visitors pay (€1 per hour) is in place in many areas of the city: watch out for the telltale blue lines. Buy parking tickets at pay-and-display ticket dispensers or purchase a €25 parking debit card (*scheda per il parcheggio*) from *tabacchi* (tobacconists). Even in restricted areas, parking is usually free after 11pm and on Sundays; check ticket dispensers for times.

Elsewhere, watch out for signs saying *Passo carrabile* ('access at all times') or *Sosta vietata* ('no parking'), and disabled parking spaces, which are marked by yellow stripes on the road.

In some areas, self-appointed *parcheggiatori* will 'look after' your car for a small fee; it may be illegal and an absurd imposition, but it's probably worth paying up to ensure your tyres remain intact.

The following carparks are centrally located: **ParkSì Villa Borghese** (viale del Galoppatoio 33, 06 322 5934/7972; €1.30/hr for up to 3hrs, cheaper after); **Valentino** (via Sistina 75E, 06 678 2597; €3/hr for up to six hours).

Vehicle removal

Your vehicle may be clamped if illegally parked: the number to call to have the clamp removed will be under your windscreen wipers. There is a hefty fine for this.

If your car is not where you left it, chances are it has been towed. Phone the municipal police (*Vigili urbani*) on 06 67 691 and quote your number plate to find out which pound it's in.

Vehicle hire

Avis *06 481 4373, www.avisautonoleggio.it*
Europcar *800 014 410, www.europcar.it*
Hertz *199 112211, www.hertz.it*
Maggiore *848 867 067, www.maggiore.it*
Sixt *199 100 666, www.sixt.it*

ESSENTIALS

Resources A-Z

Accident & emergency

The hospitals listed below have 24-hour Accident & Emergency departments – go to the *pronto soccorso* (casualty department). If your child has an accident while you're in Rome, go to the excellent Bambino Gesù hospital.

Ospedale Fatebenefratelli
Isola Tiberina (06 68 371).

Ospedale Pediatrico Bambino Gesù
piazza Sant'Onofrio 4 (06 68 591/ www.opbg.net).

Ospedale San Camillo
circonvallazione Gianicolense 332 (06 55 551/www.scamilloforlanini. rm.it).

Ospedale San Giacomo
via Canova 29 (06 36 261/ 06 322 7069).

Ospedale San Giovanni
via Amba Aradam 8 (06 77 051/ www.hsangiovanni.it).

Policlinico Umberto I
viale Policlinico 155 (06 49 971/ www.policlinicoumberto1.it).

Dental emergencies

For serious dental emergencies, use hospital A&E departments. Otherwise, see *Dentisti* in the Yellow Pages.

Pharmacies

Farmacia della Stazione
piazza dei Cinquecento 49-51 (06 488 0019). **Open** 24hrs daily.

Piram
via Nazionale 228 (06 488 0754). **Open** 24hrs daily.

Credit card loss

American Express
06 7228 0371
US cardholders *800 874 333*

Diners Club
800 864 064

MasterCard
800 870 866

Visa
800 877 232

Customs

Travellers who arrive from EU countries are not required to declare goods imported into or exported from Italy if they are for personal use, up to the following limits:

- 800 cigarettes or 400 cigarillos or 200 cigars or 1kg of tobacco
- ten litres of spirits (over 22% alcohol) or 20 litres of fortified wine (under 22% alcohol).

For people arriving from non-EU countries the following limits apply:

- 200 cigarettes or 100 cigarillos or 50 cigars or 250 grams of tobacco
- one litre of spirits or two litres of wine
- one bottle of perfume (50 grams/ 1.76 oz), 250 millilitres of eau de toilette or various merchandise not exceeding €175.

Anything above these limits will be subject to taxation at the port of entry.

There are no restrictions on the importation of cameras, watches or electrical goods. For further information call Italian customs (*dogana*) on 041 269 9311 or check www.agenziadogane.it.

Disabled travellers

With its cobbled streets, narrow pavements and inaccessible facilities in old buildings, Rome is a difficult city for disabled people. That said, many city centre buses are now wheelchair accessible and most museums and larger hotels have suitable facilities.

CO.IN (tollfree 800 271 027/06 5717 7094, www.coinsociale.it) is a non-profit organisation that gives information on disabled facilities in hotels, restaurants, museums etc and can arrange special transport for groups around the city. It collaborates with the city council on the useful www.romapertutti.it website (Italian only).

Electricity

Most wiring systems work on 220V. This is compatible with British-bought appliances (with a plug adaptor); US 110V equipment requires a current transformer. Adaptors can be bought at any electrical or hardware shop (*elettricità* or *ferramenta*).

Embassies & consulates

For a full list of embassies, see *Ambasciate* in the phone book.

Australia
Via Antonio Bosio 5 (06 852 721/ www.italy.embassy.gov.au).

Britain
Via XX Settembre 80A (06 4220 0001/ fax 06 4220 2334/www.britain.it).

Canada
Embassy: via GB de Rossi 27 (06 445 981/www.canada.it). Consulate: via Zara 30 (06 445 981).

Ireland
Piazza Campitelli 3 (06 697 9121).

New Zealand
Via Zara 28 (06 441 7171/ www.nzembassy.com).

South Africa
Via Tanaro 14 (06 852 541/ www.sudafrica.it).

USA
Via Vittorio Veneto 119 (06 46 741/www.usembassy.it).

Internet

Most of Rome's major parks (see box p77) have free wireless access. The areas covered are being extended to city-centre areas; look out for the 'Hotspot' signs.

easyEverything
Via Barberini 2 (www.easyeverything. com). **Open** 7am-1am daily. No credit cards.

Mail Boxes Etc
Via dei Mille 38-40 (06 446 1945). **Open** 9am-6.30pm Mon-Fri; 9am-1pm Sat. No credit cards.

Police

For emergencies, call one of the following helplines:
Carabinieri (English-speaking helpline) *112*
Polizia di stato *113*
The principal Polizia di Stato station is at via San Vitale 15 (06 46 861, www.poliziadistato.it). Others, and the Carabinieri's *commissariati*, are listed in the phone directory under *Polizia* and *Carabinieri*. Incidents can be reported to either.

Post

For postal information, call 803 160 (8am-8pm Mon-Sat) or visit www.poste.it.

There are local post offices (*ufficio postale*) in each district; opening hours are 8.30am-6pm Mon-Fri (8.30am-2pm Aug),

ESSENTIALS

8.30am-1.30pm Sat and any day preceding a public holiday. They close two hours earlier than normal on the last day of each month. Main post offices in the centre have longer opening hours.

Stamps can be bought at post offices or *tabacchi* (see below). *Posta prioritaria* is the equivalent of first class post. Most postboxes are red and have two slots, *per la città* (for Rome) and *tutte le altre destinazioni* (everywhere else).

Posta Centrale

Piazza San Silvestro 18-20. **Open** 8am-7pm Mon-Sat.
Other main offices: Piazza Bologna 39; Via Marmorata 4.

Vatican Post Office

Piazza San Pietro (06 6988 3406). **Open** 8.30am-6pm Mon-Fri; 8.30am-5pm Sat.

Smoking

Smoking is banned anywhere with public access, including stations, lobbies of apartment blocks, and restaurants and bars except where a clearly designated smoking room is provided. This is strictly enforced.

Tabacchi

Tabacchi or *tabaccherie* (identifiable by signs with a white 'T' on black or blue) are the only places where you can legally buy tobacco products. They also sell stamps, telephone cards, and tickets for public transport.

Telephones

Dialling & codes

■ For international calls from Rome, dial 00, followed by the country code, area code (omit the initial zero of area codes in the UK) and number. Codes include: Australia 61; Canada 1; Irish Republic 353; New Zealand 64; United Kingdom 44; United States 1.
■ Rome landlines have the area code 06, which must be used whether calling from within or outside the city. To call Rome from abroad, dial your international access code followed by 39 (Italy), then 06. Do not omit the 0.
■ Numbers beginning 800 are toll-free. Numbers beginning 840 and 848 are charged at low set rates, no matter where you're calling from or how long the call lasts. These numbers can be called from within Italy only; some of them function only within a single phone district.
■ Mobile numbers begin with a 3. GSM phones can be used on both 900 and 1800 bands; British, Australian and New Zealand mobiles work fine, but US mobiles are on a different frequency that doesn't work (unless it's a tri-band).

Directory enquiries

This is a jungle, and charges for information given over the phone are steep. The major services are: 1254 (Italian and international numbers); 892412 (international numbers, in English and Italian, from mobile phones); 892892 (Italian numbers).

Italian directory information can be had for free on www.info412.it; www.paginebianche.it.

Operator services

To reverse the charges (make a collect call), dial 170 for the international operator. If you are reversing the charges from a phone box, insert a 10¢ coin (refunded after your call).

Public phones

Rome has no shortage of public phone boxes and many bars have payphones. Most only accept phone cards (*schede telefoniche*); a few also accept major credit cards. Phone cards cost €1, €2.50, €3, €5 and €7.50 and are available from *tabacchi* (see above), and some newsstands and bars.

Time

Italy is an hour ahead of London, six hours ahead of New York, eight hours behind Sydney and 12 hours behind Wellington. As in all other EU countries, clocks are moved forward one hour in early spring and back again in late autumn.

Tipping

Foreigners are generally expected to tip more than Italians, but ten per cent is considered generous; anything between €1 and €5. Some smarter eateries now include a 10-15% service charge. In cafés and bars, leave 10¢-20¢ on the counter when ordering. Taxi drivers will be happy if you round the fare up to the nearest whole euro.

Tickets

Expect to pay *diritti di prevendita* (booking fees) on tickets bought anywhere except at the venue on the night. You can pick up concert tickets at the giant Messaggerie Musicali store at via del Corso 472 (www.messaggeriemusicali.it), and at the Feltrinelli bookshop at largo Argentina 11 (www.lafeltrinelli.it).

Hello Ticket

Ala Termini, Termini station (by platform 23), via Giolitti (800 907 080/06 4782 5710). **Open** 10am-7pm Mon-Fri.
For most concerts, plays and sport.

Tourist information

The offices of the local tourist board, APT, and the state tourist board, ENIT, have English-speaking staff. For visitors looking for more personal service, the private Enjoy Rome agency is highly recommended. Rome's city council has well-stocked green-painted tourist information kiosks (PIT) at points around the city that are open 9.30am-7.30pm daily.

APT (Azienda per il Turismo di Roma)

Via Parigi 5 (06 3600 4399/www.romaturismo.com). **Open** *Office* 8.30am-7pm Mon-Sat. *Phoneline* 9am-7.30pm daily. **Other locations**: Fiumicino airport, terminal B (06 6595 4471).

Enjoy Rome

Via Marghera 8A (06 445 1843/fax 06 445 0734/www.enjoyrome.com). **Open** *Nov-Mar* 9am-6.30pm Mon-Fri; 8.45am-2pm Sat. *Apr-Oct* 8.30am-7pm Mon-Fri; 8.30am-2pm Sat. No credit cards.

Ufficio Pellegrini e Turisti (Vatican Tourist Office)

Piazza San Pietro (06 6988 1662). **Open** 8.30am-6.30pm Mon-Sat.

Visas

EU nationals and citizens of the US, Canada, Australia and New Zealand do not need visas for stays of up to three months. For EU citizens a passport or national ID card valid for travel abroad is sufficient; non-EU citizens must have full passports.

What's on

Roma C'è

www.romace.it
Comprehensive listings for theatre, music, dance, film and nightlife every Wed, with a small English-language section.

Trovaroma

Free with *La Repubblica* every Thur; includes an English-language section on the week's concerts, exhibitions and guided tours.

ESSENTIALS

Vocabulary

Pronunciation

a – like a in ask
e – like a in age or e in sell
i – like ea in east
o – like o in hotel or hot
u – like oo in boot
c – as in cat before a, o and u;
otherwise like ch in cheat
g – as in good before a, o and u;
otherwise like g in giraffe; gl – like
lli in million; gn – like ny in canyon
h – after any consonant makes it
hard (ch – cat; gh – good)
sc – like sh in shame; sch – like
sc in scout

Useful phrases

hello/goodbye (informal) *ciao, salve*
good morning *buon giorno*; good
evening *buona sera*; good night
buona notte
please *per favore, per piacere*; thank
you *grazie*; you're welcome *prego*
excuse me, sorry *pardon*, (formal)
mi scusi, (informal) *scusa*
I don't speak Italian (very well)
non parlo (molto bene) l'italiano
do you speak English?
parla inglese?
can I use/where's the toilet?
posso usare/dov'è il bagno?
open *aperto*; closed *chiuso*; entrance
entrata; exit *uscita*

Transport

bus *autobus, auto*; car *macchina*;
coach *pullman*; plane *aereo*; taxi
tassì, taxi; train *treno*; tram *tram*;
bus stop *fermata (dell'autobus)*;
platform *binario*; station *stazione*;
ticket *biglietto*; one-way *solo andata*;
return *andata e ritorno*

Directions

where is? *dov'è?* (turn) left *(giri a)
sinistra*; (it's on the) right *(è a/sulla)
destra*; straight on *sempre dritto*;
is it near/far? *è vicino/lontano?*

Communications

dataport *attacco per il computer*;
broadband *ADSL (adiesselle)*;
cellphone *telefonino*; courier
corriere, pony; fax *fax*; letter *lettera*;
phone *telefono*; postcard *cartolina*;
stamp *francobollo*; a stamp for
England/the US *un francobollo
per l'Inghilterra/gli Stati Uniti*

Days

Monday *lunedì*; Tuesday *martedì*;
Wednesday *mercoledì*; Thursday
giovedì; Friday *venerdì*; Saturday
sabato; Sunday *domenica*.
yesterday *ieri*; today *oggi*;
tomorrow *domani*; weekend
fine settimana, weekend

Numbers, sizes & weights

0 *zero*; 1 *uno*; 2 *due*; 3 *tre*; 4 *quattro*;
5 *cinque*; 6 *sei*; 7 *sette*; 8 *otto*; 9 *nove*;
10 *dieci*; 11 *undici*; 12 *dodici*; 13
tredici; 14 *quattordici*; 15 *quindici*;
16 *sedici*; 17 *diciasette*; 18 *diciotto*;
19 *dicianove*; 20 *venti*; 30 *trenta*;
40 *quaranta*; 50 *cinquanta*; 60
sessanta; 70 *settanta*; 80 *ottanta*;
90 *novanta*; 100 *cento*; 200 *duecento*;
1,000 *mille*; 2,000 *duemila*
I take (shoe/dress) size *porto il
numero/la taglia…*; 100 grammes
of… *un'etto di…*; 300 grammes of…
tre etti di…; a kilo of… *un kilo di…*;
five kilos of… *cinque chili di…*

Booking & paying

booking, reservation *prenotazione*
I'd like to book… *vorrei prenotare…*
…a table for four at eight *un tavolo
per quattro alle otto*
…a single/twin/double room *una
camera singola/doppia/matrimoniale*
how much is it? *quanto costa?*
do you take credit cards?
si accettono le carte di credito?

Menu Glossary

Sauces & toppings

aglio, olio e peperoncino *garlic, oil and chilli*; **alle vongole** *clams*; **al pomodoro fresco** *fresh/raw tomatoes*; **al ragù 'bolognese'**… *a term that doesn't exist in Italian*; **al sugo** *puréed cooked tomatoes*; **all'amatriciana** *tomato, chilli, sausage and onion*; **alla gricia** *as above, but without tomato*; **all'arrabbiata** *tomato and chilli*; **alla carbonara** *egg, bacon and parmesan*; **alla puttanesca** *olives, capers and garlic*; **cacio e pepe** *cheese and black pepper*; **in bianco** *with oil or butter and parmesan*; **(ravioli) ricotta e spinaci** *filled with curd cheese and spinach*.

Meat & meat dishes

abbacchio, agnello *lamb*; **animelle** *fried pancreas and thymus glands*; **bresaola** *thinly sliced cured beef*; **coda alla vaccinara** *oxtail in celery broth*; **coniglio** *rabbit*; **lardo** *fatty bacon*; **lingua** *tongue*; **maiale** *pork*; **manzo** *beef*; **ossobuco** *beef shins with marrow jelly inside*; **pajata** *veal/lamb intestines*; **pancetta** *bacon*; **pollo** *chicken*; **porchetta** *roast suckling pig*; **prosciutto cotto** *ham*; **prosciutto crudo** *Parma ham*; **trippa** *tripe*; **vitello** *veal*.

Fish & seafood

alici, acciughe *anchovies*; **aragosta, astice** *lobster*; **arzilla, razza** *skate*; **baccalà** *salt cod*; **branzino, spigola** *sea bass*; **calamari** *squid*; **cernia** *grouper*; **dentice, fragolino, marmora, orata, sarago** *various forms of bream*; **cozze** *mussels*; **gamberi** *prawns*; **mazzancolle** *king prawns*; **merluzzo** *cod*; **moscardini** *baby octopus*; **ostriche** *oysters*; **pesce sanpietro** *john dory*; **pesce spada** *swordfish*; **polpo, polipo** *octopus*; **rombo** *turbot*; **salmone** *salmon*; **seppie** *cuttlefish*; **sogliola** *sole*; **tonno** *tuna*; **vongole** *clams*.

Vegetables

asparagi *asparagus*; **broccoli siciliani** *broccoli*; **broccolo** *green cauliflower*; **broccoletti** *turnip tops*; **carciofo** *artichoke*; **cavolfiore** *cauliflower*; **cicoria** *green leaf vegetable like dandelion*; **cipolla** *onion*; **fagioli** *beans*; **fagiolini** *green beans*; **fave** *broad beans*; **funghi** *mushrooms*; **insalata verde/mista** *green/mixed salad*; **melanzana** *aubergine, eggplant*; **patate** *potatoes*; **patatine fritte** *french fries*; **piselli** *peas*; **puntarelle** *bitter salad vegetable usually served with anchovy sauce*; **rughetta** *rocket*; **sedano** *celery*; **spinaci** *spinach*; **zucchine** *courgettes*.

Fruit

ananas *pineapple*; **anguria, cocomero** *watermelon*; **arance** *oranges*; **ciliegi** *cherries*; **fichi** *figs*; **fragole** *strawberries*; **mele** *apples*; **nespole** *loquats*; **pere** *pears*; **pesche** *peaches*; **uva** *grapes*.

Desserts

gelato *ice-cream*; **pannacotta** *literally 'cooked cream', a thick blancmange-like cream*; **sorbetto** *water ice*; **tiramisù** *mascarpone and coffee sponge*; **torta della nonna** *flan of pâtisserie cream and pine nuts*; **millefoglie** *flaky pastry cake*.

Miscellaneous

antipasto *hors-d'oeuvres*; **primo** *first course*; **secondo** *main course*; **contorno** *side dish, vegetable*; **dessert, dolce** *dessert*. **fritto** *fried*; **arrosta** *roast*; **alla griglia** *grilled*; **all'agro** *with oil and lemon*; **ripassato in padella** *(of vegetables) cooked then tossed in a pan with oil, garlic and chilli*. **formaggio** *cheese*; **parmigiano** *parmesan*; **pane** *bread*; **sale** *salt*; **pepe** *pepper*; **aceto** *vinegar*; **olio** *oil*.

Index

Sights & Areas

a

Ara Pacis Augustae p85
Aventine p122

b

Baths of Caracalla p122
Baths of Diocletian p109
Bioparco-Zoo p92
Borghese p90
Borgo p142

c

Campo de' Fiori p60
Capitoline Museums p53
Caracalla p122
Castel Sant'Angelo p143
Celio p115
Centrale Montemartini p126
Chiesa Nuova/Santa Maria in Vallicella p71
Circus Maximus p53
Colosseum p53
Crypta Balbi p61

d

Domus Aurea p109

e

Esquiline p105
Explora – Museo dei Bambini di Roma p92

g

Galleria Borghese p92
Galleria Colonna p100
Galleria Doria Pamphili p71
Galleria Nazionale d'Arte Moderna e Contemporanea p96
Galleria Spada p61
Gesù, Il p61
Ghetto p60
Gianicolo p141

i

Imperial Fora & Trajan's Market p55

k

Keats-Shelley Memorial House p85

m

MACRO p103
Mamertime Prison p57
MAXXI p103
Monteverde p141
Monti p105
Museo Barracco di Scultura Antica p63
Museo delle Anime dei Defunti p153
Museo di Palazzo Venezia p57
Museo di Roma in Trastevere p133
Museo di Roma p71
Museo Ebraica di Roma p63
Museo Nazionale d'Arte Orientale p109
Museo Nazionale delle Paste Alimentari p100
Museo Nazionale di Villa Giulia p96
Museo Storico Nazionale dell'Arte Sanitaria p143
Museum of Via Ostiense p126

o

Orto botanico (Botanical Gardens) p133
Ostiense p123

p

Palatine, The p57
Palazzo Altemps p71
Palazzo Barberini – Galleria Nazionale d'Arte Antica p101
Palazzo Corsini – Galleria Nazionale d'Arte Antica p133
Palazzo del Quirinale p101
Palazzo Massimo alle Terme p111
Palazzo Ruspoli-Fondazione Memmo p86
Pantheon p73
Piazza di Spagna & Spanish Steps p86
Piazza Navona p73
Portico d'Ottavia p63
Prati p153
Protestant Cemetery p126

q

Quirinale p100

r

Roman Forum p58

s

San Carlino alle Quattro Fontane p101
San Clemente p115
San Francesco a Ripa p136
San Giorgio in Velabro p58
San Giovanni p118
San Giovanni in Laterano p119
San Gregorio Magno p117
San Lorenzo p120
San Lorenzo fuori le Mura p120
San Lorenzo in Lucina p86
San Luigi dei Francesi p73
San Marco p58
San Nicola in Carcere p58
San Paolo fuori le Mura p126
Sant'Agnese in Agone p73
Sant'Agostino p73
Sant'Andrea al Quirinale p102
Sant'Andrea della Valle p63
Sant'Ignazio di Loyola p75
Sant'Ivo alla Sapienza p75
Santa Cecilia in Trastevere p136
Santa Croce in Gerusalemme p119
Santa Maria del Popolo p86
Santa Maria della Concezione p96
Santa Maria della Pace p75
Santa Maria Della Vittoria p111
Santa Maria in Aracoeli p59
Santa Maria in Cosmedin & the Mouth of Truth p58
Santa Maria in Domnica p117
Santa Maria in Trastevere p136
Santa Maria Maggiore p111
Santa Maria sopra Minerva p75
Santa Prassede p112

ESSENTIALS

ESSENTIALS